planning and design of

TOWNHOUSES and CONDOMINIUMS

By Robert E. Engstrom and Marc R. Putman

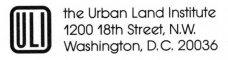
the Urban Land Institute
1200 18th Street, N.W.
Washington, D.C. 20036

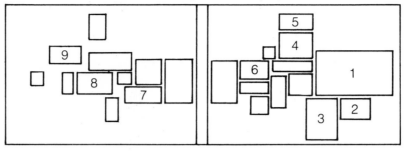

Cover Photographs

1 Scarborough, Bloomington, Minnesota (Minneapolis-St. Paul SMSA). Photograph printed with the permission of *Better Homes and Gardens* (© Meredith Corporation).

2 Summit Place, St. Paul, Minnesota. Courtesy of James Majerus.

3 Applewood Landmark, Mississauga, Ontario, Canada (Toronto Census Metropolitan Area). Courtesy of Shipp Corporation Limited. Photographer: Jac Jacobsen.

4 Sumner Village, Montgomery County, Maryland (Washington, D.C. SMSA).

5 Heritage Sound, Milford, Connecticut. Courtesy of Heritage Development Group, Inc.

6 Cedarview, Minneapolis, Minnesota.

7 Birnamwood, Burnsville, Minnesota (Minneapolis-St. Paul SMSA).

8 Orindawoods, Orinda, California (Contra Costa County).

9 Scarborough, Bloomington, Minnesota (Minneapolis-St. Paul SMSA).

Recommended bibliographic listing:
Robert E. Engstrom and Marc R. Putman. Planning and Design of Townhouses and Condominiums.
Washington: Urban Land Institute, 1979.
Second Printing with revisions 1980

Library of Congress Card Catalog Number 79-64813
International Standard Book Number 0-87420-587-5
Printed in the United States of America

About the Authors

Robert E. Engstrom, is president of Robert Engstrom Associates, Inc., a Minneapolis based, multi-disciplined firm with extensive experience in the planning, design, and marketing of single-family detached and townhouse/multi-family communities. His past experience includes all aspects of the design, development, and marketing of several well-known townhouse developments. In addition to consulting work, his current activities include the design and development of Summit Place, an urban infill and restoration development in the historic district of St. Paul and the development of a 500-acre recreation site on Lake Superior in northern Wisconsin.

Bob Engstrom is a graduate of the University of Minnesota. He is currently a trustee and chairman of the education committee of the Urban Land Institute and immediate past chairman of the ULI Residential Development Council. He was chairman of the ULI Homes Association Committee, which helped establish the Community Association Institute.

Marc Putman is director of land planning and landscape architecture with the Minneapolis firm of Robert Engstrom Associates, Inc. He has been involved with over 125 projects, encompassing tasks of environmental analysis, master planning, and detail open space, amenity, architectural, and graphic design.

He received a master's degree in landscape architecture and a bachelor of science in landscape architecture with a minor in applied arts and architecture from Iowa State University.

Acknowledgments

Many people have contributed suggestions and material for this publication. Special thanks is given to Joe Steller of the ULI staff for perceptive assistance; to the ULI Director of Publications, Frank Spink, Jr., for unusual patience; to Residential Development Council Member, George Orning, for tabulating the consumer questionnaires; and to the ULI review panel consisting of Fritz Grupe, Ron Nahas, Henry Paparazzo, Gary Ryan, John Schmidt, and Doug Unruh.

Earlier ULI publications and ULI members contributed information pertinent to successful development, especially Byron Hanke as the author of ULI TB#50. Former development colleagues provided the framework and assistance that enabled the development of numerous townhouse and open space communities; namely, Bruce Thomson, Robert Davidson, Jerald Grande, Lawrence Laukka, Daniel Herbst, James Hill, Gerald Mazzara, and William Nicholson. Architect Michael McGuire provided early insights into planning and design complexities. Dave Stone gave added dimensions to creative marketing.

Advice and imaginative assistance came from Jack Buxell, the authors' associate at Robert Engstrom Associates, Inc.

Finally, the authors acknowledge the comments and satisfaction of innumerable homebuyers, who provide the ultimate criteria for the planning and design of residential developments.

About ULI-the Urban Land Institute

ULI–the Urban Land Institute is an independent, nonprofit research and educational organization incorporated in 1936 to improve the quality and standards of land use and development.

The Institute is committed to conducting practical research in the various fields of real estate knowledge; identifying and interpreting land use trends in relation to the changing economic, social, and civic needs of the people; and disseminating pertinent information leading to the orderly and more efficient use and development of land.

ULI receives its financial support from membership dues, sale of publications, and contributions for research and panel services.

ULI Staff

Metric Conversions

meters = feet × 0.305
kilometers = miles × 1.609
square meters = sq. ft. ×0.093
hectares = acres × 0.405
(1 hectare = 10,000 square meters)

ULI Publications Review

In order to enhance the scope of this book, the manuscript was reviewed prior to publication by a committee experienced in the development of townhouses and condominiums. Drawn mostly from the Institute's Residential Council, the review committee members have contributed to the quality of the final book by evaluating the manuscript in light of their own experience in the field. While unanimity of opinion was neither sought nor obtained relative to all points, this book does reflect the views of a group of experienced professionals who gave freely of their time to participate in its preparation.

ULI Review Committee
Greenlaw (Fritz) Grupe, Jr.
President
The Grupe Company
Stockton, California

Ronald C. Nahas
Vice President
R. T. Nahas Company
Castro Valley, California

Henry J. Paparazzo
President
Heritage Development Group, Inc.
Southbury, Connecticut

Gary M. Ryan
Colorado Division Manager
M. J. Brock & Sons, Inc.
Englewood, Colorado

John L. Schmidt
Vice President
Institute of Financial Education
(affiliated with the U.S. League
of Savings Associations)
Chicago, Illinois

Douglas A. Unruh
President
Grupe Communities, Inc.
Stockton, California

Contents

Foreword

The overwhelming majority of Americans identify with and pursue the American dream. A key element of that dream is homeownership, which for the greater part of the last 35 years has been defined as proprietorship of the single-family detached house, owned in fee simple. However, during the course of our history, other forms of housing have been of equal importance in fulfilling the American dream. The row house is a form that dates back to the beginning of our nation. It was a popular and commonly found form of housing at least until the first decade of the 20th century. Because of the rise of the suburbs and, thus, the attraction of the single-family detached house, it was not until the 1960s that a suburban form of the row house, the townhouse, reemerged as a housing choice. The public's acceptance of the condominium form of ownership in the 1960s and 1970s further paved the way for the acceptance of alternatives. As the present-day movement back to cities gains popularity, the cycle will have come full circle with the restoration and infill of townhouse blocks and the condominium conversions of older buildings.

Many within the housing industry continue to support the view that single-family detached housing is still the preferred choice—that for the majority of Americans other choices are less desirable. In response to this perspective, *Planning and Design of Townhouses and Condominiums* was developed. The premise of this book is that good planning and design will make the townhouse and condominium co-equal housing choices for many.

In 1973 ULI published *Townhouses and Condominiums: Residents' Likes and Dislikes* by Dr. Carl Norcross. It was the first and remains the most definitive study of the preferences and dissatisfactions of those people who had selected townhouses or condominiums as their homeownership form. In 1975, when condominium development was booming, Congress initiated a massive study of condominium development with particular focus on what appeared to be a series of problems and abuses. A nationwide survey done at that time served to reaffirm the findings of the Norcross study, upon which this book builds.

With rising housing costs, shrinking energy resources, and significant changes in the demographics of those people entering the housing market, clearly other forms of homeownership than the single-family detached house will continue to be a growing and important segment of the U.S. housing stock. Furthermore, the ability of the townhouse and condominium forms of ownership to compete effectively with single-family detached housing will be tied to the quality of planning and design applied to them.

Much criticism has been laid to the quality of design for single-family detached housing. However, time and a modicum of tree planting may transform even the most mediocre of merchant-built housing tracts into a relatively pleasant neighborhood with desirable levels of privacy, recreational amenities, and visual attractiveness—the concerns of good planning and design. As the density of development increases, this gentle hand of time and nature is not so readily effective. It becomes, therefore, most important that townhouse and condominium developments be carefully conceived and designed from their inception. This care must reach all the way from proper site selection to the many small design details such as outdoor lighting, mailboxes, selection of paving materials, and even to concerns about modifications after initial construction. Modifications which tend to occur naturally, without community control, in most single-family detached neighborhoods must be of significant concern in maintaining the design quality of a townhouse cluster.

Recognition of the importance of good planning and design for townhouse and condominium development led the authors, Robert Engstrom and Marc Putman, to approach ULI in 1975 with the idea of doing a book that would draw upon their broad experience. The idea was to set down verbally and graphically planning and design concepts and ideas that would maximize the preferences identified in the Norcross study.

This book represents a 3-year commitment on the part of the authors to the collection, organization, and articulation of some of the best concepts in planning and design for townhouses and condominiums. It is as much a book to be looked at as to be read. In many cases the sketches, illustrations, and plans are as informative as the textual material. Captions are carefully constructed to focus the reader's attention on the precise visual message. We believe that the extent to which the concepts and ideas as set forth in this publication are applied effectively in the field will significantly enhance the quality of the built environment; and, further, that the application of the planning and design concepts in this book will assure financial success for the well-conceived project.

Frank H. Spink, Jr.
Director of Publications

1 Introduction

William Rothchild

Over the years the word *townhouse* has been used in many ways. In this book it is used as a design term, referring to the physical form of two or more single-family attached homes with a ground floor entry. Townhouse ownership may be conveyed the same as a single-family detached home, by fee simple deed of land. A community association maintains and may hold title to any common property.

Whereas *townhouse* refers to the physical form of a type of home, *condominium* is a term which refers to a form of ownership. This term may be applied to any type of housing—including townhouses, single-family detached units, and high-rise structures. This study refers to a condominium as a dwelling where the homeowner has a deed to a *volume of space* above, below, or beside another home, particularly in a garden, mid-, or high-rise structure. The condominium form of ownership provides for community association maintenance of the common

1-1   Townhouse clusters help preserve the natural environment of a hilly, wooded site. Walden Woods (Dobbs Ferry, New York)—printed with the permission of DHI Enterprises, Yonkers, New York.

property and structures surrounding the homes. In a townhouse development, ownership of the common property as well as maintenance is conveyed to the community association.

The emphasis of this study, no matter what the form of individual ownership, is on planning and design for medium density (6 to 12 dwelling units per acre) development. The study also deals with mid- and high-rise structures, as many of the principles for medium-density projects are equally applicable to these structures.

Townhouse and condominium communities cannot be built from a cookbook for design. There are too many variables throughout the design process that require numerous value judgements. Since the planning and design process combines and balances many elements, the developer should utilize a number of specialists, or, if possible, several multi-

skilled individuals with broad design backgrounds that combine planning, architecture, landscape architecture, interior design, and engineering. The importance of an interdisciplinary project development team should become apparent as this book presents some of the many variables involved in the design of townhouses and condominiums.

1-2 (top) Turned garages, private entries, variable roof lines, and interesting textures and materials provide an atmosphere of livability. 1-3 (middle) Urban condominiums: the return of the residential property owner. 1-4 (bottom) Land use variety by mixing townhouses and condominiums, here separated by garages and open space.

3

A Brief History

The townhouse has a rich American heritage. Perhaps one of the finest examples of town-home living is Louisburg Square. First partitioned in 1826, Louisburg Square is now an historic landmark on Boston's Beacon Hill. Built on land purchased from the American painter, John Singleton Copley, the 2.3-acre site with 28 townhouse lots is the oldest known American residential land development with a homes association.* The private streets, common park, and pride of the residents are some of the reasons why this development has increased in value and de-

*Homes association and community association are used interchangeably.

1-5 Private streets and a common park—new ideas found in America's first townhouse development—Boston's Louisburg Square (1826).

sirability over the years. Louisburg Square is a townhouse development that has weathered the test of time.

Row houses on single lots have a long history in the East, in San Francisco, and in other cities. However, it was the block developments with a central court (like the Forest Close development of the 1920s in New York) that provided the impetus for the few *townhouse on the green* developments that began appearing in the late 50s and early 60s. In 1961, the Federal Housing Administration approved Hartshorn Homes in Richmond, Virginia, even though these townhouses did not satisfy the usual FHA requirement of having direct street frontage for each home. The following year, the sales success of Huntington Continental in the Los Angeles area prompted the FHA to analyze this new interest in townhouses. Subsequent approval by FHA and the Veterans Administration of home mortgage financing for townhouses provided developers with a financial foundation for the rapid growth of townhouse developments.

As contrasted to townhouses, condominiums have had a more recent history. More than 85 percent of condominium units in inventory as of April 1, 1975 were built since the 1970 Census.*

The condition of the national economy in the mid-70s slowed the momentum of townhouse/condominium construction. Many poorly conceived and overbuilt developments were exposed at that time. Following a period of adjustment, the trend toward townhouse and condominium construction has continued. Less experienced builders/developers have been replaced by more experienced and sophisticated developer/design teams, and townhouses and condominiums continue to provide an increasing percentage of the new homes under development.

---

*U.S. Department of Housing and Urban Development, *HUD Condominium/Cooperative Study* (Volume 1 National Evaluation) (Washington, D.C.: author, July 1975), p. III-1.

1-6 Structures such as these are prime candidates for condominium conversion. The building in the foreground is a new infill townhouse.

An Outlook

In spite of the traditionally promoted truism that Americans desire a detached home on a private lot, today more and more homes are townhouses or condominiums. Underlying factors that will support on a sustained basis the increasing trend toward townhouse and condominium ownership include:

- a public policy approach by some major cities to aid stability by promoting ownership and encouraging an increased number of housing units to counteract a decreasing population trend;
- a decreased number of rental apartments being built due to rising maintenance, construction, and financing costs, the insidious impact of present rent controls or the threat of future rent controls, and tenant/landlord problems;
- the surge of urban infill and bypassed parcel development, redevelopment, and rehabilitation (this activity has been reinforced by buyer preferences, energy considerations, and ease of development due to existing infrastructure);
- the dramatic increases in the cost of housing due to inflation and higher mortgage interest rates; and
- the rising cost of land, especially high amenity sites.

Of these factors, inflation of our money supply, resulting in higher prices, has perhaps the most dynamic impact on the townhouse/condominium market. Rising prices have caused an accelerated change of attitude by potential homebuyers. Townhouse/condominium ownership is now considered an attractive living alternative and a means of building future equity. The recent tendency toward conversion of existing rental property has accelerated the percentage of homes under condominium ownership.

Townhouses and condominiums offer advantages such as:

- energy efficiency,
- efficient construction and land development costs,
- land conservation—by using less land for a given number of homes and preserving open space,
- lower long-term public maintenance and energy costs,
- a means of stabilizing and diversifying existing neighborhoods,
- improved environmental quality,
- a more secure home and community, and
- a lower maintenance lifestyle.

1-7 Urban restoration: new life for old neighborhoods.

In spite of these obvious advantages, the outlook for townhouses and condominiums is mixed. On one hand, current population trends and lifestyles, inflation, increasing material and energy costs indicate great demand for well-planned townhouse/condominium developments. On the other hand, the construction of townhouse/condominium homes may come under the shadow of increasing regulatory control. Although townhouses and condominiums are similar to other housing forms in that they are affected by many of the same supply and demand factors, these newer housing forms do not conform to the familiar single-family development process. Thus, a townhouse/condominium project may obtain a higher profile and increased public scrutiny. Environmental assessments, impact statements, referendums, local and state development regulations, and financial institution requirements cloud the hopes of many who would build or buy in these new environments. For instance, multi-jurisdictional units of government, such as the watershed district, the department of natural resources, and municipal government agencies, are typically involved in the approval process for even a simple drainage ditch. This multi-level process may be lengthy, involving coordination problems, and may result in added costs for the final townhouse or condominium.

While the development of townhouses and condominiums remains under a complex regulatory structure, creative and experienced developers will question more fully the added risks of this type of construction. To commit time, effort, and dollars, developers need *certainty;* not the certainty of a saleable product, but the legally definable certainty that all necessary permits have been obtained or are quickly attainable while the market for the product being developed still exists.

The purpose of this book is to clarify the planning and design aspects of townhouse and condominium development. The intention is that the anticipated increased demand for townhouses and condominiums will be met with a better physical product. At the same time, it is hoped that a clearer understanding of the development process for townhouses and condominiums will enable those involved from the public and private sectors to better meet the demand in an effective, efficient manner with units of a reasonable cost.

Martin Tornallyay

1-8 Open space and amenity features: an integral part of townhouse and condominium design.

2 Livability and Process

The townhouse/condominium development process puts carefully designed, marketable site and building plans through a sequence of private decisions and public approvals. Circumstances today are creating a more complex atmosphere for these tasks. Thus, many developers have come to recognize the increased need for skilled planning and design, and have organized teams of specialists to coordinate the various disciplines. In the decisions/public approvals process, planning and design consultants must be cognizant of the needs of the builder or developer and requirements of the marketplace. The plans they prepare must integrate budget constraints, energy conservation, livability factors, and up-to-date building and land use techniques.

Given current technological and social trends, people have been and will be changing and re-adapting their lifestyles at increasing rates. Thus, their living environments must keep pace. In the complex, multi-faceted townhouse/condominium development process, flexibility is crucial to meeting people's needs. Design should reflect the lessons of previous successful and unsuccessful efforts, blending new ideas with the proven designs of the past. Throughout the intricate design and approval process, the ultimate judge of good design and construction quality is the individual homebuyer. Larger-scale design decisions may properly be made only if they reflect and reinforce those same principles that determine the quality of life at an individual level.

2-1 Function, safety, privacy, security, identity, and social interaction are central to a carefully planned and designed project.

The Factors of Livability

With the interests of the individual in mind the factors of livability—including function, safety, privacy, security, identity, and social interaction—are central to a carefully designed, environmentally sound townhouse/condominium project.

Function and Safety

A townhouse/condominium community must basically provide shelter in a functional and efficient manner, being organized, understandable, reasonably accessible, and safe. Generally, these goals are attained by combining compatible community elements and separating conflicting factors. For instance, a number of large windows oriented toward a beautiful vista take advantage of a compatible element—a natural amenity—thus enhancing livability. Separation of roads from walkways increases safety (eliminating a conflicting factor). Garbage/trash storage separated from the entries of the home again designs function and livability into the residential surroundings.

Privacy and Security

People need the option of controlling their contact with other activities and people at certain times. Besides visual contact, this privacy should include, as much as possible, control over noises, lights, and odors. Private areas within the confines of a home, privacy from neighbors sharing a common wall, and private outdoor spaces are vital.

2-2 Whether in the city or suburbs, a townhouse/condominium community must be functional and safe.

Security is a provision for defense against intruders or strangers that violate a person's privacy. Separated, private home entries and careful window placements play a significant role in designing privacy into a housing unit. From a land planning standpoint, a single community entry will make the entire community more of a private court than a dangerous thoroughfare, enhancing both privacy and security.

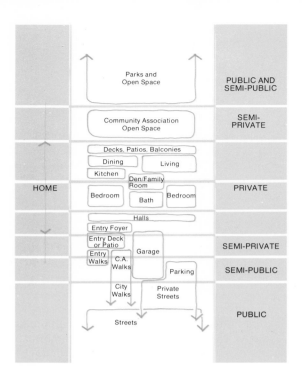

2-3   A good home plan provides for varying levels of privacy.

Identity and Character

People express their individuality through the ownership of distinctive and unique property. Their homes and surroundings play a central role in this image-setting function. The preservation of a 12-inch oak near an individual's front door lends instant character, while forceful architecture and other created site features add distinction. A carefully designed community entrance may also add special character and identity. As people are very conscious of community identity, once achieved, it will greatly contribute to the success of a development.

Community and Interaction

In a townhouse/condominium community, interactions need not and should not be forced. As mentioned previously, there must be provisions for privacy. However, those convenient opportunities for social contact that are planned and designed into the community will be recognized and used as desired. Community amenities, such as a convenience store or the deck area of a swimming pool, provide places for social interaction. Within the home itself, provision for social interaction should also be made by designing a "hearth"—dining room, country kitchen, or family room. The "hearth" should be planned for maximum family/guest interaction.

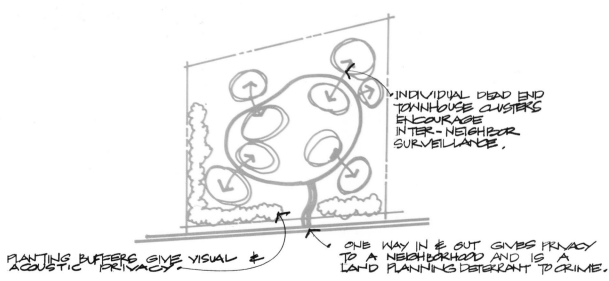

INDIVIDUAL DEAD END TOWNHOUSE CLUSTERS ENCOURAGE INTER-NEIGHBOR SURVEILLANCE.

PLANTING BUFFERS GIVE VISUAL & ACOUSTIC PRIVACY.

ONE WAY IN & OUT GIVES PRIVACY TO A NEIGHBORHOOD AND IS A LAND PLANNING DETERRANT TO CRIME.

2-4   Create a feeling of privacy and security through land plan and perimeter details.

2-5 (above left) Identity and character: a balance of natural features and good design.
2-6 (above right) Establishing a strong, visual community identity often aids marketing success. 2-7 (right) The right kind of sign helps to create community character. 2-8 (lower right) Casual interaction occurs naturally if the right facilities are planned.

Financial Value

In real estate, satisfying the elements of livability is financially valuable and results in benefits to others. If the new homebuyer's judgements are accurate, financial security will be enjoyed through long-term home value appreciation. If the builder has provided for the basic human needs as well as or better than surrounding residential alternatives, he will find success with a rapid sales pace. This should yield a ready profit to begin the process again, made easier the second time by having established an image as a developer of quality environments.

For the city or municipal government, observing these livable design elements in a new community promotes positive fiscal impacts and environmental quality. For the existing residents of a community, efforts to instill livability in newly added, surrounding townhouses and condominiums may improve land value and upgrade the visual quality of the neighborhood. Financially valuable design may thus be equated with how well the factors of livability are met. The following sections and chapters will incorporate these factors in the planning and design of townhouse and condominium communities.

Applying Livability to Development

Townhouse or condominium development requires a continuous process of asking questions, assembling a growing base of information, and then forming better and more complete answers—each building on the former. Generally, the development process consists of three major phases, each of which contain elements that may occur at the same time. Figure 2-9 illustrates the three phases. They are:

1. Supply/Demand and Land
   - the recognition that a specific market (i.e., family, single adult, retiree) exists for townhouses and condominiums, coupled with the developer's intention to react to it; and
   - the location and acquisition of land suitable for development;

2. Planning and Design
   - concept plan;
   - preliminary plan; and
   - final plan; and

3. Model Construction/Home Production
   - model home construction;
   - marketing and sales; and
   - home production/customer service.

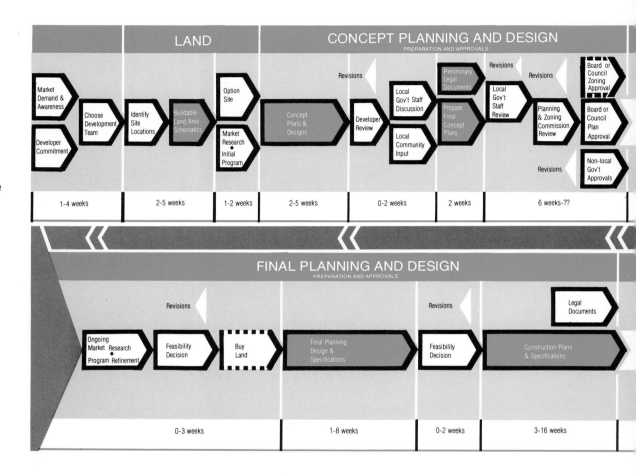

2-9 Planning and Design Sequence Chart. This chart shows the sequence of activities and approvals typically experienced in townhouse or condominium development. Several variations to this sequence are:

- The decision to exercise the option to purchase land may occur at one of several stages, but preferably after zoning approval has been obtained. In some areas, the concept and preliminary stages are combined into one step of the approval process.
- With concentrated activity and expeditious approvals, the time span from project commencement to model center opening may be shortened to approximately 30 weeks.

This chart emphasizes planning and design factors. Many other items that are part of the development process are not shown.

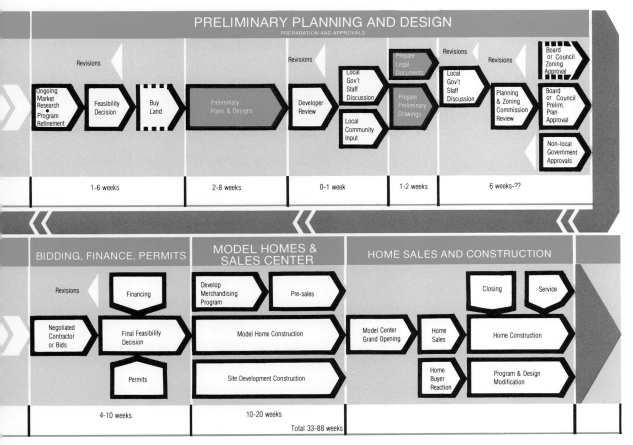

PRELIMINARY PLANNING AND DESIGN
PREPARATION AND APPROVALS

Revisions

Ongoing Market Research • Program Refinement → Feasibility Decision → Buy Land → Preliminary Plans & Designs

Revisions

Developer Review → Local Gov't Staff Discussion / Local Community Input → Prepare Legal Documents / Prepare Preliminary Drawings

Revisions

Local Gov't Staff Discussion → Planning & Zoning Commission Review

Revisions

Board or Council Zoning Approval / Board or Council Prelim. Plan Approval / Non-local Government Approvals

| 1-6 weeks | 2-8 weeks | 0-1 week | 1-2 weeks | 6 weeks-?? |

BIDDING, FINANCE, PERMITS

Revisions

Financing

Negotiated Contractor or Bids → Final Feasibility Decision

Permits

MODEL HOMES & SALES CENTER

Develop Merchandising Program → Pre-sales

Model Home Construction

Site Development Construction

HOME SALES AND CONSTRUCTION

Closing — Service

Model Center Grand Opening → Home Sales → Home Construction

Home Buyer Reaction → Program & Design Modification

| 4-10 weeks | 10-20 weeks | |
| | Total 33-88 weeks | |

Approvals That Affect Design

Asking for solutions before they may logically be derived does not recognize the step-by-step method for finding the best solutions to a design problem. If a government body requests preliminary planning or design solutions that are not logically available until further along in the development sequence, the designer must go too far on insufficient knowledge. This happens quite frequently when ordinances call for concept site plans and detailed architecture at the same time. This results in excessive time and expenditure to find architectural answers before they are appropriate or valid. The ultimate results are either higher home prices or forcing a creative developer to replace an imaginative concept with a more ordinary plan. When premature government requirements do exist, using examples of previous developments and design solutions may allude to the general character of the proposed development.

A logical development sequence will generally assure that the best product will be designed economically and on schedule. Figure 2-9 shows the design process as it logically proceeds, alluding to the importance of adapting developer and government expectations to the actual sequential method of townhouse/condominium design. Of course, there are variations in the approval process. Internally, however, the design sequence used by the developer and the design team should not vary significantly.

The Development Team

From beginning to end, the development process combines many skills and disciplines. These skills may be found in separate individuals, one firm, or several multi-disciplined consultants. One person may even possess a working knowledge and ability in two or more areas of expertise.

The Developer

The developer is the initiator of the development process who provides risk capital and managerial ability in order to develop financially viable, competitive townhouses or condominiums. There are many diverse rea-

sons motivating his decisions, but profitability is the basic criteria for his evaluative choices and actions. The pride of building a quality environment and responsibility for the welfare of the public also motivate and reward the developer's efforts.

The complexity of the mid-density development process and the commonly narrow profit margins accentuate the need for precise, timely decisions. This complexity fosters the need for assistance by other people and disciplines. Thus, the developer generally assembles a team to help understand and cope with the market and with natural and institutional limitations. One of the best ways for a developer to deplete cash flow is to hire a full staff from the start. However, circumstances may make it appropriate, if not necessary, for a developer to add skilled people directly to his staff or to employ the consulting services of individuals or a multi-disciplined firm at the outset.

Choosing the design team is basic to the success of the development process— competent, experienced team members will add tremendously to the appeal and marketability of a project. A developer must have a positive attitude toward the use of outside advice, recognizing that good design does not cost as much money as it makes in the long run.

Market Research

The developer may call upon market research aids to validate informal ideas concerning the intended townhouse or condominium market. A newer role is that of monitoring the market to assure that the buyers will still be there when the homes become available. In some areas this task has become more important due primarily to the longer time necessary for government approvals. When this is necessary, the experienced townhouse/condominium marketing director or marketing consultant may provide the best recommendations for possible program and design changes with respect to new attitudes and purchasing capabilities of people in the marketplace. The professional market analyst provides an objective overview of the market and evaluates the short-term and long-term demand.

Legal

As the legal aspects greatly influence the final design of a project, an attorney plays an important role in townhouse/condominium development. The attorney is normally responsible for reviewing and/or preparing land acquisition and option agreements, so important to the phasing of the project. An experienced real estate attorney will recognize the importance of coordinating the project phasing with the release clauses of the

PLANNING

MARKET DEMANDS, CODES, BUDGET

THE SITE

UTILITIES

ENGINEERING

Townhouse/Condominium
DESIGN

STREETS

COURTS

ARCHITECTURE

HOMES

BUILDINGS

OPEN SPACE

LANDSCAPE ARCHITECTURE

2-10   A design solution is the result of the interaction of many factors.

14

option agreements. Prior to this, the attorney may aid in judging the political climate of the locale and assist in evaluating the technical aspects of zoning and other regulations controlling the development. Informally, the attorney may open up channels of communication to key people in the city. Since the creation of a community association is central to the townhouse/condominium concept, legal expertise is particularly important in the preparation of the community association legal documents.

Finance

Financing plays a major role in what is designed and whether it may be built. Moreover, the availability of borrowed funds is perhaps the most crucial part of the entire development process over which the developer has the least control. While the cost and availability of money fluctuate greatly, the developer must attempt to borrow funds at just the right time to keep costs at a minimum. Knowledge of mortgage sources and techniques is as essential to development as is a knowledge of construction. Understanding of finance or a capable staff financial officer is a must for the successful townhouse/condominium developer. The developer also needs skill in financial and accounting management, which involves organizing material, labor, and supervisory expenditures, disbursing payment to subcontractors, and monitoring cash flow.

Design

The term *designer* is used throughout this book to describe a member of *any one* of the following three professions—planning, architecture, or landscape architecture. Each of these disciplines is described in detail below.

Planning. The townhouse/condominium land planner is a combination of a number of disciplines. This person should be familiar with engineering, economics, construction, and marketing considerations of mid-density land development and must also have a working knowledge of land inventory, analysis, and evaluation methods. A planner must additionally have an understanding of the buildings or home clusters that must be accommodated on the site. Combining this diverse input with buyer preferences demands a sensitive artistic balance.

Most importantly, the land planner must be able to give valid reasons for the selected design solutions both to the developer and in municipal presentations. Being familiar with the need for development phasing should permit accurate representations of the plan implementation. For small developments, the architect will often fulfill the planning function.

Architecture. As quality architecture is essential to a successful townhouse/condominium development, the architect must be versed in the elements of mid-density land planning, building combinations, construction, and market demands. Today's townhouses and condominiums must be more than just well built. They must, at once, be energy and resource efficient, yet offer identity and character. The role of the architect is to design these characteristics into an affordable package, by understanding how floor plans and plan types combine into buildings or clusters adaptable to the site. For the continuing or phased development, the architect's design solutions must be able to respond to shifting market demands.

Landscape Architecture. Landscape architectural design involves the exterior townhouse/condominium environment, including building arrangements, clusters, land forms, and plantings. An understanding of architecture, plant materials, grading, street design, and construction methods is most important to the mid-density project. Much of the appeal of today's townhouses or condominiums is due to their adaptability to the land. The landscape architect may play a central role in establishing this character and the environmental quality of the new community by protecting natural features and existing vegetation.

Engineering

The civil engineer should help to refine the design concepts, converting them to practical reality. In this role, technical construction and cost experience are essential. The engineer may aid in the program and information gathering stages of design by providing site and natural feature data (boundary surveys, utility data, soil tests, rock soundings, and hydrologic tests). A surveyor legally defines and accurately locates buildings, property lines, public streets, utilities, and important natural features, but it is the engineer who prepares utility installation working drawings and may also help in the preparation of grading plans and earth work calculations and in the supervision of construction.

Construction Supervision

The conversion of townhouse or condominium design from contract documents to reality is a difficult job of coordination and constant vigilance to ensure that the outcome is actually the product that was designed. The construction supervisor must be almost two people; the hardheaded ramrod who demands performance of the subcontractors according to absolute time and budget constraints and, at the same time, a sensitive interpreter of design drawings who insures that the spirit of the design comes through in what is actually built. The construction supervisor may be on the staff of the developer or the general contractor doing the construction. Design consultants may provide construction supervision as a part of their professional service.

Marketing/Sales

Marketing plays a key role in the success of most townhouse or condominium developments. The marketing director may be of great assistance in conveying to the development team current consumer requirements and in critiquing concept and preliminary designs. It is he who, involved with the design process, will enthusiastically convey the livability features of a development to the sales staff. The marketing director will generally use an advertising/marketing agency to help assemble a marketing program which generally includes schedules for media use, brochures, graphic displays, and the operation of a sales model center.

Customer Service

Followup and correction of homebuyer complaints, no matter how minor, are vital to the developer as well as to the success of a project. In the short term, a well-organized, prompt, and fair customer service program reinforces the marketing and sales effort by building referrals from satisfied customers. In the long run, a high quality product coupled with excellent customer service ensures a good reputation for later phases of the project and future projects of the developer. To guarantee customer satisfaction, a developer who is selling parcels of land to individual builders should be sure that they will meet the standards that have been set for the project. Usually the developer achieves this by enforcing design and construction guidelines as well as by limiting lot sales to qualified builders only.

The Review Process

The Developer

A developer's comments and evaluations regarding alternative plans may be either supportive of or destructive to the design process. After plans and designs evolve according to a rational design process they should be reviewed according to how well they meet the design criteria and program originally agreed upon. That is, did the designer adhere to the recommendations of the market analysis? How well have the livability factors actually been met?

During the review process, the developer must test the design proposals against economic capabilities and projections, which are tied closely to construction feasibility. For instance, the wooded area chosen for the first phase cluster may require the extension of too much road or excessive fill. The developer may weigh the cost of the road extension against choosing a less desirable location closer to the entry and committing a larger budget for model area improvements. While this type of decision may be considered very tentative long-range planning, it is the exact type of increasingly specific consideration that should be generated throughout the design process.

To gain the most from his designers, the developer should allow early concepts to be as spontaneous as possible. After a number of conceptual land plans are prepared, detailed engineering, economic, and construction limits should be applied. The architect should first be left free to explore the townhouse or condominium spatial and massing considerations. After a number of home concepts have taken visual form, production constraints may then be introduced. Similarly, the person doing site development design, usually the landscape architect, architect, or engineer, should be encouraged to ask, "What should the landscape be like—within various budget choices?" Once the best concept is distilled into a plan, it should be refined by budget and construction limits. The ultimate result should be a delicate balancing of function and aesthetics, practicality and character.

Developer reviews and decisions in actual townhouse/condominium development practice occur at intervals as shown in Figure 2-9. The developer's financial considerations, phasing, and actual design critiques grow more specific as the plans and designs start to detail how the townhouses or condominiums will look and function.

At the concept phase of planning, there are a great many unknowns. In fact, the actual political feasibility of the entire development may be uncertain. For this reason, the planning costs must be kept as low as possible. This means that the drawings or sketches must be loose and reflect the accuracy of the information on hand. Specifically, accurate boundaries and topography may not be available. These plans should really serve exploratory purposes, to encourage the free flow of ideas from the design team. Once the developer's preference for one plan or the best parts of several designs is found, density and unit counts within the various

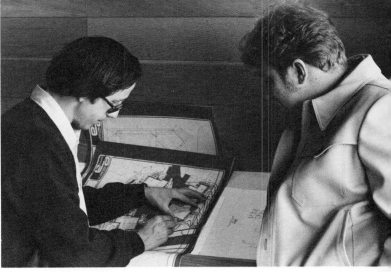

2-11 Ongoing reviews and refinements move plans from concept to final design.

phases may represent the first feasibility estimate. Moreover, these plans may serve as a basis for obtaining early city and community reaction at a fairly low cost. The concept design, if ably prepared, should identify the major constraints to development on the site, define buildable areas, show major circulation systems, open space areas, and total yield in numbers of units and types.

Once the final concept plan is selected and approved both by the developer and the various governmental agencies, the decision may be made to move into preliminary planning, design, and engineering of the site plan, buildings, and utilities. The preliminary design focuses on first phase development, determined from the final concept plan. With the acquisition of accurate site information, much greater attention to detail is possible. Specifically, emphasis is on the development of marketable floor plans and cluster or condominium building configurations. The formation of specific floor plans or building configurations allows work on detailed site

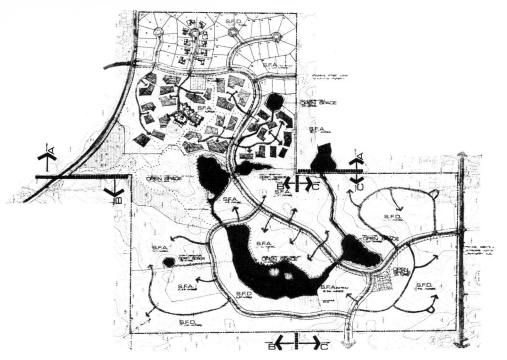

2-12   A concept plan showing the major proposal, including land uses, cluster entry locations, streets, and open space.

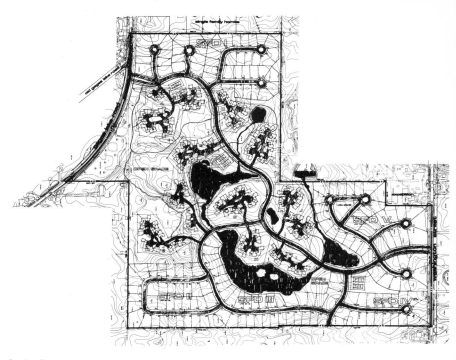

2-13   Preliminary design: a more detailed layout of buildings, streets, and open space.

2-14   Preliminary design: typical cluster layouts and building configurations.

development plans and in turn allows the completion of quite preliminary cost estimates based upon current unit costs. Preliminaries may include price ranges per square foot of townhouse or condominium, unit costs for roads, sewers, water lines, sidewalks, etc. Investigation of the cost and availability of construction materials should begin during this phase.

With the gradual refining of design into specific plans, financing packages may begin to be researched; initial appraisals may be made. When initial commitments for construction financing and/or long-term mortgages are obtained, final selection of the townhouse block or condominium building that will be the model center marks the beginning of the final design phase.

Final townhouse or condominium design re-volves around the preparation of construction drawings and specifications, the most com-plex and carefully prepared documents of the entire design sequence. Work on the final design documents normally represents 50 to 60 percent of the total design budget. De-pending upon project size and the repetition of building plans, the developer may estab-lish a design budget through a number of methods—a percentage of construction costs, a lump sum figure, or an hourly rate times a multiplier for overhead and ex-penses. The final design documents and specifications are used for final bidding, ob-taining building permits, and construction.

Government

Government reviews play a significant role in determining the livability of a townhouse/ condominium community, either encourag-ing or restricting good design. The best gov-ernment reviews recognize design as a gradually growing, complex process, best dealt with in stages—from concept design through final detail plans. As the developer's team has a leader, similarly, the government review team should also have a leader. Often it is helpful if there is a knowledgeable con-temporary planning person on the city plan-ning staff, a person who understands the total development and is able to weigh the merits of the various city staff comments. This person may help to achieve more rapid processing and approvals within the existing regulatory framework without compromising creative design.

Planning Staff Concept

The planning staff concept review meeting should reacquaint the various members of the development team with the development plan. Advice and recommendations given should be weighed for their potential of im-proving the plan. It is at this meeting that the choices between private roads or city roads, community association maintenance or city park dedications, and other developer/gov-ernment prerogatives may be discussed. The development team should learn more of the specifics of the required government ap-provals and the various local groups that, for one reason or another, wish to influence the project plan design. The developer and de-sign team may encourage visits by various municipal officials to representative projects in the area; this may be very effective in con-veying the proposed project's image and character, particularly if approvals are re-quired before the appropriate design stage has been reached.

There are probably as many opinions about how to present a townhouse/condominium plan to local community groups as there are plans themselves. Anyone familiar with the plight of a design subjected to committee planning (government or corporate) knows that it is better first to formulate what seems to be the best solution. Recommendations and considerations may then be tested against the program criteria that developed the plan. Community input, however, may re-ally help a design. Frequently, residents of a site's locale may be able to provide informa-tion that the market survey or land analysis has missed. For instance, an existing resi-dent may point out that a 50-year flood is reached just about every spring because the storm sewer inlet inevitably plugs with debris—this type of information cannot be found on the best topography plans.

Information should be presented to in-terested existing residents of a community and other community groups on an informal basis or in a public hearing. During these meetings, two objectives should be ac-complished: (1) to show local residents the commitment of the developer to plan, de-sign, and build the best development possi-ble under the existing market and regulatory conditions; and (2) to gather data with the genuine intention of incorporating valid comments or criticisms into the plan. Par-ticipating community groups should begin to recognize the credibility of a design gener-ated by valid market, land, and livability criteria. Occasionally, citizen groups that were originally organized to oppose an en-croachment into their community will mature into positive influence groups that will sup-port a well-designed development.

Concept Plan Approval

Townhouse/condominium approvals gener-ally come under the heading of multi-family, planned unit development, or similar de-velopment procedures. In this context, initial approvals must be a resolution of good faith by the local government, must stipulate a total density, and are normally conditional, based upon the project's character. The de-veloper, bound then by the constraints of the general concept plan, has the necessary assurance to begin the complex and costly process of more detailed design, development, and construction.

After possible revisions of the concept plan, the planning staff normally will make a review and recommendation to a planning board or commission. The planning staff's primary role is to evaluate the quality of the proposed plan according to reasonable standards of design and to study the relationship to the municipal infrastructure. The planning commission's review normally takes at least two meetings. Care should be given to assure viewing of the overall concept—not the specific details. Here again, the need for design evaluation criteria is obvious.

Final concept plan approval usually comes from an elected local administrative body, a city council, town board, or county commission. With the final concept approval guaranteeing a specific density land use, and, therefore, a basis for development financing, the developer is in a position to commit the time and money to the preliminary design of the first phase townhouse/condominium clusters noted on the concept plan.

Preliminary Design

A number of decisions must be made during or prior to the preparation of a preliminary design. The design team must arrive at mutually agreeable standards and specifications with the various government departments and agencies involved in the development process. The items to be agreed upon may include: right-of-way dimensions, street widths, turnaround diameters, horizontal and vertical road curve requirements, street gradients, street drainage sections, standard or mountable curbs versus no curbs at all, sidewalk requirements, storm sewer and sanitary sewer sizing. Meetings must also be held with maintenance, street, park, and fire officials to discuss their specific requirements. It is not unusual, however, for the developer, the design team, and possibly even the staff planners to disagree with these local departments. Properly, it is up to the planning or administrative body to arbitrate and decide which solutions are best from an overall standpoint.

At this stage of the design process the reviewers of a proposed development should strive to understand the factors and program that produced the design. Preliminary staff review should aid the developer and the design team in filling in any omissions in the presentation package. Often, this evaluation is forwarded to the administrative body and planning commission.

Many potential conflicts may be resolved ahead of the planning commission review meeting. If differences have developed, this is the time for various proponents to be heard. Commonly appointed as an independent evaluative body, the planning commission must be aware of improved design and land planning techniques. At this preliminary design stage, advocacy of improved livability may make or break a well-designed townhouse or condominium development. Ideally, these reviewers will hold a similar concern for people's safety, privacy, security, purchasing capabilities, and other factors so vital to the success of a townhouse/condominium community.

With the forwarding of the planning commission review and the approval by the administrative body, detailed construction documents may be started. Because these final documents require so much time, effort, and funds, the more factors and design parameters that are settled at a preliminary or concept stage, the less the chance for expensive delays and revisions. Both the developer and the governmental reviewer should have the ultimate goal of attempting to keep home costs as low as possible. This, of course, is assisted by an expeditious and flexible approval process and an awareness of cost-effective site planning architectural and engineering design.

FOOTING AND
FOUNDATION PLAN

2-15   Townhouse block foundation and upper level plans are part of typical final design/construction documents. (Figure continued on the next page.)

21

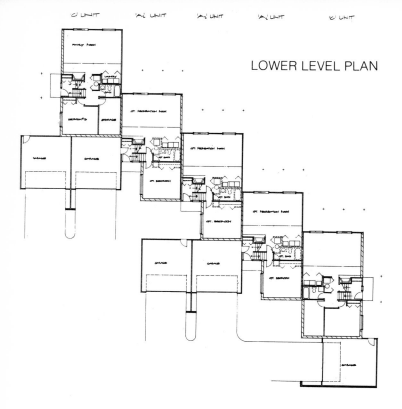

LOWER LEVEL PLAN

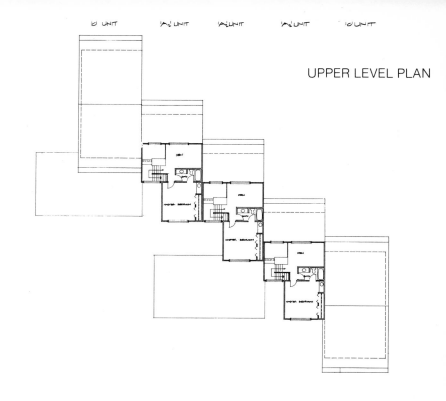

UPPER LEVEL PLAN

2-15   Figure continued from the previous page.

MAIN LEVEL PLAN

Construction Documents

The architects, landscape architects, and engineers working on the final designs, specifications, and material selections must know under which building code the townhouse/condominium project will be reviewed. While the requirements between various building codes are similar, the disparities between them are significant enough to cause potentially long and costly delays in approvals from both government lending institutions and local building inspectors. The development team should know the submission requirements and schedules of the various lending agencies and public administrative departments.

Approval of the final plats and drawings normally comes from the local administrative body or staff and amounts to a check to assure that the final plans are in conformance with the concept and preliminary representations.

Design During Construction

Townhouse/condominium development is sufficiently complicated to require a team for design. Even with the combined expertise of a design team, during construction there will still be unforeseen difficulties and opportunities for better design solutions appearing. As construction details apply to each townhouse or condominium unit, refining even a single detail may multiply into significant savings for a development.

If properly combined, the site design drawings may serve a construction coordination function. A composite site plan of the development drawn at a scale of 1 inch to 20 feet should show virtually all improvements, including area landscaping and sprinkler system, on a single sheet. It is drawn after all other plans have been approved for construction. The purpose of this plan is to check for any design conflicts or encroachments. It has many practical uses in the field as site work progresses. The combined or composite plan should show:

- all building locations, including expansion area, if any;
- swimming pool, playground equipment, fences, lighting, and walks;
- sanitary sewer, water, storm sewer, electric, gas, and telephone lines;
- carport or garage footings and foundations;
- paving, curbs, and gutters;
- lot numbers and street addresses; and
- finished floor elevations.

When completed, the composite should be used by the field superintendent, subcontractors, material suppliers, and deliverymen as follows:

- to mark locations for temporary buildings and material stockpiles;
- to indicate job progress (work completed and scheduled);
- to instruct deliverymen; and
- to check field improvements or changes during construction.

With such a complete drawing, previously undetected design conflicts may be resolved, thus avoiding costly delays during the development and construction period.

3 Program Determinants

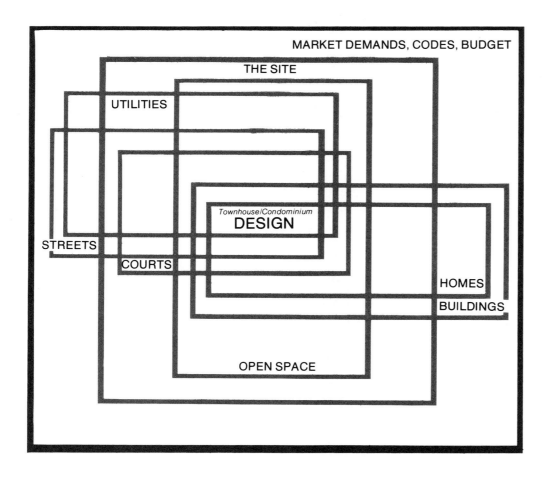

MARKET DEMANDS, CODES, BUDGET

THE SITE

UTILITIES

STREETS

Townhouse/Condominium
DESIGN

COURTS

HOMES

BUILDINGS

OPEN SPACE

3-1   Finding the design solution by combining and overlapping the pieces.

Townhouse/condominium success depends on the accuracy and the acquisition at the proper time of design determinants in the development process. Such an approach holds down research and design costs and encourages solution finding through a gradual process, moving from the general (concept planning stage) to the specific (preliminary to final design stages). It may be a costly error for a developer to gather too much information or too detailed design solutions too early in the development process.

The nature of the planning and design program will determine the livability, marketability, and profitability of a townhouse or condominium development. In addition to such standard program determinants as price range, number of bedrooms, unit square footage, and the unit count and mix, there are many other equally strict limits to planning, such as site boundaries, easements, setbacks, and road widths. The townhouse/condominium development program is then actually a complete list of guidelines, limits, and performance requirements. Naturally, the plan that best fulfills the greatest number of program requirements constitutes the best design.

It is far easier to compile, research, and modify a comprehensive listing of all the design limits and aspirations for a project than it is to revise a set of final working drawings or, worse yet, a cluster of unsold units later on. An organized list of program determinants is a scorecard for designers, a method of evaluating how well their plans and designs will meet the developer's designs. Without a detailed program in mind, the scope of the design task and contractual obligations becomes a hit and miss, hard-to-qualify project.

The criteria for livability form the basis for a specific developer/design team list of program determinants. A large amount of livability input is derived at the beginning of a project . . . the concept stage of design. As the planning and public approval processes often take months, careful attention must be given to keeping the program current with changing conditions. For instance, the anticipated buyers may lose their ability to obtain mortgages by the time final construction drawings are completed and building permits given, which may necessitate a price restructuring and perhaps a redesign.

Figure 3-2 shows many of the basic program elements which affect the planning and design process. It lists the kind of information necessary for each involved sector during the various phases of townhouse/condominium design. Notice that the market research and site acquisition stages precede the three design phases.

3-2 Basic Program Elements for Planning and Design

| program sources | Project Phase | | | | |
	market research	find; acquire site	concept planning & design	preliminary planning & design	final construction, design, market
THE MARKET (buyer demands)	• income ranges • growth sectors • target market • absorption rates • capture estimates	• prominent natural features with market appeal	• ownership preferences • purchase capabilities • reassess capture ratio • scale of building • unit sq. footage • price range • number of bedrooms	• is market information still valid? • refine buyer profiles • refine unit mix to price range	• is market information still valid? • market response to evaluation of first phase • advertising; marketing program
THE LAND (physiographics)	• market appeal of location	• site problems • approximate boundaries • covenants & deed restrictions • easements • site positives	• U.S.G.S. topo base-10' interval, interpolate 5' or 2' intervals • county soil survey • aerial photo • traffic inventory • peripheral land use • adjacent utilities • water features • geology; preliminary soundings • plat map	• tree surveys • accurate water table calculations • 1' or 2' contour interval topo • soil borings • detail rock soundings • boundary survey	• later phase soil tests
THE DEVELOPMENT TEAM	• commitment to develop townhouses or condominiums	• site inspection • buildable land use schematics • checklist	• scale and number of units • product types • rough development costs • amenities • phasing	• costs of homes • development and home cost estimates • financing availability • model center location • unit design, bldg design • preliminary community association documents • detailed road plan • detailed phase one development plan	• final costs & budgets • financing & mortgage package • sales program • phase 2; etc. plans, reviews, adjustments • contract plans & specs
THE GOVERNMENT	• other projects on record for development permits issued	• ordinances/density • political/design climate • utilities, services	• specific ordinances & requirements • services, capacity, extensions • codes	• engineering requirement • existing utility plans & profiles • density constraints; requirements	• bldg codes • inspections • engineering, energy specifications

Market Awareness and Research

The developer's decision to build townhouses or condominiums may originate as an experienced hunch—a mental summation of the economic trends, building activity, and desires within a specific market area. To validate market awareness, the developer must make an approximation of the market sector and the current competition within the sector. Transportation, employment, and development patterns, along with housing types and locations in greatest demand, should be studied with the results illustrated on a market area map. This information is necessary both for making the commitment to develop townhouses or condominiums and finding the best site.

Readily available information is usually adequate for identifying the growth sector in a community. Properly, market research helps in selecting the site; detailed research should continue after the site has been found and before option contingencies are removed. This market data, coupled with design graphics, may be used for informal presentations to lending institutions and governmental approval bodies.

Market research should take two forms: an investigation of the activity within the local site and market sector and a study into longer-term indicators of continued market strength. Market information that may be quickly and economically compiled may come from several sources:

- local competition,
- building permit information,
- multiple listing service sales statistics,
- discussions with the lenders, builders, developers, and realtors, or
- census data.

As developers are the first to state that townhouse and condominium development is a competitive business, they should know the competition's product, prices, and quality. Since price rises change the value of existing homes and what the buyer can afford, it is important to know *when* the competition built their homes. Home prices may rise significantly as additional phases of a single development are completed.

The methods of surveying the competitions' products may be pretty simple, since examples may be well displayed in merchandising centers or under construction. Getting an overall picture of the total housing supply for an entire market area is a much more complex job. For new housing, this may be gained by comparing the number of building permits to new occupancy permits, utility hookups, or service billings. These numbers will show the difference between the "actually sold" and "sold" stickers on a competitor's sales plat. These statistics should permit the developer to estimate the market absorption rate. A developer must then judge what part of this absorption rate may be captured. In a moderate-sized metropolitan area, it is possible for an established developer with a good reputation and a variety of housing types to capture over 25 percent of sales in a market area. Most builders, however, say that capturing 2.5 percent of a major metropolitan area is an ambitious program.

In market areas where the Board of Realtors has a multiple listing service, statistics are usually available that show home sale prices by geographic sections, the percent of listings sold, and the length of time it took for the listings to sell. This data is an excellent indicator of market activity in a given community or growth sector.

Another indicator of potential housing demand is census data and the projected population growth within the market area. However, do not apply national or state trends to local conditions; the latter have a habit of changing just at the wrong time or perhaps they never followed the general trends to begin with. Housing demand comes from local markets, whereas national trends are based on averages of numerous market areas—many of them significantly different from the target market.

Longer-term indicators such as the vitality of employment and industry in the area may be researched through utility companies, employment agencies, the Chamber of Commerce, and other civic groups. The type of employment that is available will tell a lot about the price and type of townhouse or condominium that should be designed and built or if they should be built at all. Consumer surveys indicate that townhouses and condominiums have been a primarily white collar housing solution catering to the "empty nester," professional couples, and single buyers.

The number of households and their makeup tells even more about the form of housing that might be desired or acceptable. People of different ages and lifestyles demand different housing forms and floor plans. Knowing the income ranges of these groups adds to the potential of providing the right product for the market's purchasing capabilities. Single households, increases in female employment, and acceptance of two incomes for mortgage qualification by lending institutions, indirectly increase housing demand by raising the income level of families. These factors are longer-term indicators of potential housing demand.

Although market research indicates the needs and capabilities of homebuyers within the market area, it is not a working drawing for development. Limited by its very nature, it may only provide information about *past* solutions. Using successful competitors' designs is an excellent place from which to start in terms of testing new market data and site constraints. Exact copying with minor changes, however, will automatically put the product, once constructed, 3 to 6 months behind the competitor's newly refined home designs. The rule is to study a design concept, but make it better by innovation. It is properly the role of the creative individuals involved in the land development process to understand and apply the implications gleaned from market research, along with other equally important livability design parameters.

Site Acquisition

The selection of townhouse or condominium land is as important as any other program or design determinant. Primarily, the site's size and cost must fit the financial and management capabilities of the developer. Secondly, the land's shape, surroundings, and features must be able to complement townhouse/condominium building configurations.

Specific information must be gathered on each potential site to permit a comparative analysis and evaluation of a number of different sites. Figure 3-3 shows a list of some of the common factors to be considered in buying land for townhouses and condominiums.

Location

Once marketing research has helped to determine the price range, home, and structure type, the general location selected for the site is perhaps the key factor to its success. The presence of schools, shopping facilities, and residential homes of quality may help to decide the establishment of new housing in different cost brackets. The higher the true value of the land (not artificially inflated by underlying zoning) the greater the potential for townhouse/condominium success. Construction of townhouses or condominiums makes the most sense when an economic advantage is gained by dividing a $30,000 per acre cost by eight townhouses or fifteen

3-4 (above) and 3-5 (below) Townhouses and condominiums are well suited for high amenity sites. This water-oriented development consolidated dock design and reduced disturbance of slopes and vegetation, improving the visual quality of the lakeshore. Careful building and site design enables more homes to enjoy the water views.

3-3

Townhouse/Condominium Land Buying Checklist

- ☐ Location, access
- ☐ Owner
- ☐ Price, conditions, terms
- ☐ Legal description and plat
- ☐ Gross area, net buildable area
- ☐ Frontage
- ☐ Improvements
- ☐ Current income
- ☐ Ordinance and code restrictions
- ☐ Attorneys and appraisers fees
- ☐ Type of title
- ☐ Natural site features with market appeal
- ☐ Relationship to off-site features
- ☐ Type of listing and commission due

- ☐ Price per lot, per acre, per front foot
- ☐ Liens, taxes, assessments
- ☐ Utilities—location, availability, and hookup charges
- ☐ Easements
- ☐ Protective covenants
- ☐ Lot sizes, density, setbacks, rights-of-way
- ☐ City, county, state, metropolitan, national regulations
- ☐ Community facilities
- ☐ On-site structures for potential use
- ☐ Features of archeological or historical significance

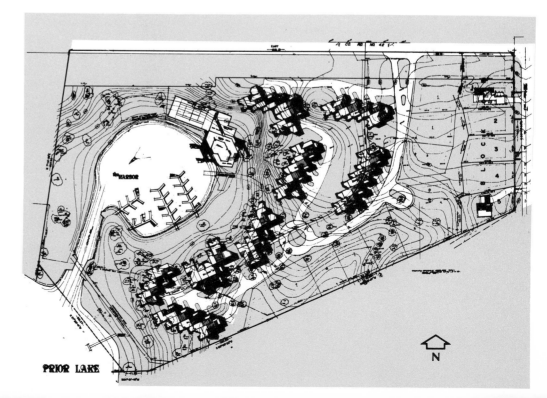

PRIOR LAKE

N

condominiums instead of four single-family detached homes. However, development risks are greatly multiplied by attempting to challenge existing strict zones of a differing residential type. In many communities across the country, buyers are still most used to conventional detached housing and will accept a townhouse/condominium development only in a high amenity-oriented location; i.e., lakeside, riverside, with excellent views, and so on.

Savings on common wall construction cannot offset the disadvantages of a bad site. A good location is best even though the land may be expensive. Unfortunately, in some areas the most desirable land is not available due to the classical zoning map approach of placing multi-family housing as a buffer between a highway and single-family detached communities. Ironically, this outdated zoning approach places the most people in the most undesirable locations and fewer people (living in detached homes) closer to natural amenities and open space. An ideal townhouse/condominium site should be close to natural amenities and buffered from the noise, pollution, and danger of highways and high volume roads. The typical location for much townhouse and condominium development has been on separate parcels in the suburbs. Urban infill land and sites within larger developments are alternative locations for this kind of development.

Infill Sites. The impact of higher energy costs on homebuyers plays a significant role in assembling a complete development pro-gram. Land that has been previously by-passed is now seen in many cases as preferable to suburban or exurban locations. Close-in sites are becoming valuable as much for economic reasons as they are for convenience factors.

The flexibility of townhouse and condominium design permits clustering, resulting in the reduction of total land coverage. This allows building on a smaller site with unique features, normally thought to have poor development potential for single-family detached homes. Frequently, the very reasons a site was bypassed for detached housing (steep slopes, narrow buildable area, varied shape) may make it attractive for townhouse or condominium construction.

For the established community, the opportunity to offer more varied housing choices to its residents is an asset. Providing new housing for older neighborhood residents may free the existing, often more moderately priced older homes for growing families, when older couples desire the differing lifestyle of a new townhouse or condominium. Development on infill sites also reinforces the existing commercial and retail activity, promoting new vitality and diversity and reversing the stagnation of commercial enterprise. Often, the infill of a new project will signal the restoration and revaluation of a declining community, a cornerstone of a sound tax base. For the developer, infill sites normally offer a ready-made market from existing residents and friends, meaning reduced marketing costs and a shortened sellout period. The existing infrastructure

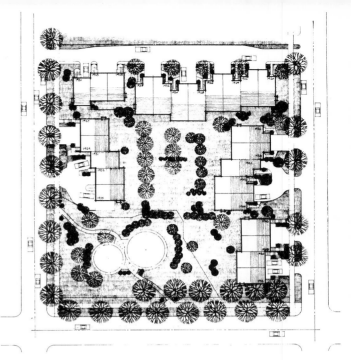

3-6   This former elementary school site is an example of an infill site that presented an opportunity to the developer and the community. Designed with the cooperation of the neighborhood, an area of extreme topographic change was dedicated as a small, public park. Marketing virtually took care of itself in this central city development.

3-7   Close-in condominium communities may draw the majority of buyers from former homeowners who desire to stay in the area.

Edmund C. Flynn

provides services without a land development time delay, ultimately resulting in lower front-end and interest expenses.

Unfortunately, an infill site may pose one or more problems. The site's smaller size may limit the design flexibility normally possible on a larger parcel of land. The site may, of necessity, be located near detracting features and uses, have poor soils, or a high price. Existing residents may be sceptical of new development, or government controls may be inflexible. In some cases, a built-up municipality may not be accustomed to reviewing the more creative type of development, or may not have the ordinances that permit the vital flexibility. Therefore, ordinance changes or variances may be required. To counterbalance difficulties, imaginative and accommodating planning and design solutions are required. In fact, having to design around a number of constraints may result in a more interesting development.

The Larger-Scale Community. A developer may set his sights on a larger-scale project of three hundred acres or more. Assembly of a large section of land will permit the control of the new neighborhood's surrounding environment simply by making it a part of the project. This is normally done most economically by acquiring options on land anticipated for inclusion in a development. Each parcel is then purchased as it is needed.

In many states, larger-scale communities are developed by entities that rely on builders to purchase parcels of land on which to construct homes. The smaller sites sold to the builders are served by an overall infrastructure of roads, utilities, and amenities installed at the front end, usually by a large development company. The small, low-volume builder may then capitalize on the marketing advantages and reduced risk of a smaller site within a larger development.

Site Services and Restrictions

Knowledge of streets, highways, and mass transportation routes plays a key role in selecting a proper townhouse/condominium site. If traffic congestion is a possible problem, more detailed investigation of traffic capacities (as discussed in the Site Inventory section) should be completed. Zoning, public relations, and marketing difficulties may be avoided by acquiring an accessible site that does not substantially change the existing traffic patterns.

3-8   A modern solution in a traditional neighborhood.

In most cases, the availability of utilities is fundamental to beginning a plan and design for townhouses and condominiums. In land acquisition, the availability of utility services once a project is begun should be guaranteed. Because the current emphasis of sanitary sewage treatment and processing is on centralized systems, service extensions are crucial to site selection. Municipal policies toward providing services must be known. Higher prices and political pressures have made the smaller-scale, individual sewage treatment or storage and disposal systems a cost-effective replacement for the complicated and costly centralized systems. Very large developments may have an internal treatment system to provide the assurance of available services for a long-term build-out period.

Capacities of utilities that bypass or cross a site should be known as well as the easements and rights-of-way provided for them. Other restrictive or protective covenants should be carefully researched prior to the commitment to option or gain control of a piece of land.

Because the type and administration of land use regulations are pivotal to even beginning a townhouse or condominium project, the political climate governing design of a parcel of land must be appraised before purchase. Specifically, the developer must understand the approval procedures. Is there a PUD or similar provision for the land? Are the existing ordinances free of rigid, outdated regulations? Are there organized community groups with a record of opposi-

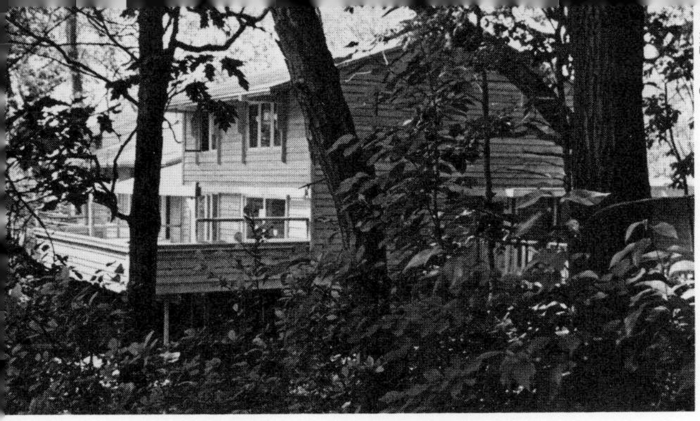

Gary Elliott

3-9 A site with existing trees provides a finished-looking environment which may improve the sales pace.

tion to or support for townhouse/condominium development in the area?

Development Potential

The development potential of a piece of land should be determined in a preliminary land inventory. This abbreviated (less costly) land inventory, analysis, and evaluation is commonly all that is necessary at the land shopping stage. Natural restrictions and constraints to development are the emphasis of this part of the selection process. The principle areas of this general inventory and analysis should focus on anticipated problems with soils, hydrology, geology, and vegetation. The obvious goal is to avoid extremely high development costs later on by uncovering normally unforeseen problems, such as the need for special footings and foundations on low-bearing strength soils. While townhouse/condominium construction may adapt to many site constraints, an understanding of the building capabilities and limitations of the land should be assessed here. The preliminary land inventory should also note high-quality plant material on a site, locating major tree groupings or shrub clumps with amenity value for preservation.

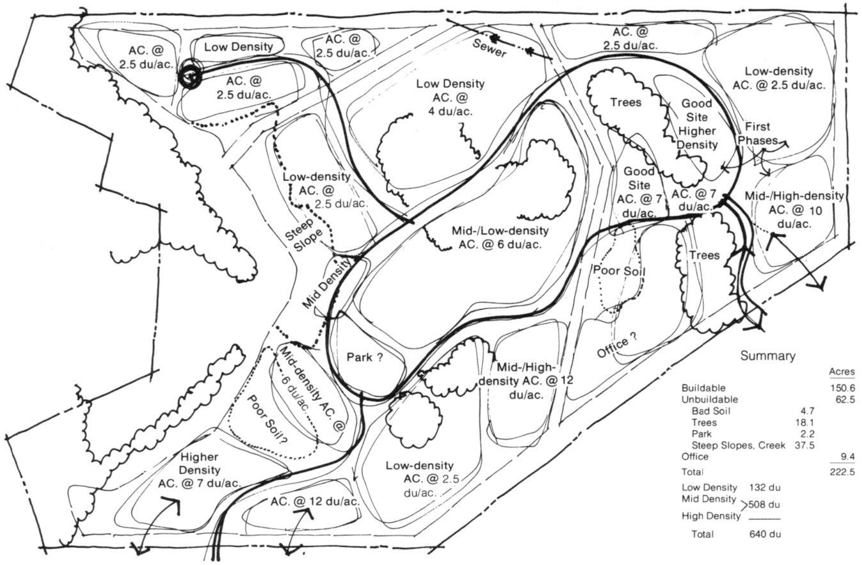

3-10 Schematic plan studies provide information on the buildable area and achievable density.

Schematic Planning

The aggregate of the aforementioned investigations should combine graphically in preliminary land use schematics. The experienced developer enlists design input at this early stage to estimate the actual developable land on the parcel under consideration. For even a small site, purchasing one week of a land planner's time for the purpose of preliminary land use schematics is inexpensive compared to the potential of wasted option dollars or the interest costs incurred while carrying land later found unsuitable for townhouse/condominium construction.

Loose sketches should provide density estimates based upon some casual evaluations of the site features and constraints. Site planners must draw upon experience gained from proven projects in assembling even these loose plans. The plans should be at a scale of 100 feet or 200 feet to the inch for sites of under 100 acres. For sites over 100 acres, a scale of 1 inch equals 200 feet or 400 feet is appropriate. Any larger scale (1 inch equals 50 feet, 40 feet, 20 feet) is likely to require additional expense in unneeded detail. The only elements that need be shown are possible major vehicular circulation routes and buildable land areas. Rough area calculations multiplied by expected marketable densities should yield an estimate of total units.

When the preliminary land use schematics are completed, a decision to seek control of a site may be made. Option periods should allow adequate time for detailed market studies (three to eight weeks), the first phase design (three to ten weeks), and government approvals (eight weeks or more). The partial release clauses of the land purchase contract should be made to coincide with the land use schematic's phasing plans. Open space requirements and the size of the initial community association will influence the phasing plan and release clauses.

Site Inventory

Following site acquisition, a more thorough assessment of the site is necessary before beginning more detailed design. The more complete the information, the more explicit the program, the better the design. The more factors that are inventoried and understood, the more likely the final design will recognize positive factors and neutralize potential problems or even turn them into assets. The inventory may also serve as an excellent generator of community group comments and input while graphically validating the quality of a plan.

Inventory drawings should be at a scale large enough to be usable in preliminary concept plan layout and in public presentations. The use of these drawings communicates developer concern for a proper design process. It not only yields a better design plan, but demonstrates the basis for decisions that might otherwise be called arbitrary. For instance, the reason for a particular road placement would not be so obvious were it not for the graphic display showing bad soils flanking the road on one side and a large oak tree and bedrock on the other.

While much information may be gained, interpreted, and evaluated on paper or second-hand, there is no substitute for actually see-ing these abstractions and symbols on the site. Having a complete mental image of the actual site features is a crucial part of the design process, even at this early stage. Many parts of a site plan may be determined by inventorying a site's natural features. The more subtle aspects, like concealed shallow rock formations or leachable sand deposits in clay, are as important to the developer as knowing utility hookup locations.

The "nuts and bolts" of assembling a site inventory and evaluation begin with building on the general data and experience used in land purchase decisions. As shown by the program checklist (Figure 3-2), extremely detailed site information may not be necessary at the concept design stage.

A site's boundaries are available on plat maps filed with the city or county or may be approximated from property descriptions. While these drawings are generally not 100 percent accurate, they are appropriate to this level of planning and design. Once acquired, they should be enlarged to the same scale as the other site inventory drawings so that all elements may be combined in transparent overlays, helping to guide the planning process.

Land Use Regulations

A comprehensive job of site evaluation incorporates existing governmental controls. Since it is not unusual to find land particularly suited for townhouse or condominium construction zoned exclusively for single-family detached homes, the type and flexibility of land use regulations are major program determinants. For instance, to know that the typical setback regulation of 20 to 35 feet does not apply to private court roads or that the distance requirements between buildings need not be more than 10 feet is important.

Before beginning design, required road rights-of-way (typically 40, 50, or 60 feet) and paving width requirements (commonly 20 to 36 feet) must be known. Cul-de-sac lengths, diameters, property line and dedicated road setbacks, density or land use intensity requirements, first floor area minimums, if any, park or open space areas and percentages, water, sanitary, and storm sewer standards are some of the other specifications that must be evaluated in terms of townhouse/condominium construction. The various land delineations, such as commercial, business, watershed easements, property line setbacks, through-road setbacks, etc., should

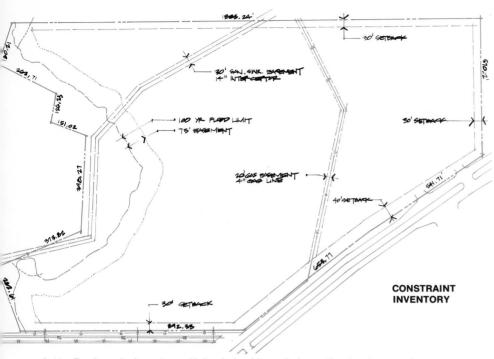

CONSTRAINT INVENTORY

3-11 Begin a site inventory with basic land boundaries noting legal constraints.

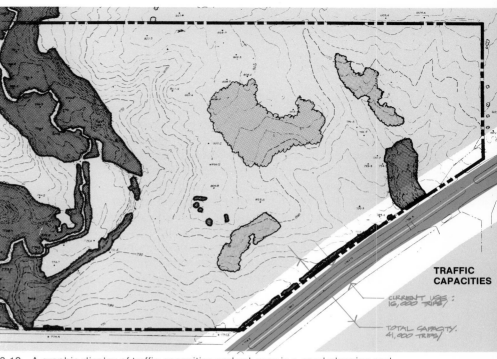

TRAFFIC CAPACITIES

CURRENT USE: 16,000 TRIPS/

TOTAL CAPACITY: 41,000 TRIPS/

3-12 A graphic display of traffic capacities and volumes is a good planning and presentation tool. The relative widths of the lanes read as a bar chart of current traffic and available traffic capacity.

be shown on the site inventory base at the outset and may be used as a separate exhibit in presentations.

Adjacent Uses

It is preferable for the townhouse/condominium site to be adjacent to open space systems, cultural facilities, and other features that offer direct benefits to future residents. A certain amount of value may also accrue to a site by being adjacent to a well-designed single-family residential area. On the other hand, adverse off-site influences should be recognized for their negative impact on a site.

Proximity to private or municipal recreation facilities should be considered for its value. While it is redundant and sometimes a waste of amenity dollars to duplicate facilities, overused nearby municipal tennis courts (for example) may suggest the inclusion of on-site tennis facilities for residents. Where appropriate, provision for pedestrian and/or vehicular connections to off-site facilities should be made.

The general idea is then to spread the value of compatible off-site uses within a site and to buffer, turn the project's back on, or screen incompatible influences or uses. The site analysis plan should serve as a note pad for the potential impacts of such considerations.

Traffic Analysis

When the number of people to be housed upon a given site increases, adequate access becomes important. The first step is to accumulate data giving an accurate picture of the average daily trips on peripheral site roads. Additional information about peak traffic loading of short duration and high volume is particularly important in intersection design. A graphic presentation comparing the current use of these peripheral roads to the total carrying capacity of the highways will yield an accurate picture of a site's eventual impact on the peripheral transportation systems.

The anticipated traffic from a higher density development is a common negative zoning argument. However, "The number of vehicle-trips per person is almost independent of density or size of dwelling units. Thus, traffic generation varies directly with the number of persons living within a particular unit of area. Although the number of vehicle-trips per person tends to remain fairly constant, the number of persons per dwelling unit generally decreases in high-density housing, so that the number of vehicle-trips per dwelling unit tends to decrease with higher densities."* Figure 3-13, showing actual trip generations for various residential land uses provides one source of objective data for planning. Increased traffic is often a concern for existing residents. However, cost-effective highway or public works departments usually do not build additional lanes or roads until the vehicle per hour design capacity is exceeded.

Figure 3-13 is an interpolation and summarization of the data obtained from five principal sources: *Trip Generation by Land Use*** by the Maricopa Association of Governments, Maricopa County, Arizona; *National Cooperative Highway Research Program Report #121*; trip generation data from the *Institute of Transportation Engineers*†; the *Tenth Progress Report on Trip Ends Generation Research Count*‡ by the San Francisco District of the California Department of Transportation; and the ULI Publication, *Residential Streets*.§ The number of dwelling units covered by the various studies is impressive. The ITE and Maricopa County summaries include over 200 studies each, covering 146,500 dwelling units. Each of the references should be consulted for additional information on trip generation by vehicle and by person.

3-13

Summary of Residential Trip Generation Data			
		Trip Generation Rate (daily trips)	
Land Use	Density	Typical Range	Typical
single-family detached	1-5 du/ac.	7-13	9.5
townhouses and apartments	5-15 du/ac.	5 - 8	6.5
mid-rise and high-rise apartments	15-60 du/ac.	3 - 7	5.0

* Highway Research Board, *National Cooperative Highway Research Program Report #121* (Washington, D.C.: author, 1971) p. 32.
** Maricopa Association of Governments, *Trip Generation by Land Use* (Maricopa County, Arizona: author) pp. 3-25, 185.
† ITE Trip Generation, *Institute of Transportation Engineers,* Topics 200-270, (Arlington, Virginia: author, 1976).
‡ State of California Department of Transportation, *Tenth Progress Report on Trip Ends Generation Research Count* (San Francisco: author, 1975) pp. 1, 2, 8, 9, 11, 138-144, 153.
§ ULI, ASCE, NAHB, *Residential Streets: Objectives, Principles, and Design Considerations* (Washington, D.C.: author, 1974).

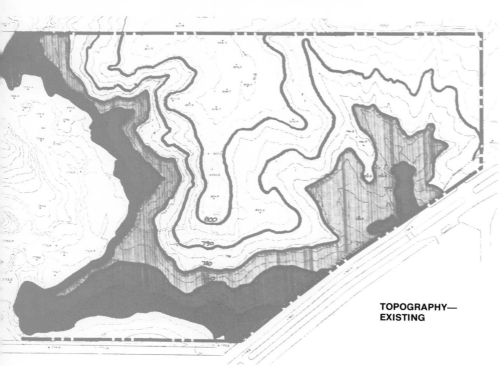

TOPOGRAPHY— EXISTING

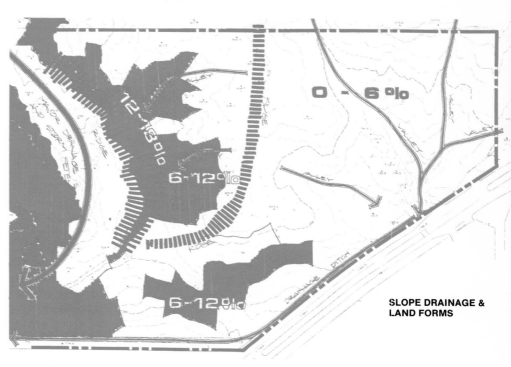

SLOPE DRAINAGE & LAND FORMS

3-14 Shading a site's topography is a graphic aid to understanding the land's limits and potentials.

3-15 Ridge lines, drainage swales, and other site planning determinants should be noted to aid in street and utility design.

This summary information for residential decision making should be used as a general guideline due to some data limitations described herein. The various summaries often include studies from the same data base, with some of the studies now becoming somewhat dated. Townhouses and condominiums are usually listed as apartments, with no differentiation made between ownership and rental. There is a geographical concentration of the trip studies, with very little information comparing suburban and urban locations. In addition, comparisons are not made with variables such as the availability of public transportation, the presence of recreational amenities within the development, length of trips, location of employment, and proximity of shopping, church, and school facilities.

Traffic rates are stated in terms of an average weekday trip per unit or an average daily trip per unit. Saturday traffic tends to be somewhat higher and Sunday traffic slightly lower than the weekday rate. When measured according to the value of the dwelling unit, higher value homes have more trips than lower value homes.

Topography

A topographic plan is basic to site analysis. A quick and inexpensive place from which to start is a United States Geologic Survey map. The USGS 7½-minute series maps (1 inch equals 2,000 feet) may have a 10-foot contour interval and are usually readily available. For the conceptual design stage,

graphic interpolation or infilling of 5-foot or 2-foot contour interval lines between the 10-foot lines may be sufficiently accurate. For later design stages, more accurate information is necessary. Many communities have 2-foot contour interval topography available, which is much better for initial planning. The topographic base, coupled with the property boundaries, acts as the underlay for slope and drainage analysis.

For preliminary and final stage planning, a local engineer or land surveyor should be retained to provide a graphically accurate, field-verified boundary survey. The 1- or 2-foot interval topography map of the site may be field verified at the time the boundary survey is made. Normally, these maps are guaranteed accurate to within 1 foot.

Utilities

A detailed study of the utilities and services information that was gained prior to site acquisition may be a major site design determinant. Sanitary and storm sewers should be inventoried and evaluated for location, elevation, easements, size, capacity, condition, and the exact center line, manholes, cleanouts, and easement widths. The water line's location, capacity, valves, and hydrants should similarly be noted on a plan, as well as storm sewer, power, gas, and telephone lines. In general, utility access to a site is not as great a constraint with townhouses or condominiums as with detached housing; services may be run in the streets or in open space with a far greater degree of flexibility.

Drainage/Surface Water

Water movement should be indicated on the slope and drainage plan, along with notations of water features and their high and low levels. The relative elevation of the water table may be noted on the plan, as well as minimum basement or finished floor grades. This is best discovered from soil borings and comparing the recent rain history to earlier weather records in order to anticipate high water table elevations. The existence of floodplain areas on a site introduces a new set of rather complex considerations; knowing the cycles and levels of both the 50-year and 100-year projected storms becomes important design data.

Soils, Geology, and Aquifers

Soil tests are costly, but failing to take at least several borings in key locations may be even more costly. Analyses of strategic locations, chosen from land use allocations in schematic plans, are relatively inexpensive to assure a workable concept plan, compared with the costs of large-scale excavations and filling later on. More borings or back-hoe digging may be required in the preliminary and final design phases.

Construction problems resulting from poor soils may be very expensive. Similar costs may result from trying to build on geologic conditions improper for townhouse or condominium construction. For instance, the existence of bedrock quite close to a site's surface may drive the price of utility installation (and the homes served) beyond what the market will bear. At the concept plan stage of design, a few strategically placed borings or seismic test soundings should establish adequate information for the preparation of plans. For detailed design, a complete grid of seismic rock soundings, yielding a geologic topography map, may be required. Efficient utility layout is simplified by being able to see the subsurface structure as a contour map. Information on soils, geology, hydrology, and topography is often available through the municipal planning office and soil conservation service.

An important physical site feature is the aquifer, a water-bearing stratum of rock, gravel, or sand. Aquifer recharge areas are points where surface water enters to eventually recharge deep well water sources. The presence of this type of hydrologic feature may call for a more detailed inventory and evaluation.

Trees and Vegetation

The existing plant material is a good indicator of a site's soil types and development capacity. For instance, cattails, willows, and other wetland trees and vegetation indicate that the land is poorly drained and normally high in organic content. Several hand-auger soil borings to verify these suspicions may save thousands of dollars. Within building sites, hand-auger soil borings may signal a need for expensive compacted fill.

The right kind of plant material in the right places, however, will enhance a site's value. Sales records indicate that a home built close to existing trees will bring a 2 percent to 10 percent lot premium over similar homes sited on open land. More importantly, this kind of vegetation will increase a townhouse's/condominium's sales pace and the probability of success.

Existing trees and shrubs should be iden-

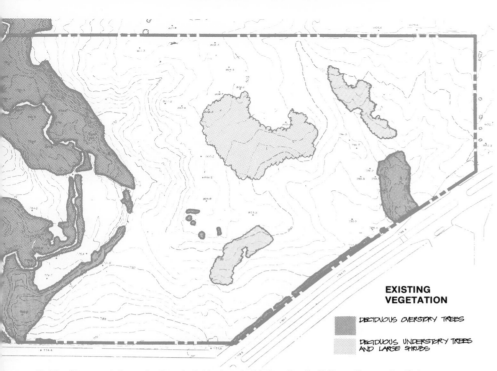

EXISTING VEGETATION

▨ DECIDUOUS OVERSTORY TREES

▨ DECIDUOUS UNDERSTORY TREES AND LARGE SHRUBS

3-16 Show existing plant material to locate high value building sites, potential parks, or open space locations, and to help clarify possible poor soil conditions.

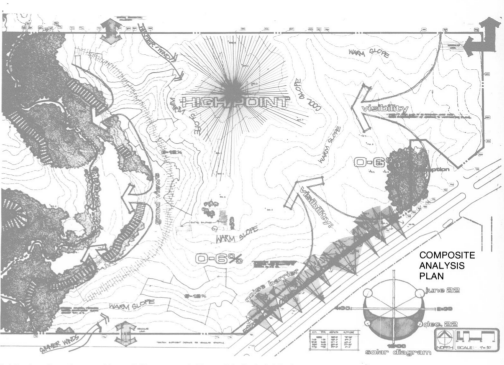

COMPOSITE ANALYSIS PLAN

3-18 In planning and in public presentations it is helpful to have a composite analysis plan noting the site features and influential plan aspects.

tified by type, or preferably by name, and evaluated for impact on the development. The basis for the plant material inventory is the topography plan that typically notes tree groupings. (See Figure 3-16.) For more detailed tree and shrub locations, a printable film or mylar transparency of the aerial photography used in generating the site's topography is invaluable. At scales of 1 inch equals 100 feet, this photograph allows accurate locating of larger individual trees and water features. At larger scales, i.e., 1 inch equals 30 feet, smaller individual trees within stands, shrubs, and other small site features become visible.

Wildlife

A side effect of the more recent open space planning concepts is the problem of interfering with as well as the potential for preserving wildlife habitats. While difficult to quantify, there is perceivable value to all in the preservation of wildlife. Although a detailed inventory of habitats and movements within a site is beyond the appropriate scope of concept plans, the presence of floodplains, marsh areas, natural grass, hedgerows, or forested sections does indicate animal habitats, and the conservation of wildlife will prove immeasurably beneficial.

3-17 Others may profit from improved residential environments.

4 Project and Site Planning

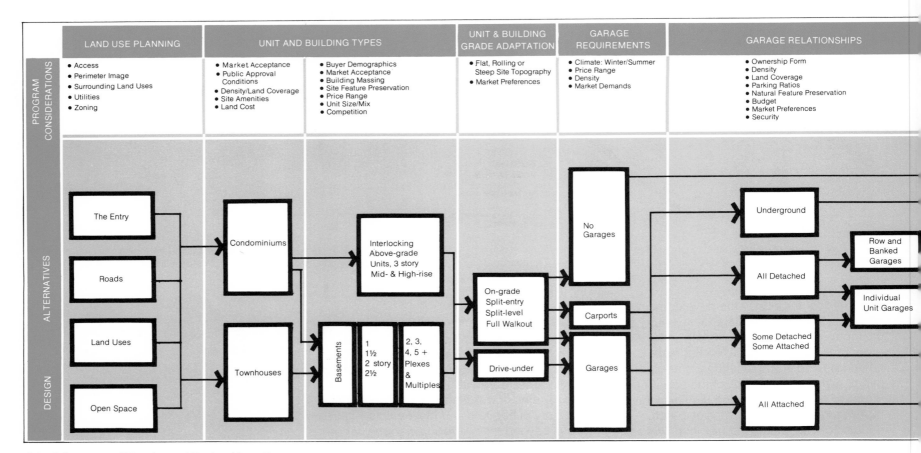

LAND USE PLANNING	UNIT AND BUILDING TYPES		UNIT & BUILDING GRADE ADAPTATION	GARAGE REQUIREMENTS	GARAGE RELATIONSHIPS
• Access • Perimeter Image • Surrounding Land Uses • Utilities • Zoning	• Market Acceptance • Public Approval Conditions • Density/Land Coverage • Site Amenities • Land Cost	• Buyer Demographics • Market Acceptance • Building Massing • Site Feature Preservation • Price Range • Unit Size/Mix • Competition	• Flat, Rolling or Steep Site Topography • Market Preferences	• Climate: Winter/Summer • Price Range • Density • Market Demands	• Ownership Form • Density • Land Coverage • Parking Ratios • Natural Feature Preservation • Budget • Market Preferences • Security

4-1   A Sequence of Planning and Design Alternatives.

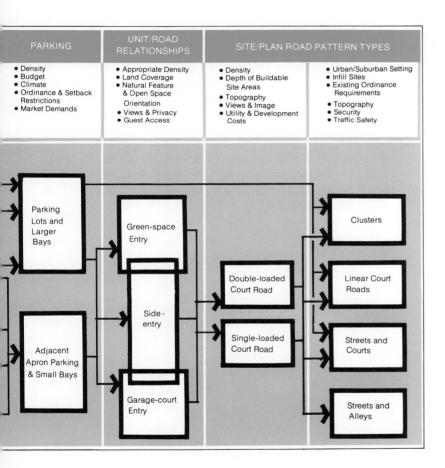

PARKING	UNIT/ROAD RELATIONSHIPS	SITE/PLAN ROAD PATTERN TYPES	
• Density • Budget • Climate • Ordinance & Setback Restrictions • Market Demands	• Appropriate Density • Land Coverage • Natural Feature & Open Space Orientation • Views & Privacy • Guest Access	• Density • Depth of Buildable Site Areas • Topography • Views & Image • Utility & Development Costs	• Urban/Suburban Setting • Infill Sites • Existing Ordinance Requirements • Topography • Security • Traffic Safety

Parking Lots and Larger Bays

Adjacent Apron Parking & Small Bays

Green-space Entry

Side-entry

Garage-court Entry

Double-loaded Court Road

Single-loaded Court Road

Clusters

Linear Court Roads

Streets and Courts

Streets and Alleys

What follows is a brief discussion of land use planning considerations which sets forth the design principles necessary to allocate proper uses and circulation within a parcel of land for townhouse/condominium phased development. Primary questions that heavily influence the final planning and design solution are:

- what are raw land costs;
- what density yields are achievable;
- what ownership form is necessary and marketable,
- what are basic home floor-plan types, interior, and construction requirements;
- how important are garages; and
- if garages are necessary, must they be attached?

Figure 4-1 shows design alternatives that may typically satisfy various market, site, cost, aesthetic, or amenity program requirements. The central elements of the design process—project and site planning (handled in this chapter), building site design (handled in Chapter 5), and building design (handled in Chapter 6)—are integrated and viewed here in the context of the design alternatives chart.

Land Uses

Following the formation of the design program, in which market, site, and governmental limits upon development are identified, land use planning for the townhouse/condominium site may begin. In preparing a preliminary concept site plan, basic land use designations must be indicated. These uses are determined by the approach the development team has taken relative to existing land use controls. The concept site plan should show major and minor road locations and begin to suggest a *graduated* use or hierarchical road system separating various land uses. After settling on the land use types for a site, concept planners can move toward several solutions—applying the developer's various program requirements to different areas within the site. In many cases, new projects are a considerable improvement over older developments because of new materials and greater environmental design sensitivity.

On a small site, concept planning may proceed all the way to complete construction drawings. On larger sites, where phasing is necessary, the concept site plan will divide parcels of land into logical zones for first and later phases of construction. In either case, an experienced developer will have planners build from the schematics that led him to buy the land in the first place.

Concept drawings should be a small enough scale to discourage extremely detailed and expensive considerations. Furthermore, since these concept plans should be an outgrowth of site analysis, the ability to overlay preliminary sketches cuts design time and expenses and easily communicates the reasoning behind the planning. Therefore, concept plan sketches should be of the same scale: usually 1 inch equals 50 feet for projects of less than 50 acres, 1 inch equals 100 feet for projects of 50 to 200 acres, or 1 inch equals 200 feet for projects of over 200 acres.

4-2   Ridgeway Center (Memphis, TN): A mixture of uses based on proximity to a highway, high value/low amenity land, and protected interior property.

Mixed Land Uses

Today's approach of mixing land uses and building types on a single piece of property is, in a way, the rebirth of the older, more energy-efficient, socially interactive town environment. Good planning provides for more than one type of land use within a community or development. This adds to functional convenience, character, and identity, and may involve mixing single-family detached homes or commercial/institutional uses with townhouses and condominiums. Some early planned unit development (PUD) ordinances permitted locating commercial facilities exclusively for the benefit of the residents within large, high-density development. This usually is an economically unworkable concept. Commercial facilities should be located where merchants may draw from a large trade area. A mixture of shops that cater to the convenience needs of residents may make a more functional, safer community, enabling walking or bicycling to replace convenience auto trips. Energy saving is an automatic by-product. Additionally, this community asset may be very important to older persons in suburban areas, who normally must rely on a car to shop. While financial benefits are clearly present, retail and office facilities are usually included in a concept plan for architectural more than financial reasons.

In a typical suburban location, townhouses should not be used to infill higher density mid-rise or high-rise development. A small number of townhouses will be overpowered by the scale of the surrounding buildings, and prospective buyers will be concerned about loss of privacy and lack of identity. A good way of mixing land uses is to establish separate "mini-neighborhoods," with open space, courts, or parking areas as spacial dividers.

4-4 Mixing commercial and residential uses: safety, convenience, and fewer car trips.

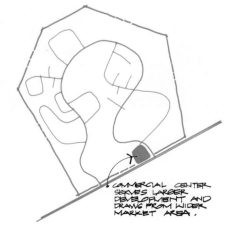

COMMERCIAL CENTER SERVES LARGER DEVELOPMENT AND DRAWS FROM WIDER MARKET AREA.

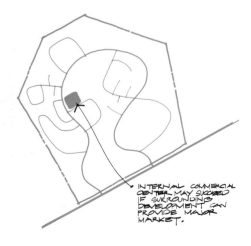

INTERNAL COMMERCIAL CENTER MAY SUCCEED IF SURROUNDING DEVELOPMENT CAN PROVIDE MAJOR MARKET.

4-3 Highway traffic enables merchants to draw from larger trade areas. Self-contained shopping areas within a new development usually have difficulty drawing people from outside the project.

41

Community Image

A community's character is partially established before a person actually enters the development. The boundary or perimeter uses give a first impression of the inside of the project. A project that complements the surrounding land blends compatible uses, while screening incompatible land uses.

The entry to the site itself from peripheral streets furthermore plays a significant role in determining one's first impression of the community. Obviously, this must be a consideration early in the site selection process. Entry roadways are discussed in detail later on in this chapter.

4-5 (above) The entry to a community should subtly express quality and openness. 4-6 (right) The use of open space in this project allows a blend with mid-rise housing without overpowering the townhouses.

Final Concept Plan

A professionally prepared, artistically rendered concept plan and supportive material also contribute to a development's image. Care should be taken to make all of the displays, graphs, plans, market analysis conclusions, off-site evaluations, and natural feature inventories as clear as possible. Public presentations may be made using 35-mm slide or overhead projectors, display boards, published booklets, or combinations of these. The concept plan presentation should be as orderly and well-thought out as the developer's actions must be during the entire design process.

In a number of concept plan review sessions, a request is made for displaying the final character of the project. As mentioned earlier, this is "putting the cart before the horse." The design process cannot work that way. Character illustrations of comparable projects may be shown, but it must be remembered that photographs of previous projects suffer from the same basic problem as market research: they demonstrate yesterday's solutions and ideas—products that were suited to yesterday's conditions. The same design principles should still apply today, but their application and the visual appearance of the product should possibly be altered to suit current needs.

Other than for the concept review session, the final concept plan and supportive materials may serve two other functions. The concept plan may be used in preliminary meetings with various lending institutions. Secondly, in many areas of the country, medium- and larger-scale projects are required to submit environmental impact statements (EIS). This is almost always true when planning with water resources. With some reshuffling of the concept site plan, it becomes usable for environmental impact statement requirements. Integration of appropriate EIS type of data directly into the planning and design process is a more constructive approach. The alternative—using EIS's as a delaying political strategy or to reflect inflexible governmental regulations—only creates additional costs that must be borne by the consumer.

Although it is sometimes convenient to publish in booklet form the market conclusions, site inventory and evaluation, and reduced-scale final concept plans, this booklet cannot replace larger-scale drawings. Usually, the larger the drawing, the better it communicates and the lesser the likelihood that misunderstandings or delays would occur. As a townhouse/condominium community is developed phase-by-phase, the detailed preliminary or final site plans may be reduced and inserted in the land use concept plan.

At an early stage, general information about roadways, open space, and utilities is shown on the plan. In order to include this information, a detailed knowledge of these elements is required. Thus, each of these elements is discussed in the following sections.

Roadways

Planning for Graduated Use

The housing growth occurring in the late 1940s and throughout the 50s focused strong political and market demands on government and developers to provide paved streets. In most cases, builders and developers answered this demand by merely extending existing city streets in a homogeneous fashion. Because the new neighborhoods were almost exclusively served by city street extensions, the municipalities controlled roadway design. Standards set by the municipalities were patterned after highway specifications, the only generally accepted road design standards at that time. Little research toward the short- and long-term cost-effectiveness of existing design standards was done. The only design modifications made were in answer to new load requirements for truck traffic and improved maintenance requirements. The impact of road standards on residential environmental quality was not even considered.

It was not until the 1960s that increased environmental sensitivity and growing cost-consciousness caused people to challenge rigidly applied road standards. Increasing site development costs, a concern for preserving the natural environment, and changing buyer demands stimulated this interest in both a site's natural features and a buyer's purchasing capabilities, resulting in new street design standards for townhouse/condominium communities. Today's best professional townhouse/condominium designs attempt to create an integrated

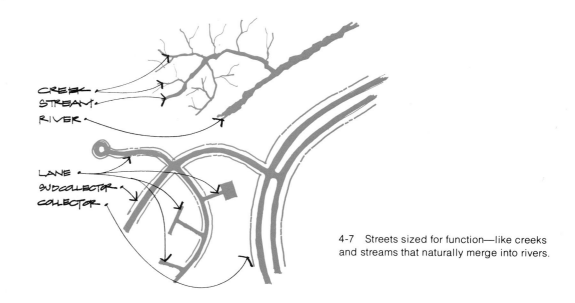

4-7 Streets sized for function—like creeks and streams that naturally merge into rivers.

whole—an environment where street design, cost, and maintenance considerations are sensitively balanced with pedestrian circulation, open space, and the homes themselves.

Street design and fitting streets to traffic requirements is an integral part of the livable townhouse and condominium development. Well-designed streets affect the design impact of the entire community and are a pleasant contrast to the uniform, gridiron road patterns of older residential developments—which were expensive, destructive to topography and plant material, and largely devoid of variety or character. Unfortunately, subdivision regulations, which have specific and generally excessive requirements for street widths, pavement thicknesses, and other items are somewhat prohibitive to new

street design. These restrictive regulations aim at high quality development. The net effect, however, has been specifications calling for very costly roads and excessive land coverage. The newly designed streets are functionally sized, designed for graduated use, and parallel the natural form and efficiency of small brooks flowing into creeks and streams eventually merging into rivers. The concept of varying street size according to function should be indicated on concept plans and refined in preliminary and final drawings. Depending on the size of a development, once the entrance area is chosen, concept site plan street design may begin with placement of a collector or subcollector. Further breakdown into lanes, places, or courts may take the form of looping streets, *Ts,* or culs-de-sac.

Where appropriate, new street patterns for townhouses and condominiums should be extensions of existing circulation routes. This may require that a community arterial be extended through a development. Local home access roads, however, should discourage through-traffic. An efficient yet aesthetic balance has been achieved in many new developments. Newly designed streets should be functional and safe, with the proper provision for service and emergency vehicles. Homes will be far more secure, private, and possess a greater neighborhood character as a result of placement on streets designed exclusively for residential use.

New street designs have been viewed by many government maintenance and engineering departments as reductions in good design standards. Private ownership of roadways has been an escape valve for this dilemma. Many municipalities, however, sensitive to the contemporary needs of people, have moved to adapt their street design standards, maintenance equipment, and procedures to permit flexible street requirements for PUD developments, rather than superimposing a standard ordinance.

The use of community association-owned and -maintained private street systems has worked even under the burden of what is double taxation. Once a development is built utilizing private streets, the homeowners not only pay their own voluntarily contracted maintenance crews, but also are forced to pay the identical mill rate as the person in the next neighborhood whose streets are maintained by the city. The homeowner, in effect, must subsidize the cleaning, upkeep, and, in winter climates, plowing of another's roads. This condition obviously puts the private street development at a competitive price disadvantage with those projects that build publicly-maintained streets.

In the long term, there appear to be several actions that would eliminate some of these cost allocation inequities. The people who are forced to pay twice for the maintenance of their local residential street could be granted a lower millage tax rate. This would provide an equitable tax structure for those who choose to maintain their own local streets. The indirect result would be to reduce the cost to local government by potentially removing much of the future municipal street maintenance burden.

A more complex yet workable program would be to alter the maintenance budget section of the tax rates to reflect actual costs incurred by the maintenance department on a neighborhood basis; rewarding the easier to maintain areas with lower rates, just as the private maintenance companies vary their billing system for the different townhouse community road patterns they service. The result would ease the burden of maintaining more intricate road patterns. Roads that cost more to maintain would pay more to the city maintenance department; those that cost less would pay less. City engineers and maintenance personnel would no longer be bound by budget constraints to press for the most easily maintainable street configurations. Increased maintenance charges would limit the overly complex street designs that are hard to maintain. The impact on street specifications would be dramatic. Streets would be economically acceptable from both a private and government standpoint, while also aesthetically varied.

The intent is that private street systems not be the only alternative—municipalities should review their standards from a broader perspective than just maintenance and traffic capacity in order better to realize roadway planning for graduated use.

4-8 The narrow width, curved pattern design of this street discourages through-traffic.

Street Planning

A smooth flowing alignment of collector streets may do much to create a favorable feel and image for a townhouse/condominium residential development. Stepping down the capacities scale of roadways will save on cost and require less ground. Gradually steeper grades and tighter curves are not only possible but desirable to help hold down speed.

The preliminary design of the street system is based upon the graduated use circulation plan shown on the final concept plan. The details must be jointly agreed upon by the regulatory agencies and the developer's design team. A decision to go with a mixture of municipally-owned and -maintained collector streets and subcollector routes combined with privately owned courts, necessitates a partnership between a local community's

4-9 Excessive road widths in a residential area are expensive and dangerous—signs do not discourage speed.

engineering and maintenance departments and the developer.

The site planner must also take into consideration the site inventory and evaluation. The presence of low bearing soil capacity will indicate where the roads should not be placed. Today more than ever before the high cost of construction demands an efficient street system—letting the land dictate road placement will reduce street construction expense. From accurate topography, soil, and other natural feature inventories, the site planner is able to lay out roadways with greater confidence. The design of flowing, curvilinear streets is not a designer's fantasy come true, but rather, a practical result of very real determinants.

Residential roadways should not be constructed to enable rapid travel between various parts of a community—a street system for a new development should respect the function of residential roadways by making provision for arterials or intercommunity roadways. Within the actual residential areas, however, roads should emphasize character, safety, and convenience—not speed. These streets should signify their function through narrower widths and specifications, not merely through signs for lower speed limits.

A significant impact of improved street planning is on security. A community with one or two entries, having homes clustered in small, perceivable neighborhoods or "mini-neighborhoods," is an environment designed for natural surveillance. Crime is deterred where there are few, easily blocked avenues of escape. As cars cannot easily cut through a development, residents become familiar with the cars that enter and exit, learning those belonging to neighbors and recognizing more easily those of strangers. Furthermore, a community association is a natural institution for managing a centralized surveillance system to monitor crime and other emergencies (See also Chapter 7).

In general then, a road's function and environmental impact are based upon certain standards, each of which must be considered in the design of streets for townhouses and condominiums:

- character of the development,
- trip generation,
- vehicle ownership,
- pavement widths,
- gradients,
- edge treatments,
- curb types,
- drainage configurations,
- soil bearing capacities,
- construction costs, and
- right-of-way dimensions.

4-10 (top) The entry road may very well set the character of the entire community. 4-11 (bottom) Select a development entry with adequate sight distance. A poorly located entry with reduced sight distances detracts from community image.

The Entry Road

As mentioned earlier in this chapter, the approach to a townhouse/condominium site is the first encounter with the development, and entry placement significantly determines a community's image and visual character. It is in concept site planning that an actual location is chosen for the entry. Although a project normally has some flexibility in locating the main entrance road, its final selection must first consider function and safety. Adequate sight distances are the primary consideration. Locations of existing vegetation or interesting land formations should also help to position the entry and set the community's image. Generally, a well-designed townhouse/condominium entry road might include earth work, plantings, and signage to create an element of surprise and openness.

Although smaller townhouse/condominium communities generate neither the traffic volume nor the amenity budget to warrant a double entry road, for larger communities the use of a divided section of road that merges after a short distance into a project's collector or subcollector route may set a positive image and provide a safer intersection. The center island that results from the double lane access is a convenient spot for project signs, low shrubs, high overstory plantings, and character lighting. It is desirable to place signs and plantings as close to the collector road as possible. Adequate sight distances, however, are maintained by keeping a 10- to 15-foot distance back from the road edge.

For larger projects the pavement width of each lane should permit movement of two cars. For developments of under 50 units, a single lane pavement width provides adequate access and egress. Proper turning radii are a minimum of 15 feet. Signage, lighting, and plantings are still appropriate and necessary for the single entry road.

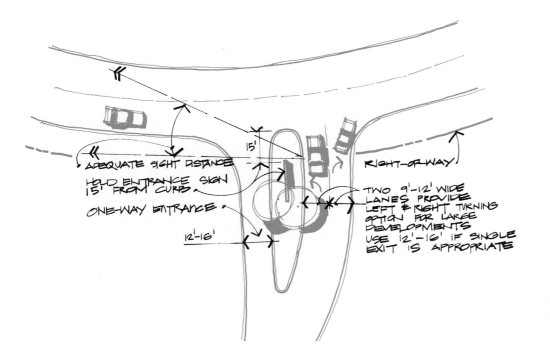

ADEQUATE SIGHT DISTANCE

HOLD ENTRANCE SIGN
15' FROM CURB

ONE-WAY ENTRANCE

12'-16'

15'

RIGHT-OF-WAY

TWO 9'-12' WIDE
LANES PROVIDE
LEFT & RIGHT TURNING
OPTION FOR LARGE
DEVELOPMENTS
USE 12'-16' IF SINGLE
EXIT IS APPROPRIATE

4-12 (left) Adequate sight distances are
maintained by holding open a 10- to 15-foot
distance from road's edge. 4-13 (below)
Design an entry for safety, function, and
character.

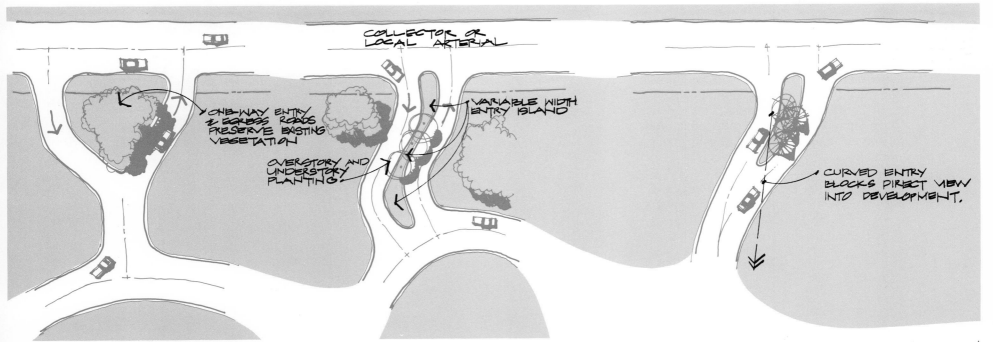

COLLECTOR OR
LOCAL ARTERIAL

ONE-WAY ENTRY
& EGRESS ROADS
PRESERVE EXISTING
VEGETATION

OVERSTORY AND
UNDERSTORY
PLANTING.

VARIABLE WIDTH
ENTRY ISLAND

CURVED ENTRY
BLOCKS DIRECT VIEW
INTO DEVELOPMENT.

Collectors

Adequately designed collector streets may be a development's key organizational element—the backbone of the site plan. A large project of over 25 acres or more may require two sizes of collector roads, calling for variations in pavement width and design speed. The design speeds of even major collector roads should reflect their primary use as residential rather than arterial roads, with speed limits of under 30 miles per hour. Overall speed may be controlled both by horizontal and vertical curve engineering standards. (See the later section on design speed.) Normally, a smooth, large-radius, 2 to 5 percent sloped roadway design feels like a residential collector route and does not need speed limit signs. A 36-foot-wide pavement is commonly used for collector streets—wide enough for two moving lanes with on-street emergency parking lanes.* Montgomery Village, in the Washington, D.C., metropolitan area, has a 36-foot curb-to-curb width collector, providing a more than adequate travel area for 300 homes. However, trends in land development have seen a reduced number of homes on smaller sites and with smaller-width loop roads.

---

* NAHB, ULI, ASCE, *Residential Streets: Objectives, Principles and Design Considerations* (Washington, D.C.: author, 1974), p. 32-33.

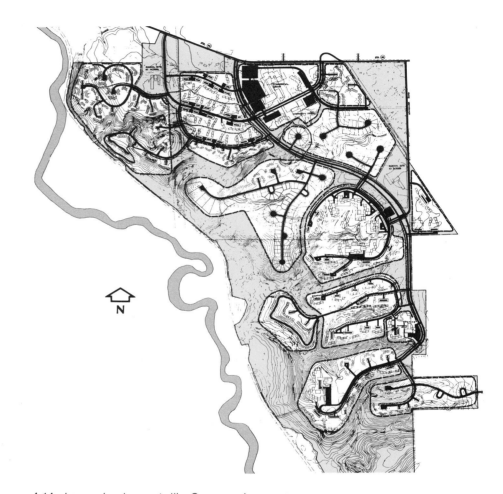

4-14 Larger developments like Greenwood Village near Cleveland use a greater number of road sizes.

Subcollectors

A look at the cars on the road today indicates that the small car is becoming popular. With this trend in mind, a 30-foot- or 32-foot-wide pavement constructed today will prove unnecessary for most drivers of tomorrow—in several more years Americans will have luxuriously wide and expensive residential streets for efficiently narrow and moderately priced automobiles. The increase in the number of small automobiles may well make 24-foot-wide pavements acceptable for future subcollector roads, even though in many cities the present use of this width for residential streets is now considered too tight. Twenty-four-foot subcollectors are standard for residential streets in Winnepeg, Canada, which has an average midwinter on-the-ground accumulation of approximately 60 inches of snow. This street size seems to work well when coupled with good signage and enforced parking regulations.

A 26-foot-wide residential subcollector assures one freely moving lane, even when parking occurs on both sides of the road. The level of resident inconvenience occasioned by the lack of two moving lanes is remarkably low; no appreciable difference in driving convenience is noted between a 26-foot-wide and a 36-foot-wide pavement, unless a developer lays out distances in excess of three blocks between dwellings and collector streets.* Typically, the elimination of sidewalks permits the maintenance of interesting side slopes that would ordinarily have to be graded to the rights-of-way.

Subcollectors should not be designed as parking lots. Granted, on infrequent occasions, a narrow road will find cars lining its sides. However, provision for infrequent circumstances returns little benefit for extremely high costing roads—the primary function of residential streets must be access to property, not rapid movement. In the residential context, collector and subcollector roads are intended for traffic movement *within* the community. Individual home driveways, therefore, should not have direct access to collectors or subcollectors, and parking should be limited to emergency and overflow uses.

---

* *Residential Streets*, p. 32.

4-15   This 24-foot-wide road in Minneapolis has effectively provided a sole access to 60 townhouses for over a decade.

Loops, Lanes, and Courts

The streets that directly serve today's townhouses and condominiums must recognize the psychological need of people for a "sense-of-identity." Residents want a neighborhood with security and privacy, normally achieved through locating fewer homes on streets *designed* for slower speeds. While small, short-length loop roads may fulfill this basic need, one of the many forms of culs-de-sac or clusters may provide an efficient turnaround configuration.

Narrower roads serving fewer homes mean smaller immediate neighborhoods, giving residents a greater sense of identity and pride. By having to conform to the lifestyles of fewer people, individualism is enhanced. Reduced car speeds through *planning* rather than just signage efficiently designs safety into a neighborhood. Roads designed for lower speeds remove some of the uneasiness that parents may feel when their children step out the door. Streets beside townhouses and condominiums should require slow enough speeds to permit even the most unwary driver to react to children in the street. This is equally valid for the elderly.

The tremendously popular turnaround or cul-de-sac was originally constructed out of necessity. The physical features of certain areas did not allow streets to run all the way through. Thus instead of designing dead ends, streets were simply rounded out to create turnaround spaces for vehicles. When sales proved that people actually preferred living on these culs-de-sac, planners began designing them even though there was no physical reason to do so.*

Because culs-de-sac have no through traffic, street widths may be dramatically reduced. A 20-foot-wide pavement is generally the minimum which offers year-around utility and convenience where snow and ice control needs are foreseeable. This width pavement is suitable for culs-de-sac up to about 300 feet long—it would allow parking on one side and would be sufficiently narrow that drivers would not be tempted to park on both sides. A 20-foot width would also meet minimum construction, amortization, space, and maintenance requirements. As the one disadvantage of a 20-foot-wide pavement is that it will not accommodate parking on both sides of the street, off street parking, proper signage, and surveillance are necessary. Since loops, lanes, or courts wider than 22 feet tempt drivers to park on both sides of the road, severely restricting traffic flow, an excess 2 feet of width may be undesirable for these roads.**

In many cluster housing situations, the court, lane, or loop roadway serving homes is normally far shorter than 300 feet. Prevalence of the mini-neighborhood concept further re-

stricts the number of homes placed along these roadways. In light of the resultant reduced density of houses, it is economically and aesthetically desirable to reduce pavement widths further. Thus, many new projects have been built with 18-foot- and 16-foot-wide pavements. Although nominal inconvenience and additional maneuvering is occasionally required, homeowners' reactions indicate that the trade-off of convenience for safety, identity, and economics is sensible and worthwhile. For smaller clusters of homes, a 16-foot-wide paving width is adequate even

---

* Barry Smith, "New Forms for Cul-de-Sacs," *Journal of Home Building,* NAHB Report #2 (Washington, D.C.: NAHB, February 15, 1968), p. 78.

** *Residential Streets,* p. 26.

Les Turnau

in winter climates. In many situations, this width is particularly suited to one-way circulation around landscape islands or parking bays and is useful in difficult terrain, where cross-pavement ground slopes are severe. On the rare and isolated occasions that parking does occur along one side of a 16-foot-wide road, there will be adequate clearance for other cars to pass. Inclusion of a one-way loop as a secondary entrance will help to alleviate the worst imaginable situation, when road clearance is reduced by snow and parked cars. Community associations may also assume the authority of towing away parking violators on these roads.

A small cluster or grouping of townhouses/condominiums may not warrant a formal turnaround facility. Although the hammer-head or *T* roadway configuration prohibits continuous entry into and uninterrupted flow out of a court, experience has shown that the residents of homes fronting on this type of roadway do not consider it to be a planning deficiency.

The turning capabilities of vehicles that will frequently utilize loops, lanes, or courts should be a major factor in systematically determining roadway turnaround diameters. Unfortunately, for many years subdivision ordinances have tended to discourage investigation of vehicle turnaround capabilities. As a result, 80-foot, 90-foot, or even 100-foot-

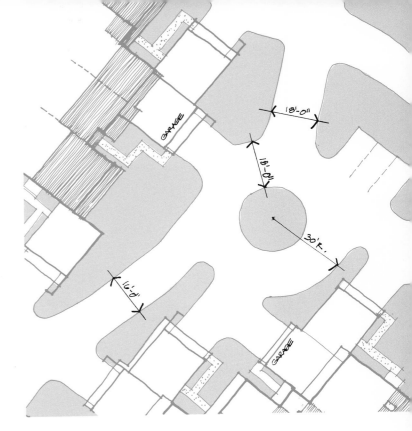

diameter turnarounds of uninteresting asphalt or concrete have been constructed, regardless of natural conditions, the number or type of homes to be served, or the preferences and capabilities of homebuyers. A thorough investigation of necessary turnaround sizes, aimed at keeping to the absolute minimum size requirements, is particularly important for townhouses and condominiums, where high density living makes maintenance of adequate open space areas so vital. Given the actual turning capabilities of various automobiles, a 60-foot diameter should accommodate virtually every car and most delivery trucks. However, as the larger service and emergency vehicles that infrequently enter a townhouse/condominium court must also be considered in determining the size of turnarounds and roadways, a discussion of these vehicles and their requirements follows in the next section.

In summary, it is important to balance cost-effective design with initial expense, construction and maintenance considerations, aesthetics, amortization, and long-term maintenance requirements. The obvious advantages of narrower turnarounds and street widths for loops, lanes, and courts are:

- use of less pavement;
- less water runoff;
- fewer storm sewers required;
- less land consumed due to narrower rights-of-way;
- slower traffic and increased safety; and
- less asphalt material, maintenance time, and expense required—thus conserving petroleum resources.

4-16 (left, top) and 4-17 (left, bottom) As children will play in the streets, driveways, and parking lots, even with nearby tot lots and open space, roads adjoining homes must be designed for lower speeds.

4-18 (top) A cluster of townhouses built with 16-foot and 18-foot pavement widths that has proved functional and provides space for landscaping. 4-19 (bottom) A high-amenity island in the center of a cul-de-sac.

53

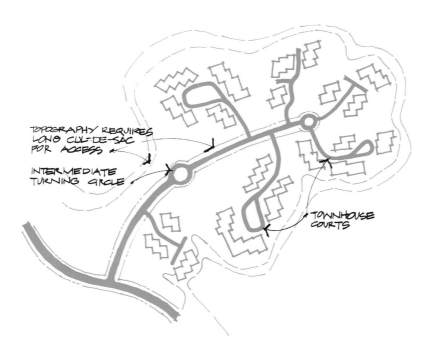

TOPOGRAPHY REQUIRES LONG CUL-DE-SAC FOR ACCESS

INTERMEDIATE TURNING CIRCLE

TOWNHOUSE COURTS

4-20   A large, intermediate turnaround serving long, non-looping residential courts.

Service and Emergency Vehicles

School Buses. School bus sizes and turn-around requirements must be considered in the design of a residential cluster street system for townhouses and condominiums. Most new communities containing graduated-use streets should contain a separate and safe pedestrian circulation system of paths funneling to sheltered benches at bus pickup points, which are best located close to collector routes. A loop road system with numerous clusters or mini-neighborhoods funneling into it will eliminate the need for school buses to enter housing clusters. On the roads where school bus access and turnarounds are required, the necessarily large turning radius needed (normally 100 feet in diameter) will yield a large center space on which the construction of a significant landscape feature may be warranted. A long cul-de-sac of 1,000 to 1,200 feet may necessitate an intermediate turning circle for buses. From a safety standpoint, buses are the only class of large vehicle for which backing maneuvers would seem unadvisable due to the driver's difficulty in seeing behind the bus.

Fire Trucks. More stringent than bus requirements, fire equipment turning radii requirements must be accommodated in townhouse/condominium site planning. Fire engines must go directly to an alarm by the quickest, most efficient route. Rarely will a fire truck be required to use a dead end, turnaround, or minor subcollector, unless a fire occurs on one of these roads. Knowing the most direct access route and being totally familiar with addresses within his jurisdiction is as important to the fireman as actually knowing how to fight a fire. Thus, it would be extremely rare for a fireman to mistakenly use a minor access road—the rare instance when this might occur would not justify standardizing extremely large and costly pavement diameters. An emphasis on larger, legible, well-designed street name and number signs would reduce the likelihood of this kind of error.

The high cost of very large fire trucks, their frequently limited maneuverability, and high maintenance costs have accelerated the trend toward use of smaller vehicles with smaller turning radii. Except for high-rise condominium projects, there is little need for very large hook and ladder or pumper trucks (requiring a large turning radius) for most low-rise townhouses and condominiums; although the turning radii selected for a new development's roads must, of course, depend on the type of equipment that a municipality already possesses. Older fire equipment, which have turning diameters as large as 110 feet, make backing movements mandatory in culs-de-sac and even at some intersections. Where backing movements are necessary, guidance and traffic control are handled by the accompanying firemen. A 70-foot turnaround diameter is adequate according to actual turning tests of a typical suburban community pumper.

Responsive local governments, seeing the widespread popularity of the mini-neighborhood and the cost efficiency of smaller pavement diameters, should size new fire equipment to residential requirements. Some communities are beginning to use smaller standard truck sizes on which various forms of fire fighting equipment may be mounted. The use of smaller trucks, having turning diameters in the 60- to 80-foot range, will save the future residents of townhouse/condominium communities many times over what it would cost to build around the requirements of larger equipment.

Furthermore, a close look at the statistics of fatalities associated with residential fires shows that most of the deaths are caused by smoke inhalation. Accordingly, electronic smoke detectors are much more effective in saving lives than fire trucks; the statistic would best be altered by installing smoke detectors rather than by widening streets and eliminating cul-de-sac islands and culs-de-sac. Thus, much of residential fire fighting is reduced to the function of property value protection (secondary to saving lives, but still important). In keeping road width requirements within the minimum range, the dollars that a resident saves from reduced pavement expense, mortgage interest, and taxes (in long-term city maintenance) will more than pay for a home's fire insurance policy.

Moving Vans. If a developer has succeeded in establishing a well-designed townhouse/condominium community that satisfies its residents, moving vans should be fairly infrequent visitors. In addition, even the largest trucks are extremely maneuverable tractor-trailer rigs, driven by professionals familiar with narrow streets. Moving vans, like fire trucks, also carry additional riders to aid the driver with backing maneuvers.

Trash Collection Trucks. Depending on the make and model, trash and refuse collection trucks may require turning radii of 55 to 57 feet.* With the guidance of loaders, a driver's backing movements present no significant problem—not enough to warrant large and costly paving diameters for a 180 degree turn.

_____

* _Residential Streets_, p. 42.

In many communities, garbage collection is managed by a private collection contractor able to set his price relative to the costs incurred in servicing different residential housing types. When a community association contracts with a single garbage hauler, a minimum number of collection trips and greater efficiency result in a lower collection price per living unit. Many refuse collectors for townhouse/condominium communities use small three-wheel vehicles for house-to-house collection, later returning to a centrally located compaction truck. The collector-court road system is particularly suited to this efficient method of garbage collection. For townhouses or condominiums at grade, rather than centralized units, individual garbage cans may be kept in garages or in fence-extension enclosures. Either of these possibilities would eliminate the mess that may develop at common garbage collection facilities.

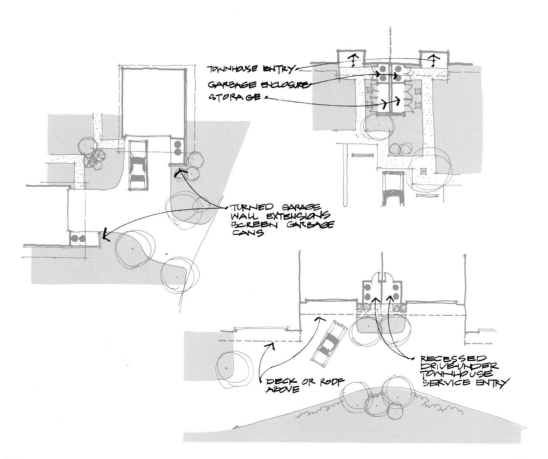

4-21 (left) and 4-22 (above) With individual trash collection points, a townhouse or condominium is more like detached residential housing.

Snow Plowing. In snow areas, snow removal from smaller residential streets is usually the lowest of plowing priorities. However, plow maneuverability within any size turnaround or cul-de-sac is essential. New developments in snow removal equipment aimed primarily at increased efficiency and decreased cost are leading to the use of smaller, more maneuverable vehicles, of which a cost-conscious, market-responsive community association should be fully aware.

Perhaps one of the greatest snow removal difficulties involves planted median strips or landscaped islands. For median strips, the blade type used on trucks must consider the design of the curb or paving edge. Also, plowing guide markers should be part of a community's comprehensive signage or graphics system. Careful motion studies should be made of the vehicles that will clear snow from culs-de-sac or loops and the results used in street design for efficient snow removal from parking and planting areas.

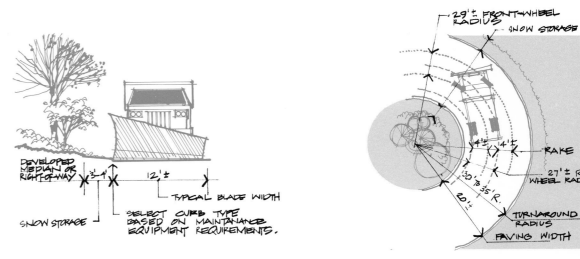

4-23 (left and right) Design for the moving, turning, and plowing capabilities of maintenance equipment.

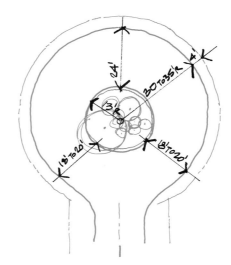

4-24 Increased width at the back of a cul-de-sac allows maneuvering space for more rapid snowplowing.

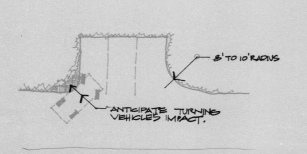

8' TO 10' RADIUS

ANTICIPATE TURNING VEHICLES IMPACT.

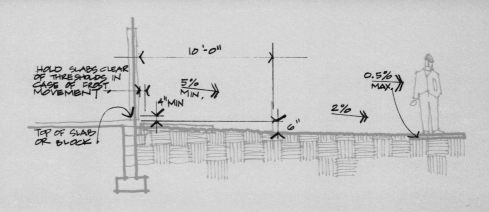

HOLD SLABS CLEAR OF THRESHOLDS IN CASE OF FROST MOVEMENT.

TOP OF SLAB OR BLOCK

10'-0"

5% MIN.

4" MIN

6"

2%

0.5% MAX.

Engineering Details

Street design details influence the overall character of a townhouse/condominium community. They create the initial impression of a community at its entrance and may also lend a feeling of safety to the residents.

A civil engineer's technical expertise in detailed design of streets is particularly important for those portions of a townhouse/condominium community road system that will be dedicated to a city or municipality. The engineer must be familiar with the city's street design procedures and requirements. Perhaps at this stage more than any other, an engineer's advocacy of improved, cost-effective roadway design may have its greatest impact.

Design Speed: Horizontal and Vertical Curves.
In the past, residential street design resulted from two rather disconnected mathematical processes. First, the concept roadway sketch was refined into a hard line plan.

In order for the roadway to be surveyed and built, tangent lengths and radii were overlapped on the plan; then the horizontal curve minimums were superimposed according to the design speed of the road. From the profile of the road, the second mathematical alignment or vertical curve was applied to a plan and profile sheet. Again, the curves were mathematically based upon the design speed of the road. Often, conforming to one or both of the mathematical limits had a devastating effect on existing grade and plant material and on the safety of the townhouse/condominium community residents.

A 30-mile-per-hour vertical curve is of little value when extensive land clearing is necessary and it involves the loss of significant land forms and natural foliage. The fact is that most roads may be driven at 10 mph over the design speed without much danger to the driver. In designing roads, it should be remembered that mathematical design speeds represent higher actual speed limits.

Tightening both horizontal and vertical curvatures (in effect, using lower design speeds), is particularly desirable for roads built in rolling wooded areas. While this seems a sacrifice of safety standards for aesthetics, reduced sight distances are a natural speed limit sign. People involved with the planning, design, and engineering of residential roads should keep in mind that a road designed for residential functions should need no speed limit sign—the structure of the road itself should warrant a reduced speed.

A plan for collector routes may be drawn separate from building site considerations, but because court road design and building site planning are so interrelated, they are best drawn as coordinated elements. In the preparation of these detail designs, close attention must be paid to the preservation of existing plant material and the maintenance of existing grade. More important than conforming to a minimum design speed curva-

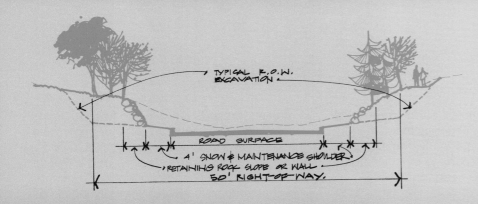

TYPICAL R.O.W. EXCAVATION
ROAD SURFACE
4' SNOW & MAINTENANCE SHOULDER
RETAINING ROCK SLOPE OR WALL
50' RIGHT-OF-WAY

4-25 (far left) Plan larger radii in court areas to reduce sod and vegetation damage and maintenance costs. 4-26 (middle) Use adequate slopes to provide a margin for construction errors. 4-27 (right) Create interest, save vegetation and site development dollars by minimizing the right-of-way grading.

ture, roads should be checked for adequate vehicular clearances and function during inclement weather.

The Figure 4-28 lists some roadway specifications that have worked well in townhouse and condominium developments with winter climates. Since this is the most severe design condition, these same specifications should be suitable in other climatic circumstances and may be subject to modification particularly in the area of maximum slope. In final road design, reduced street widths and closely designed court turnarounds require attention both to turning radii and internal slopes.

A minimum of a 4-foot radius should be utilized when linking a parking apron to a residential court. A minimum slope of 6 inches in the first 10 feet around buildings or 5 percent is recommended and, in some cases, required by government lending institutions. From this slope perimeter, minimum pavement drainage gradients

4-28 Roadway Specifications

Street Type	Right-of-Way Widths	Pavement Widths	Minimum Pavement Slopes	Maximum Typical Slopes
Subcollectors, Loops	40' - 50'	20' - 24'	Concrete 0.3% Asphalt 0.8%	8%*
Loops, lanes, places, courts	pavement width	16' - 24'	same as above	12%*

* In certain unusual situations, where adherence to these grades would cause excessive cutting, filling, or destruction of existing plant material, street and court sections of limited length may be steeper.

should exceed 0.5 percent. In practice, it is preferable to use a minimum of 2 percent. This gives an adequate tolerance in case of construction error, assuring proper flow.

Numerous methods of slope retention for road cuts and embankments make it possible to preserve a much greater portion of natural topography and vegetation than is typical for single-family detached residential development. An effective practice is to grade only the street width plus a 4- to 5-foot portion of the right-of-way.

This, however, requires a coordinated approach to engineering utility locations. That is, most right-of-way requirements are excessive in relation to the utility and street surface requirements. Allowing for a reasonably flat area of 3- to 4-feet wide before beginning the back slope to the retaining wall or to existing grade provides ample width for utilities and snow storage in even the heaviest snow areas. Provision for sidewalks in appropriate locations requires an additional 4 to 6 feet of flat area.

Curbs. There are several reasons why standard, raised concrete curbs are not desirable for many condominium or townhouse clusters. First, because clusters normally have very tight radii and intricate paving shapes, the use of curbing requires time-consuming, expensive installation. Secondly, because the roadways within most mini-neighborhoods are designed to keep speeds quite low, there is no need to use curbs as protection against vehicles going outside of the roadway. The third reason is more subtle—the presence of concrete curbs within a residential cluster conveys a feeling of urbanism. Townhouse/condominium developments should generally have a more suburban, natural design scheme—

noticeable, light-colored curbs draw a line around open space and may make a court interior seem denser. Finally, the use of inverted crown court roads to channel stormwater eliminates the need for curbing.

For townhouse/condominium collector and subcollector roadways, one of two basic concrete curb sections is desired—either the rolled/mountable curb or the straight battered curb. For subcollectors, the former curb type has a decided advantage over the latter since it permits court or driveway placement at any location along its length. This is particularly valuable in townhouse/condominium communities that depend on phasing. As design changes in response to

market demands are basic to the concept of cluster housing, flexibility in locating courts and driveways for later additions is important. A battered curb is a preferred collector road edging, since the collector is a central, higher volume roadway. Normally, housing should not front on collectors, further reducing the need for curb cuts.

Another alternative is to place precast concrete curb sections on the edge of asphalt roadways. This may be a cost-effective solution, providing the durability of cast concrete curbing without the difficult and expensive forming requirements. Still, however, concrete curbing should be limited to areas subject to intensive use, i.e., entries and the inside circumference of turnarounds.

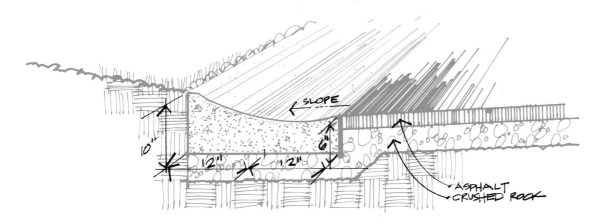

4-29 (left) and (above) A rolled or mountable curb section for subcollectors and loops maximizes development flexibility by eliminating the need for curb cuts.

Roadway Cross-Sections. Residential road surfaces may provide economical storm drainage collection and disbursal. For townhouse and/or condominium residential courts, the use of inverted crown section is one preferred type for storm drainage. This drainage swale permits an inexpensive, flexible method of diverting storm drainage into either catch basins or onto open space dispersal areas. When no road curbing is used, it is preferable to harden and thicken the edge of the pavement to prevent deterioration.

The inverted crown roadway section, however, is difficult to form and without at least a 1 percent slope may deteriorate over time due to ponding in more shallow pitch sections. For some site planning situations, an alternative is the use of a chemically hardened, formed asphalt or concrete curb on one side of the court. A flat roadway pitched to this curbing then channels the water to storm drains or dispersal areas. This roadway section is economical and easy to build, but it is not durable. An asphalt or concrete curb may also be formed on both sides of the roadway using a crowned road.

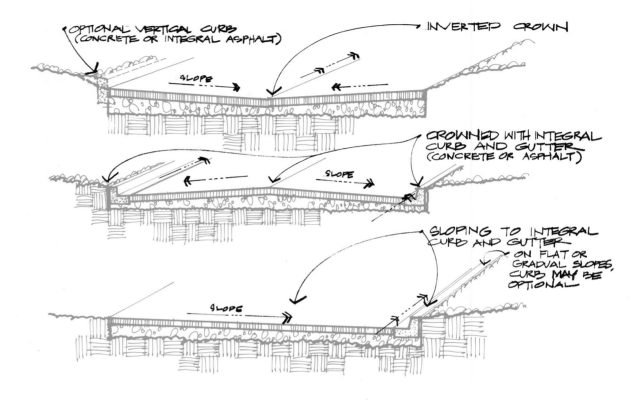

4-30   Court road types for stormwater drainage: inverted crown, crowned with curb, and sloping flat surface to one curb.

Open Space

In site planning for townhouses and condominiums, the need for open space must be recognized and provided for. Local government requirements for low housing density and large lots are, in part, a response to this need. Ironically, by carefully designing open space, an actual higher density of people is effectively possible. A uniform spacing of townhouse/condominium buildings a set number of feet from each other is an inefficient use of land when considering today's lifestyles and environmental values, high land costs, and existing long (and expensive) street and utility runs.

From the natural resource inventory and building group layout an open space system for townhouses and condominiums may be planned. The open space plan should provide for four basic types: private outdoor space, semi-private home entry spaces, community association semi-public space, and public open space. Although private and semi-private open spaces are discussed in Chapter 6 (Building Design) and details related to specific open space features are discussed in Chapter 7 (Amenities), open space as it relates to site planning is handled in the following section—since planning for open space should be an integral part of project site planning.

4-31 (top) Private outdoor space: a desirable feature for every home. 4-32 (upper middle) Semi-private home entry spaces buffer the home from noise and pedestrian traffic. 4-33 (lower middle) Passive or active community association recreation areas should be located near the homes. 4-34 (bottom) Public open space provides access to city assets—in this case, the waterfront.

Public Open Space

Even on lower cost land, a uniform scattering of buildings between equally sized open spaces is not the best site planning answer. On the contrary, tighter spaces along roadways or areas constricted by garage walls may be widened within entry courts and tightened again at entering walkways to accentuate and vary open spaces.

A complete, effective open space system should tie together a number of diverse recreational activity areas, strengthen a sense of community, and help to create a true neighborhood. Planning for public open spaces means recognizing and distributing the value of natural and built amenities to as many homes as possible. The knowledge that a community contains public open spaces has a good psychological effect on residents. However, there is no substitute for direct access to the open space—being able to actually see vistas, views, field game areas, walking paths, or simply landscaped countryside from one's own windows. Thus, for an open space system to be cost-effective, the site plan must expose as many homes as possible directly to the outdoor area. The value of this approach is easily borne out by a look at the premiums that normally accrue to homes with the best view or the closest proximity to high-amenity spaces, such as a lake or golf course fairway.

Building footpaths, sidewalks, and walkways is another way of spreading open space among the majority of residents, while at the same time creating a safe pedestrian linkage system. Being able to separate pedestrian flows from vehicular traffic is both aesthetically desirable and functionally safe. Additional discretionary time and renewed interest in physical fitness has made jogging, biking, and cross-country skiing more popular. Also, a new respect for the natural environment adds a greater demand for wooded pathways. In contrast to the rather spotty placement of amenities in earlier developments, today's site planning for connected open space permits a more logical framework within which to structure preserved natural vegetation, tennis courts, swimming pools, tot lots, sitting areas, and other townhouse/condominium amenities features. (For more details about each of the aforementioned amenities, see Chapter 7.)

Public field game areas for soccer, softball, baseball, football, and so on are subject to the same planning limitations as swimming pools or tennis courts—this open space should be visibly close but must not interfere with the zone of privacy surrounding a person's home. The best way to protect against pathways' and activity areas' infringing upon privacy is to separate them both vertically and horizontally. The capability of a community association to sponsor a number of local sports teams adds reason for site planning field game activity areas. Planning for townhouse/condominium open space areas should reinforce and extend neighboring and community values.

An interesting potential of public open space is an improved atmosphere for the personal and social development of children. An open space system that encourages spontaneous interaction between various age groups in a neighborhood is a desirable feature. With centralized, safe public play areas, parents generally permit their children to range farther from home, thereby promoting a child's sense of independence and personal growth.

Les Turnau

4-35 (far left) The pathway system should link major amenity features within the open space system. 4-36 (above) An active public recreation area on the periphery of a development may complement semi-public, community association open space. It also provides visual relief for a higher density development. 4-37 (left) Suburban open space requirements are different. Larger open space areas could be dedicated to the city to reduce community association maintenance responsibilities.

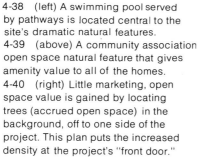

4-38 (left) A swimming pool served by pathways is located central to the site's dramatic natural features.

4-39 (above) A community association open space natural feature that gives amenity value to all of the homes.

4-40 (right) Little marketing, open space value is gained by locating trees (accrued open space) in the background, off to one side of the project. This plan puts the increased density at the project's "front door."

Martin Tornallyay

Natural Features

In the selection of townhouse/condominium land, the presence of natural features on a site is one of the most important criteria. A plan for maximum livability respects a site's natural features. *Where* the natural features are included within the site is almost as important as *whether* they are included at all. A frequent and unfortunate occurrence is the placement of open space natural features some distance from the majority of homes and from the primary access/entry approach to a site. Open space natural features should permit the majority of residents to appreciate nature in their leisure. A greater amount of open space is not always better than less open space. More amenity dollars more cleverly spent on less area may result in a greater impact than the same amount of money spent on a larger amount of space.

Whether natural or built, pathway systems are not cheap. Like roads, pathways are most economically built if they respect a site's natural features and land forms, working with the environment rather than obliterating it. This makes for economical construction by avoiding retaining walls and extensive earth moving.

4-41 Preserving existing trees beside the homes provides pleasant views.

The preservation of a site's natural features generally requires increased density elsewhere on the site. A classic error in planning is to put the accrued density in an area visible from the entry. Thus, the buyer or passerby initially observes a much greater density than is actually characteristic of the site. This problem is eliminated by obtaining land with significant natural features both at the site center and entry areas. Where this is not possible, it is preferable to obtain property that permits the installation of a strong entrance approach with adequate central open space. Having primary open space only at a site's edge may make the land appear to be owned by someone else. A more subtle consequence is that while it may be linked by pathway systems, peripheral open space becomes inconvenient for residents to use and suffers from a lack of owner/user surveillance so vital to the care and security of the townhouse/condominium community. From a development phasing standpoint, it is usually desirable to penetrate wooded areas with buildings and utilize the lot premiums accrued from these extremely marketable locations to help pay for amenity improvements in other open areas. Moreover, creating some extremely marketable locations helps the developer acquire the initial momentum that does so much to assure a development's financial success.

Since open space is not free, the developer and designer must remember the value that prospective buyers place on created open areas. On the other hand, although a new homebuyer's eye may be caught by a large expanse of open space, today's knowledgeable buyer realizes that he will be paying a part of the area's maintenance for years to come. For every acre of land left open, the developer must increase the price of homes on the site. The proper balance of open space to housing comes in recognizing that too little open space will reduce home value, and therefore, the profitability of the development. The income hoped for by placing additional homes in areas that should be left for open space may be lost many times over through added marketing expenses and a slowed sales pace. Thus, like so many areas of the development process, the open space system must be planned with both short-term values and long-term burdens in mind. This is especially true in arid climates where too much sod and landscaping may become a disproportionate maintenance burden.

As an accent to maintained open space areas, small pockets of undeveloped, unsodded land, planted or designed to grow wild, will provide several benefits. Since mowing is not required, the community association may save on maintenance costs.

4-42   Within Lincoln Park, mini-parks and streetscape open space improvements by the city of Chicago have helped provide an atmosphere for construction and rehabilitation of the surrounding townhouse/condominium community.

These areas may also serve as wildlife habitats, with year-round activity, for example, from fruit-bearing shrubs or trees attractive to birds.

Buyer profiles should influence open space design as much as they do home planning. A large number of older buyers may warrant more undeveloped, natural open spaces, whereas a development on a tighter site for an anticipated large number of children will call for an entirely different design (emphasizing active play areas). In urban areas, intensively developed open space may provide both streetscape and recreational value. Open space facilities in urban areas should be developed in partnership with municipalities, since the facilities will benefit a larger area.

Pathways

A basic tenet of open space is that it be designed where natural features exist. Moreover, it should be the spatial link with homes, the visual and recreational amenities of a development, and, where possible, with off-site facilities. If the overall amenity package permits, vehicular conflicts with open space pathways should be eliminated. In some communities, pedestrian open space walkways are totally separated from streets by underpasses or overpasses. Such walkways are a desirable but costly open space, requiring higher housing unit densities and/or larger amenity budgets. If, for instance, an overpass or underpass is built along a major route to a school or other constantly used facility, the expenditure may be fully warranted and prove cost-effective because of increased livability and value.

Under normal circumstances, however, it is not economically feasible to dig a ditch or build a bridge every time a pathway crosses a street. A far more economical method of emphasizing a pedestrian crossing point at a street is to change the texture of the road to aggregate or pavers. An even more economical solution of painted crosswalk stripes may be used at pathway termini. Additional safety would result from adding texture to the roads ahead of the crosswalks.

Older standards requiring sidewalks on both sides of the street are unnecessary for townhouses and condominiums. With the special provision of off-street circulation routes, most minor streets need no sidewalks at all except when a link to a walkway system from a street is appropriate, or where part of a pathway runs adjacent to a road. If a sidewalk is required to be placed within a public right-of-way, a variable width right-of-way or easements will permit a curvilinear alignment that may enhance a particular landscape design theme. Repetitive use of design elements like signs will strengthen community identity.

Les Turnau

4-43 (top) An underpass: expensive but cost-effective if serving repeatedly used facilities like schools or shopping areas.
4-44 (bottom) This golf course, designed in conjunction with a townhouse development, is divided by a collector street. An underpass allows a direct open space link.

4-45 This large-scale development has most of its pathway system (shown in black) separated from the community's roads.

Pathway Details. Detail design of open space walkways is primarily concerned with the width, curvatures, and gradient of pathway systems. Walks dedicated to the local government should be 4-feet wide or whatever ordinances require. Where paths are an integral part of a larger common path system, they should be consistent with the design of the whole system. A 4½- to 5-foot width provides a comfortable space to two people on a leisurely stroll or gives safe clearance for bicycles passing from opposite directions.

Experience with paths designed as pedestrian open space routes shows that some are now as heavily used by bikers as by people on foot. Pedestrian and bicycle traffic separation is a growing safety trend. Within a townhouse/condominium project this separation would only be required where connection with public pathway systems is anticipated. Where necessary, variable alignments of bicycle and pedestrian paths that run in the same direction are desirable. In the case of the two different kinds of paths running parallel, the pedestrian system could have steps at grade changes—a natural way of separating it from the bike path. Generally though, steps in multi-use pedestrian walkways should be avoided, unless built with handrails and lighting.

There are a great variety of paving materials for open space walkways. While some soil types may alone be compacted to provide a reasonably hard surface, a coating of some type is usually preferred. A footpath receiving infrequent use may be surfaced with wood shavings, bark chips, or some form of crushed gravel. Then if use warrants, a community association may later pave a pathway with hard-surfaced material. On shorter sections of open space pathways, wood rounds, wood paver blocks, or a polyester-bound aggregate material laid directly on the soil may be appropriate.

A limestone or similar packing gravel base is, perhaps, the most cost-effective surface material a developer may use. Gravel base mixture will usually pack itself into a firm surface, stable enough for walking, jogging, and biking. If, at a later date, the developer or community association decide to pave the surface, the aggregate will serve as the compacted base for asphalt. While concrete may be used in tighter, more urban projects, asphalt surfacing seems to lend itself to the rolling land forms often seen in suburban open space design.

A maximum walking path longitudinal slope typically should not exceed 15 percent. Average sustained trail grades should not exceed 5 to 8 percent.* Where possible, grade sections of 1 to 4 percent will permit unlabored walking. Normally, it is best to locate a pathway so that its grade increases

---

* California Public Outdoor Recreation Plan Committee, *California Public Outdoor Recreation* Part 2 (Sacramento, California: author, 1960), p. 85.

4-46 (left) Separate bike and walkways are a result of the nationwide emphasis on biking and jogging. In some climates, they provide for alternative uses during the winter. 4-47 (right) Keeping the pathways separate from the streets is one way to provide function and safety.

gradually. A minimum transverse slope of 0.5 percent will provide positive walkway drainage. The transverse slope should not exceed 0.75 percent per foot because greater slopes are hazardous under icy conditions and at night.

These guidelines, set forth as general standards, certainly cannot take into account all of the diverse determinants that may influence a project's pedestrian circulation system. For instance, a central feature of the pathway route may involve several flights of steps to an overlook area above. Here, as with so many other site planning considerations, the land, climate, market, and economic conditions should dictate proper design.

4-48 (above) Privately owned play pieces last a long time since the kids "own a piece of the action." 4-49 (left) Private parks reduce the need for municipal parks and place recreation areas nearer to users.

Public Park Dedications

The community association typically owns a part of the immediate and intricate open space of a townhouse or condominium community, but in some cases, a public park dedication is required. While it is sometimes appropriate to have a mix of publicly-owned and privately-owned open space, it should be remembered that the level of maintenance provided by a municipality for publicly-owned open space rarely measures up to the level of expectation of townhouse/condominium residents.

Where public park dedications are required, a balance must be found between the interests of the existing community and the new residents. The open space objective should be to provide facilities within easy walking distance. Municipalities have often used an inequitable approach in reviewing public park dedication requirements for townhouse/condominium private open space and recreational facilities. The 5 percent "cash or land" dedication does not properly recognize the role of privately financed areas. Privately financed parks, structures, and other amenities for townhouse/condominium residents remove most of the burden of having to use public facilities. For this reason these residents should not be required to pay for municipal facilities they have already purchased privately.

Sometimes nearby residents and municipalities will request that community association-maintained land be dedicated for parks, access to lakeshore, or other high amenity locations. This usually will have a negative impact on a townhouse/condominium's perceived value. Inevitably, nonresidents will fail to recognize the boundaries between the public park and community association-owned property, resulting in public use, and perhaps abuse, of private property. Moreover, the identity and inherent security of a townhouse/condominium community or group of mini-neighborhoods sharing ownership and maintenance responsibilities is threatened by the presence of public facilities. This is not to say that pathways, open space systems, and sitting area facilities are never open to nonresident use. Community associations may permit visitor use as long as they treat the facilities with the same respect as do residents. For certain activities like boating, fishing, and swimming, the community association may charge nonresidents user fees which may help in any maintenance costs.

Taxation of Open Space

Over a decade ago it was suggested that the value of townhouse/condominium open space properly should accrue to the bene-fited property owners. The property owner should be taxed only on the basis of the fair market value of his home, with no tax on the open space itself because his home's value is partially based on the open space. Any additional or separate taxing of this space is double taxation. While this approach seems so reasonable and does not penalize either the buyer of a townhouse/condominium open space community or the taxing entity, there are instances where the tax assessor insists on a system of double taxation. Under this inequitable approach, open space is taxed at an acreage value in addition to the home's value. This would be the same as taxing a single-family detached home and re-taxing the backyard area separately. Obviously, any home's value is dependent upon surrounding open space, whether it is the backyard of a detached home or community association-maintained land.

A state statute directing assessors to follow a more equitable approach should be enacted to insure a uniformly administered tax sys-tem. In some cases the assessor may have a valid argument for taxation at a so-called market value, if the open space has some underlying zoning that would permit a higher land use in the future and is located in such a manner that it could be easily sold off by the community association at a future date. This obstacle may be overcome if the de-veloper executes an open space easement on the subject land, assigning away to a mu-nicipality for a given period of time the de-velopment rights of the underlying land.

DECLARATION OF OPEN-SPACE EASEMENTS AND COVENANTS

THIS INDENTURE, made and entered into this _____ day of _____, 19_____, by and between _____ (developer) a _____ corporation ("Grantor"), and THE CITY OF _____ (hereinafter called "Grantee").

WITNESSETH:

WHEREAS, Grantor is developing certain real estate for a residential community known as _____; and

WHEREAS, Grantor desires to set aside within said community cer-tain areas as permanent open spaces to provide enjoyment for the res-idents in said community; and

WHEREAS, Grantor has deemed it desirable for the efficient preser-vation and enhancement of the values and amenities in said commu-nity and to insure the enjoyment by the residents of certain rights and privileges in said open spaces, to create an agency, the _____ Association, which shall own and maintain said open space exclusively for the benefit of the residents in said community; and

WHEREAS, Grantor and Mortgagee desire to assure The City of _____ County, _____, that the open space to be maintained by the _____ Association shall be permanently devoted to the common enjoyment by the residents of _____ and shall not be developed except as hereinafter provided;

NOW, THEREFORE, for and in consideration of the premises and the sum of One Dollar ($1.00) to Grantor in hand paid, receipt whereof is hereby acknowledged, Grantor hereby grants and conveys unto the Grantee and Grantee hereby accepts a perpetual estate, interest and open space easement in _____ (legal description of open space) _____

Said estate, interest and open-space easement shall be of the nature and extent hereinafter specified and shall constitute a servitude upon the above-described areas which shall result from the restrictions hereby imposed upon the use of said areas, and to that end and for the purpose of accomplishing the intent of the parties hereto, Grantor and Mortgagee covenant on behalf of themselves, their successors and as-signs:

1. That no structures or improvements of any kind will be placed or erected upon the areas above-described until application there-for, with plans for such structures or improvements, together with a statement of the purpose for which the structures will be used,

has been filed with and written approval obtained from the Grantee. Provided however, that there shall be reserved to Grantor, its successor and assigns, the right to construct such recreational and service structures, improvements and facilities which do not unreasonably interfere with any utility services of the City of _____ located within the plat of _____ as are necessary and appropriate to the full enjoyment by the res-idents in said community.

2. That in the event that the _____ Association or any successor organization, shall at any time fail to maintain said areas in reasonable order and condition, the City of _____ _____ County, _____, may enter upon said area and provide the necessary maintenance. The cost of such maintenance shall be defrayed out of the as-sessments which the _____ Association has levied or is entitled to levy pursuant to a Declaration of Covenants, Condi-tions and Restrictions recorded contemporaneously herewith and Grantee shall in respect to the costs of such maintenance have the right to be subrogated to the rights of the Association in re-spect of its right to levy assessments and to all the remedies for collection and enforcement of the same; provided, however, that said entry and maintenance by The City of _____ _____ County, _____, shall not vest in the public any rights to use the above-described open space areas and facilities unless and until the same are voluntarily dedicated to the public by the owners.

TO HAVE AND TO HOLD unto the said City of _____, _____ County, _____, its successors and assigns, forever.

IN WITNESS WHEREOF, Grantor and Grantee have hereunto set their hands and seals all as of the day and year first above written.

(DEVELOPER)   THE CITY OF _____

BY_____   By_____
Its President   Its Mayor

Sample open-space easements and covenants form furnished by Rob-ert L. Davidson, Attorney-at-Law, Doherty, Rumble & Butler, 3750 IDS Tower, Minneapolis, Minnesota 55402.

Utilities

Lines on concept site plans should indicate the positioning of existing utilities at the earliest possible time. Detailed engineering considerations of water supply, sanitary sewer, invert grades, and storm drainage capacities play a major role in many decisions, from initial land acquisition to final site plans. Thus, good communication between engineers and other members of the design team is a must in planning for utilities.

Sanitary Sewers

The engineer's role in the planning and refinement of a townhouse/condominium sanitary sewer plan is dependent upon the interdisciplinary abilities of the other members of the design team. For instance, if the person preparing the site plans has a grasp of the civil engineering considerations of sanitary sewer design, the task of the engineer is to evaluate these plans for their function, cost-effectiveness, and efficiency in serving homes. The engineer should review these plans and propose revisions, if appropriate. There obviously must be a give and take between the members of the design team to arrive at the best possible, "livable" community. In preparing engineering plans, an engineer must know the procedure for enabling the connection of sewers to the existing municipal sanitary sewer system, as well as the schedule of dates the city may have established for sanitary sewer installation. An engineer must judge the basis for the city's sewer assessments and the methods of allocating the cost of mains and trunks that pass over and extend beyond the site's boundaries.

In light of the potential impact of sewer moratoriums on the people who are or will be in serious need of housing, sanitary sewer engineering may take on new significance. Alternative sanitary disposal methods, such as individual unit storage/processing and smaller-scale centralized systems, should become part of the engineer's design expertise. These systems may save existing taxpayers of a community the potential short-term burden of paying for additional sewer extensions while enabling new families to appreciate the benefits of townhouse/condominium living. These private sewerage systems enable development of small parcels or pockets of neighborhoods, resulting in a much more diverse and interesting community.

In sewerage-related and other site service considerations, the engineer should adopt and conscientiously promote the general design approach advocated by the developer and the other members of the design team. For example, if a site warrants preserving existing plant material, this must be stated at the outset of the development process and considered in the design of site services. The impact of a unified approach among design team members becomes gradually more important as more specific detail designs are developed and finalized. Because the installation of various site services normally requires drastic site alteration, the engineer must continually test his specific engineering designs against the developer's overall budgetary and aesthetic goals.

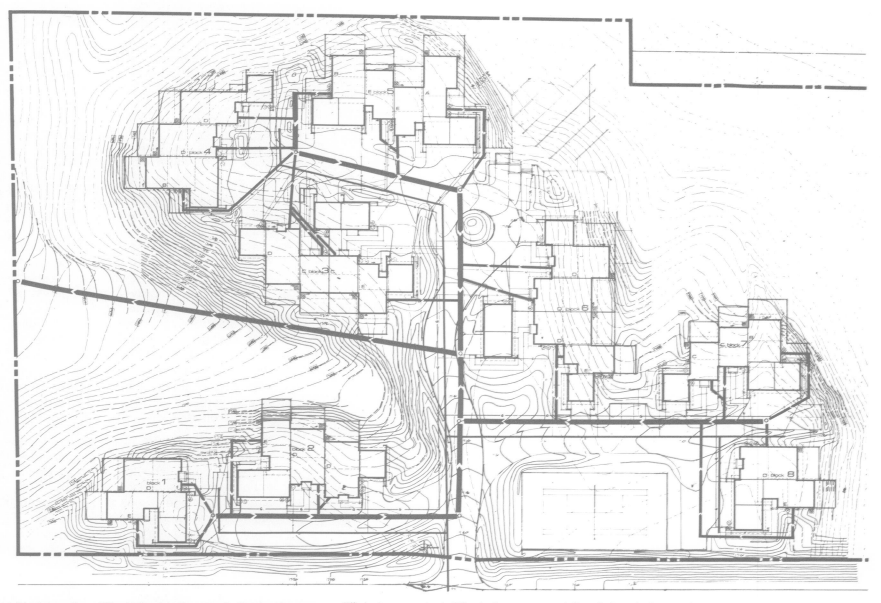

4-51 Integrating utility design into the overall site planning process. Efficient, economical utility design may save dollars that are better spent elsewhere—on amenities. (A proposed utility layout.)

Stormwater Management

As mentioned previously, storm drainage evolves with road pattern and cluster designs. Dollar savings in resources and energy through modern design of storm sewers is closely tied to improved street standards. Stormwater runoff may be decreased by reducing road pavement surfaces, right-of-way widths, and driveway lengths. The engineer's role in stormwater drainage design is to work with the design team, prepare the mathematical computations of anticipated runoff, and calculate the resultant water levels for existing and proposed collection basins, retention ponds, offsite drainage swales, storm sewers, and streams. These improved methods of anticipating water level involve retention ponding to balance out peak surges. Normally, streets constitute the primary storm sewer system, conducting water above ground as far as 800 feet. With the recommended velocity in the deepest part of the gutter limited to 10 feet per second, this water is then brought to dispersal points where it may be spread over open space and is permitted to percolate into the soil.* "Overland flows should be over and through turf or other flow retardants such as groundcover or forest litter. This is one reason why natural vegetation should be preserved whenever possible. Slopes of overland flow area should be as flat as possible, but maintaining natural topography and groundcover should take precedence over regrading to achieve flat slopes."**

In the past, stormwater management meant storm sewers, but today it is much more than a matter of piping drainage water onto someone else's property. Stormwater management is an important part of the entire water resource system. On some sites, 50- or 100-year flood levels determine the limits of road and building placement.

Problems that have resulted from the earlier rather simplistic approaches to storm drainage, i.e., reduction in groundwater levels, increased well depths, and increased flood damage downstream, have spawned new approaches to handling the rains. Improved, more environmentally sound solutions attempt to provide an equitable balance between initial cost and maintenance expense, convenience and risk of damage. New approaches to stormwater management emphasize a combination of construction and natural engineering solutions. While occasionally more complex than older solutions, the new solutions may generally reduce townhouse/condominium development cost

---

* ULI, ASCE, NAHB, *Residential Storm Water Management: Objectives, Principles and Design Considerations* (Washington, D.C.: author, 1976) p. 41.
** *Storm Water Management*, p. 43.

and the impact of storm drainage on other people's property. Another side benefit of new, improved storm drainage management is that by maximizing surface drainage while minimizing pipes in the ground, maintenance by street sweeper removal or surface excavation of silt is possible, rather than costly cleaning out of the underground pipe system.

In an ideal design solution, the water falling on a given site should be absorbed or retained on-site, to the extent that after development the quantity and rate of water leaving the site would not be significantly different than if the site had remained undeveloped. In other words, to offset the greater runoff rate due to newly added impervious paving and roof surfaces, dispersal onto open areas or into retention basins or channels must be employed. This, of course, need not be an inflexible rule. Provision for increased or decreased runoff rates should be able to be made in independent, voluntary agreements between abutting and affected property owners.

In some cases, where large natural drainage swales exist, overall site planning and engineering design should respect and even enhance them as landscape features. Constructed drainage swales should reflect their natural counterparts by looking less like artificially surveyed, trenched ditches. From a practical construction standpoint, a minimum slope for a sodded or established turf drainage swale is 2 percent. Under exacting construction standards, a 1 percent drainage swale will assure flow, yet the slightest variation during construction will result in ponding and possible moisture damage to the lawn. These slope specifications should be shown on the preliminary and final grading plans.

Like drainage swales, stormwater retention ponds should be treated as elements of design and accented by variations in shape, size, slope treatments, and plantings. Stormwater flumes may, with careful design attention, be transformed into landscape features containing trickling water or noisy waterfalls. In some cases, it might be desirable to augment the flow of stormwater with an artificial recirculating supply. A permanent water level should be maintained within a waterproof lower section of the basin, with the remainder taking up the necessary storm retention volume.

As detail design refinements for streets and parking areas are completed on the site plan, the engineering calculations of runoff, pipe sizes, and swale depths may need to be readjusted. Erosion protection and specific soil retention details, such as planting, riprap, or small siltation check dams, should be included in engineering recom-

4-52 Storm drainage retention basins and swales are an important part of site planning.

mendations for the landscape architectural design of the site.

Siltation swales, basins, or dams should be provided for construction runoff. These may simply be ditches, dug 90 degrees to the main flow or straw bales placed to intercept silt before it enters the road gutters, catch basins, or existing drainage swales. Where excavation takes place well in advance of final construction, seeding should supplement these basins.

Water Supply

The engineering design of water mains for a townhouse/condominium project must be based on standard construction details for the surrounding municipal water system. Normally, water main sizes are based upon firefighting requirements. Design team members should seek the input of the local fire chief for the placement of hydrants on the preliminary site plan. Hydrants are typically spaced at 300-foot intervals.

4-53 Utility meters may be screened.

Power and Gas

As the residential homebuyer of today is sensitive to the visual character of his environment, the building industry has responded by placing utilities underground. Power and other utility companies have found that, in most cases, vandalism and maintenance are greatly reduced. Moreover, the townhouse/condominium environment is safer without overhead power lines.

Technological advances in protective wire coatings, faster, more durable trenching equipment, and sensing devices that permit quick location of breaks, contribute to the various utility companies' acceptance of underground services. While common trenching appears to be a practical, cost-saving partnership, conflicting installation schedules and concern over maintenance lead some companies to dig their own ditches. Here, again, the use of underground sensing devices makes repeated trenching a relatively safe procedure.

Unfortunately, in areas where charges for the installation of services are on a per-unit basis, the utility company may not consider installing lines for townhouses and condo-

4-54 Locate meters in as few, centralized locations as possible and out of direct line of sight from the court road.

miniums more efficient than servicing a single-family detached subdivision. Eight homes clustered on one acre, however, require less pipe and wire and less ditching per unit than a development of one to three homes per acre.

Care should be given to the location of pad-mounted transformers. While compared with their pole-mounted predecessors they are almost beautiful, pad-mounted transformers are better placed at the ends of community blocks or separate from traveled pedestrian routes. These transformers may be sunken below grade or screened with an architectural feature or shrubbery.

The placement of power and gas lines is difficult when they must frequently be laid through areas of future additions. Although this should be avoided wherever possible, if unavoidable, townhouse/condominium block configurations should be constructed to accept different home types as market preferences shift. Platting the narrowest easements where possible is recommended.

Construction

Final Engineering Design. Utility installations are normally one of the first phases of site development construction and are almost always extensions of existing municipal services. Where it is customary for the city to own and maintain these utilities and services, townhouse/condominium residents should not be penalized because some of the utilities are installed on private easements. The developer, designer, or engineer must closely coordinate utility installation procedures and scheduling with the final design of buildings, roads, open spaces, and natural features. In a more subtle way than does the planning architecture or landscape architecture, utility designs may convey a development's theme and spirit. Careful design of utilities will save existing land forms or plant materials.

Homebuyers today have come to expect the most modern, functional utilities—properly functioning water, storm sewers, sanitary sewers, and electrical systems. Thus, designing the most efficient, low-cost but properly functioning utilities is important. Every dollar saved through careful final engineering design—cutting out every foot of unnecessary sanitary and storm sewer, reducing pipe diameters wherever possible, and eliminating every unnecessary manhole or catch basin—may be spent on higher impact, people-oriented amenities. Sewer runs should be as straight as possible, since every turn requires a manhole. The most efficient location of sanitary sewer service, therefore, may cut diagonally across street rights-of-way or use direct routes on separate easements. Stormwater should be carried for maximum distances over land or on the streets, distributed over the land as much as possible.

Surveys, Staking, Field Checks, and Revisions. Once construction drawings are completed, approvals granted, and bids in, staking of buildings may begin. Normally, the four corners of the platted building envelope are staked for on-site review prior to foundation line staking. At this point, conflicts with existing topography or plant material may be recognized and revisions made. Because of the interrelated nature of townhouse or condominium block design and the parking/court plan and grading, significant changes are difficult without considerable changes to the drainage system.

At this stage one should be prepared, however, to make on-site corrections in open space grading design and amenity placement, including pathways, tot lots, and other site features. It is not unusual for existing topography to vary from that shown on survey drawings, despite the fact that these drawings commonly guarantee accuracy to within one foot. Frequently, better judgements about the relative placement of amenity features may be made on site once new construction has defined the outdoor spaces. Preconstruction conferences anticipating this type of flexibility should establish the change order procedure.

5 Building Site Design

Parking

Parking is one of the more difficult site problems of townhouse and condominium design. When a greater density of homes is served with less paving, when more people are housed on less land, and when the number of automobiles they own remains about the same, a townhouse or condominium cluster may take on the appearance of an urban parking lot. Or, it may suffer from what has become a near-fatal townhouse/condominium disease known as "the garage court syndrome." To avoid the plague of the parking lot, people have sacrificed entry doors to their homes for 4-paneled, 16-foot-wide garage doors arrived at via 20-foot-wide asphalt walkways.

5-1 Good design tames the visual impact of the car, parking, and garages.

Good site planning and design will create a livable environment for easily marketable townhouses or condominiums. It will add to the value of individual homes while still allowing an increased density of homes per acre. A look at the majority of financially successful, award-winning projects in recent years points up at least one common characteristic—in each project, designers had broken up, screened, divided, or in some way visually reduced the prominence of parking lots or garage courts and thus had cured the ailment that may cripple a development's financial success.

5-2 (top) and 5-3 (bottom) The garage court syndrome may be a small problem . . . or a big one.

5-4 Where higher density or land forms require linear parking, angle and break sections into smaller bays. If the ground is flat with no trees, use even smaller pieces of space.

Garages

Early marketing input should establish the sales value of garages, the number required, and the importance of attaching them to individual homes. These decisions become major determinants for site planning and the design of building blocks.

In almost all ownership market areas, the provision of two covered parking spaces per unit is very important. In all market areas, a two-car garage may solve a lot of problems. Many developers advocate thinking twice before foregoing two-car garages in most price ranges. Variations to this rule would depend on prices and market demands. For example, retirees in Palm Springs would want either a two-car garage or one carport and one garage. In Washington, D.C., however, moderate-costing units may have either a two-car attached garage or open bay parking.

Attached/Detached Garages. In parts of the country where homebuyers require covered parking spaces, skillful planning may incorporate garages in the design of a more interesting living environment. On the other hand, the presence of garages means additional land coverage and greater setback distances—usually resulting in larger cluster sizes and possible problems with convenient access from parking bays, courts, or spaces. One-story garages or carports may, however, complement the architecture of the homes themselves by helping reduce the scale of the larger buildings typical of townhouse/condominium communities.

In most cases where residents want a garage, they would prefer to have it attached to their home. This desire is not always 100 percent achievable for many reasons, the main reason being that homes are not wide enough to provide room for both an attractive entrance and a double garage. However,

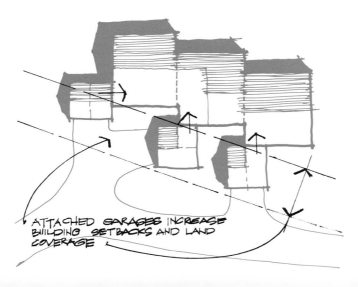

ATTACHED GARAGES INCREASE BUILDING SETBACKS AND LAND COVERAGE

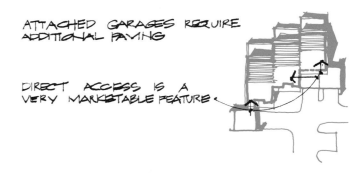

ATTACHED GARAGES REQUIRE ADDITIONAL PAVING

DIRECT ACCESS IS A VERY MARKETABLE FEATURE

5-5 and 5-6 Attached garages take up building and paving space, but provide better security and convenience.

there is a valid basis for seeking to attach garages. A home is simply more functional if it is not a long walk from the car to the front door. Bringing groceries or just one's self from a separate parking area to the home may be a major accomplishment during inclement weather.

Security is also a growing design influence for urban and suburban townhouses and condominiums. Being able to enter one's home from a garage directly attached to the home is very desirable in the minds of many homebuyers, particularly in urban infill sites. The functional convenience, privacy, and individuality afforded the owner of a home with an attached garage are strong reasons for the developer and his design team to consider their use. Norcross's buyer preference study found that almost 60 percent of the easterners surveyed preferred being able to park as close to their homes as possible. This desire, however, was tempered with the

concern that the environment should not be "spoiled" in achieving this proximity. Over one-fourth of those surveyed said they would be willing to walk as much as 150 feet.*

If the walk to the homes is pleasant, a market may accept separate garage areas as compared with attached garages. For design flexibility, a combination of both attached and detached garages as close to the individual homes as possible is desirable. A more understandable, and therefore marketable, plat is achieved if all or most of the garages are deedable as contiguous pieces of land with the homes. Where direct attachment is impossible, the access door of the detached garage should be placed as close as possible to the home entry door. Connections with decorative arbors, wall extensions,

---

*Norcross, Carl, *Townhouses & Condominiums: Residents' Likes and Dislikes* (Washington, D.C.: Urban Land Institute, 1973) p. 61.

5-7 One-story garage and carports may help reduce the scale of the larger townhouse or condominium buildings.

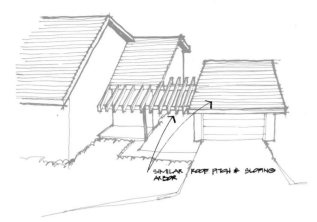

5-8 Arbors or fascia extensions visually tie buildings together.

or roof rafters make the home/garage relationship even more private and individual. An expansion of site planning choices with such program variations as turned garages relieves the forced regularity of straight townhouse blocks. Moreover, variation may break the linear mass of a building while creating a private entry or patio space.

In certain market areas, a detached cluster of garages is acceptable due to climate, environmental, or economic factors, and may foster a very open feeling of community. Sometimes individual garages are banked and placed adjacent to parking bays. Buildings of banked garages should vary in size and length from the residential structures, becoming a visual contrast to the homes rather than a uniform repetition of the same form. Using smaller garage clusters reduces the scale of parking bays and permits these parking areas to be placed closer to the homes they serve. This planning technique adds another architectural form to accent and vary a project's visual image. Lower scale garage buildings bring architectural detailing closer to eye level and within human scale, making people more comfortable, while at the same time helping to integrate larger residential structures and natural land forms.

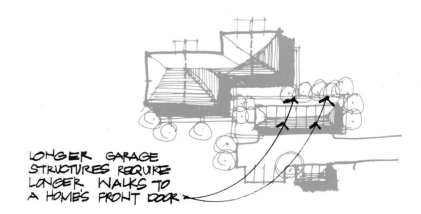

5-9 Banked garages and parking.

5-10 (top) and 5-11 (bottom) Banked garages in smaller clusters permit saving natural features, as well as reflect building architecture at a smaller scale.

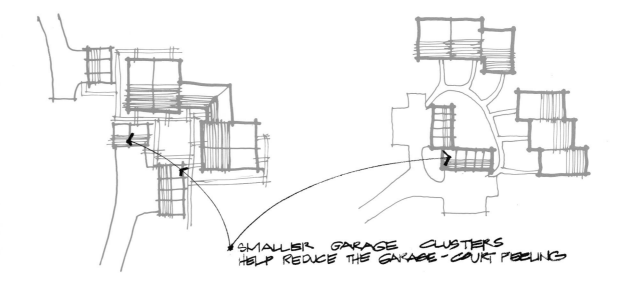

SMALLER GARAGE CLUSTERS
HELP REDUCE THE GARAGE-COURT FEELING

5-12 To reduce the walking distance, smaller garage clusters may be located closer to the homes than larger garage structures.

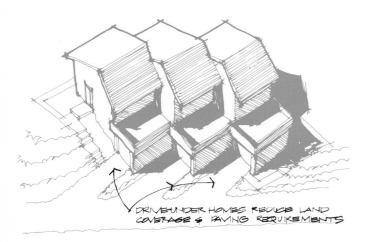

DRIVE-UNDER HOMES REDUCE LAND COVERAGE & PAVING REQUIREMENTS

Drive-under and Underground Garages.

The townhouse/condominium development utilizing drive-under units exclusively may achieve marketable densities of 6 to 12 units per acre. Homes with either a full drive-under or split-entry adaptation automatically create rolling land that depresses the road relative to adjacent open space and structures. With proper grading and maintenance, the feeling is gained that the community was built into the land rather than merely superimposed on the surface. There are, however, problems that develop from the repeated use of the same mass or volume. Repetition makes individuality and identity harder to achieve.

A unique townhouse or condominium form, the *quadrominium* or *quad,* often has attached drive-under garages. These homes, with garages grouped at the end of a building containing units above, require a condominium ownership form.

For certain expensive, high amenity sites, where densities of at least 10 to 20 units per acre are marketable, underground parking may be the only viable alternative. Without the extra site area retained through underground parking, the majority of open land is reduced to paving.

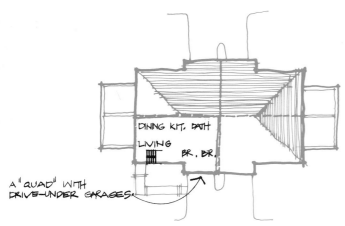

DINING KIT. BATH

LIVING BR. BR.

A "QUAD" WITH DRIVE-UNDER GARAGES.

5-13 (top) Low land coverage; each home has an attached, drive-under garage. 5-14 (bottom) A *quad* home with all attached, drive-under garages. 5-15 (right) The entrance on the green-space side of those drive-under units causes some convenience problems especially in buildings of over four units.

5-16 (top) The grade change created by the drive-under garages makes the structure appear to be built into the land. 5-17 (bottom) A condominium with garages grouped at the end of the building.

Garage Doors: Perception of Density. Automatic garage doors are the logical accessory of attached garages. They are convenient features, providing functional and security benefits. It also appears that people attach a certain distinction or status to the use of automatic doors. Though seemingly an accounting or marketing decision, the inclusion of automatic garage doors in the sale price of a home is actually a design solution—one that will strongly complement any well-planned cluster, improving the visual quality and decreasing perceived density. Keeping garage doors closed and the majority of cars out of sight conveys the subtle feeling of lower density and a better maintained neighborhood.

Designers should avoid using two garage doors for a two-car garage. The reason for this is subtle but significant. Two garage doors convey the illusion of a higher density—one double-car door is better. Two single-car garage doors should only be used if they complement a specific architectural style.

5-19 (above) Density perception through counting garage doors: on the left—one home; on the right—four narrow units or two wide ones? 5-20 (top) Automatic garage doors help to reduce the feeling of density—people are more likely to keep their doors closed. 5-21 (bottom) Single-car garages usually leave exposed automobiles due to second car ownership or use of the garage for storage.

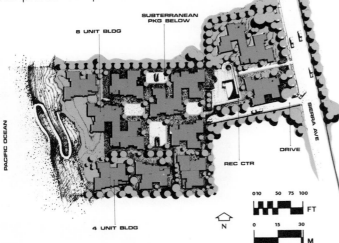

8 UNIT BLDG

SUBTERRANEAN PKG BELOW

PACIFIC OCEAN

SIERRA AVE

DRIVE

REC CTR

4 UNIT BLDG

0 10 50 75 100

FT

N

0 15 30

M

5-18 Underground parking permits maximum use of a high amenity site.

Parking Areas

The omission of garages from a townhouse/condominium complex has to have a very strong budgetary justification. However, as costs continue to rise, cost constraints may justify omitting garages from some developments.

The use of open bays or parking lots may be appropriate in higher density developments, normally designed for rental with the possibility of future conversion to townhouse ownership. For townhouse densities lower than 10 to 12 units per acre, clustering of parking courts rather than lining all court roads with parking spaces is preferable, particularly where this will coordinate with private spaces or unit entries.

The undesignated, large common parking lot provides a maximum parking capacity and reduces site development costs. It is normally used for townhouse/condominium densities of over 10 units per acre—unless an underground parking structure is built. The benefit of lower cost, however, is not appreciated from the perspective of the driving distance into the housing clusters or from the houses that overlook expanses of paving. Often, land conserved by building a large, common parking lot is added to remote open space or provides space for more units, resulting in a perception of higher density. Buyers would prefer to retain landscaped open space close to their homes. A plentiful supply of open space definitely contributes to environmental quality, and placing more

homes on a given piece of land may help lower the price of each home, but, first and foremost, a townhouse/condominium community is perceived by homebuyers, residents, and visitors from its roadways and across its parking areas. The disadvantages of a large common lot in this light are quite apparent: the living environment feels like a "carscape." Moreover, since much of the activity in these lots takes place between 6 and 8 o'clock in the morning and 4 to 6 o'clock in the evening, the undesignated parking lot becomes a racetrack for the best parking spot.

Parking lots for the livable townhouse/condominium development must be broken up visually into mini-lots. Curving or radiat-

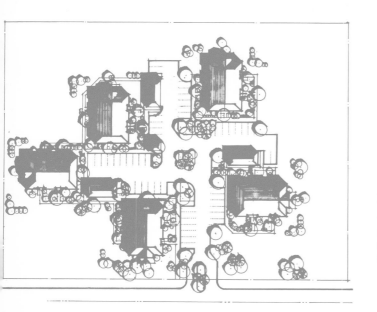

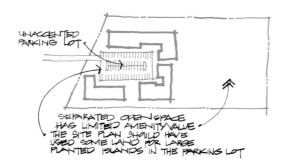

5-22 (left) This back-to-back townhouse plan shows T-roads used for garages, but do not line the road with them. 5-23 (above) Do not be too "efficient" with the parking layout. It will save construction costs but may hurt marketability. 5-24 (right) In warmer climates, the impact of parked cars may be reduced with shrubs.

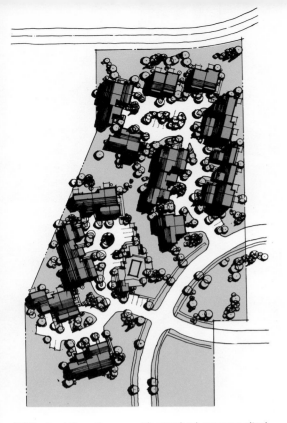

ing parking spaces, shaped to fit existing or created land forms, and curving roads interrupted by planted islands, lighting fixtures, signage, or mailbox structures all help to bring a more human, residential scale to what may otherwise become a discount store-like parking lot.

Whether garages or parking areas are used, one very effective plan for curing garage and parking problems of appearance and function is to angle the residential access courts relative to the building blocks, garages, open spaces, bays, or parking lots. This gives the person driving into a townhouse/condominium community or cluster a variety of views and prevents seeing the same view of more than several garage entries, parking spaces, or cars at once. Interest is created

by alternate opening and tightening of the spaces a person passes through while traveling on a court road. Jogged and offset homes and buildings parallel to the garages or parking spaces accentuate this interesting effect.

Garage or home sidewalls are a contrasting element, and thus prime locations for surface treatments like brick, diagonal siding, or stone, as well as for backdrop like trees, shrubs, or ivy. Integrated, varied setbacks with offset building forms in a residential court that is sloped with existing or created grades will help yield a residential environment of variety, visual interest, and surprise. This is the antithesis of the site planning approach that yields barracks-like standardized blocks.

5-25 (top) Townhouses with attached garages sited along a private court and clustered around a cul-de-sac. 5-26 (bottom) Vary the views by angling the roads, creating tight and open spaces to drive through.

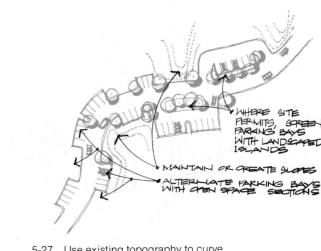

5-27 Use existing topography to curve parking bays, add islands for interest.

On-Street/Off-Street. Basically there are two parking area design options: on-street or off-street. On-street parking is fostered by streets that are wider than necessary, lack of off-street parking, inadequate signage, or lack of enforcement. In most cases, safe, cost-efficient roadway design calls for the elimination of on-street parallel parking from arterial streets, collectors, and even lower-use courts. Parallel parking may be used on minor residential streets where bays or lots are not feasible. It is preferable to have narrower streets with parking bays than to have wide streets with parallel parking. Where ad-

jacent parking is not possible, it is best to designate parking for each resident as close to his home as possible.

In either case, the goal is to break up large masses of cars into groups of less than 10 to 20. The perceived density is lowered by interspersing open space, islands, or garages. Plant material, earth forms and shaping of the road to fit grade variations further contrast what could otherwise be a sea of asphalt or concrete. Paving material changes may also add subtle but effective character to a parking area.

David Frazen

5-28 (left) Parking area paving may add character. 5-29 (top) In parking area design, divide cars into smaller groups. 5-30 (bottom) Place landscaped islands in visually prominent spots.

Joseph W. Molitor

Apron Parking. This kind of parking system places one or two spaces immediately in front of a designated garage. While this is a desirable and marketable site design approach, it should not be viewed as an inflexible requirement for an entire cluster or development.

Peripheral Parking. The isolated or peripheral parking area is sometimes used for bypassed sites or irregular-shaped parcels. This system is not recommended for a typical suburban location where other more functional and attractive alternatives are possible. This parking type has, however, a valid application on high amenity sites. Many times peripheral parking is both practical and even necessary in intensively used, "character" recreational communities, such as ski villages, where pedestrian traffic is emphasized along extensions of commercial/residential malls.

5-32 Large, remote, peripheral linear parking courts reduce pavement coverage on erosive slopes. Natural amenity of site offsets long walking distances and parking bay sizes.

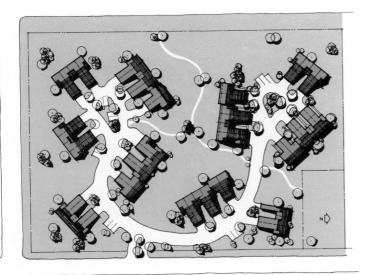

5-31 A site design with designated apron parking for each townhouse.

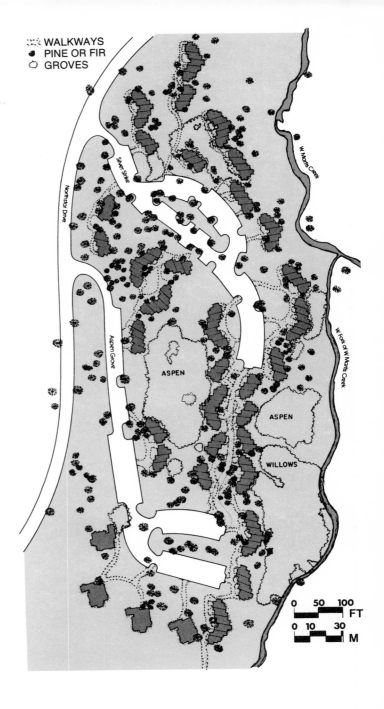

WALKWAYS
PINE OR FIR
GROVES

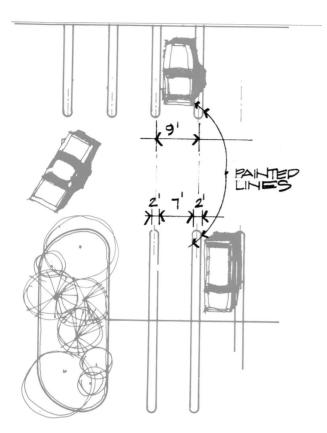

PAINTED LINES

5-33 Attention to parking details: the use of double line spaces improves the likelihood of efficient parking.

The Parking Space

Throughout the concept design stage, a standard parking space is normally drawn as 10-feet by 20-feet deep. However, for the preliminary and final stages of detail site planning, specific dimensions must be shown. Parking layouts should reflect the trend toward smaller cars. "All the domestic car companies are so heavily committed to downsizing programs that a whole new concept of the full-size car would result by the mid-80s. Already, in wheel base and weight, the new intermediates could be classed with the older compacts.* Depending on the difficulties a site planner may encounter in fitting a proper number of spaces into a plan, switching from a 10-foot- to a 9-foot-wide space may be warranted. Planning experience indicates that a switch from a 20-foot depth to an 18-foot depth will cause few inconveniences, particularly where the court road is not parallel to the garage face.

Designation of all spaces with painted lines is an important element of a functioning parking bay or lot area. A double line better insures an accurate, even spacing of parked cars. It may seem a small detail but the lined parking lot also gives a more organized and neat appearance. Further visual interest, pavement cost reductions, and stormwater attenuation may result if tire stops and permeable rock areas are placed at the ends of parking spaces. These will add texture and color to the paving surface. Since no paving is necessary behind them, tire stops may trim 2 to 4 feet of pavement from parking bays.

How Many Spaces? The number, size, and location of parking spaces for a townhouse/condominium development should be influenced by a number of variables: (1) constituent family sizes and ages; (2) income levels; (3) project density; and (4) proximity to adjacent parking facilities. Local subdivi-

*Wards 1978 Automotive Yearbook, 14th ed., Library of Congress #40,33639 (Detroit: Wards' Communications Inc., 1978), p. 150.

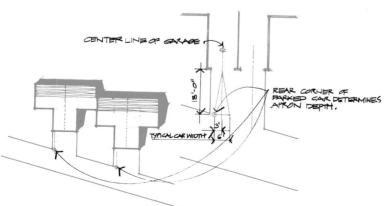

CENTER LINE OF GARAGE

REAR CORNER OF PARKED CAR DETERMINES APRON DEPTH.

TYPICAL CAR WIDTH

5-34 (left) Reduced apron parking depth does not adversely affect parking convenience and function. 5-35 (right) A parking bay with car stop and rock for attenuating stormwater runoff.

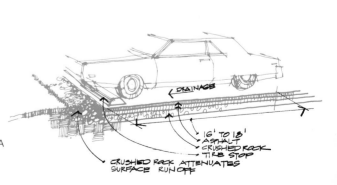

DRAINAGE

16' TO 18' ASPHALT
CRUSHED ROCK
TIRE STOP
CRUSHED ROCK ATTENUATES SURFACE RUNOFF

sion ordinance requirements are often another inflexible determinant.

Today more and more American families own two or more vehicles. Whether this trend will continue due to the greater percentage of women working or be curtailed by future energy limitations is unclear. Although a definite trend is developing toward the use of smaller cars, influencing parking space sizes, the number of necessary parking spaces for a townhouse/condominium development will probably remain constant.

Ordinances that call for more than two covered or uncovered spaces per home displace the proper role of design. When an excessive number of spaces must be placed in front of or near a townhouse or condominium building, these controls dominate the site planning process. The unfortunate results are twofold: the cost of the homes rises unnecessarily due to reduced density and greater paving cost, and access routes to the

community begin to look like used car lots. The limited and often futile task of "design" is then to squeeze in open space in an attempt to relieve the visual impact of wide expanses of pavement.

While most communities provide a process for variances, an ordinance inflexibly requiring a certain quantity of spaces fails to recognize that the types of homes and residents are a more meaningful design criteria for setting parking ratios. An extreme example may be noted in comparing the requirements of certain developments for the elderly—where less than one space per unit is adequate.

In deciding the appropriate number of spaces, the garage or carport should be included in the total parking space count. Ordinances calling for the exclusion of garages from required ratios are, in effect, calling for much higher parking ratios than will actually be needed. In complexes with garages and basement storage, overflow guest parking

should be provided at the rate of one-third space per home, in separate guest parking areas. In projects with garage but no basement storage, more overflow guest parking is usually needed, because part of the garage ends up being used for storage. This may be accomplished with larger common parking bays or aprons in front of the garages. The entire problem may be solved by providing more space in the garage for adequate storage.

Recreational Vehicle Parking. Parking bays or lots may become a convenient storage area for recreational vehicles, boats, and old cars. This is particularly detrimental for two reasons. One, additional vehicles use up parking spaces designed for guest use, causing conflicts with the use of designated spaces. Secondly, storage of old cars and recreational vehicles creates a feeling of higher density. One solution is to provide a common storage area for recreational vehicles that is maintained by the community association.

5-36 (left) and 5-37 (middle) A townhouse court is for parking, not boat storage: enforce community association covenants.   5-38 (right) If on-site storage of boats and recreational vehicles is to be permitted, designate spaces or create separate storage areas.

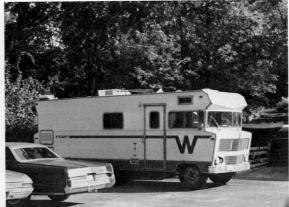

Building/Road Relationships

There are essentially two basic kinds of unit building and parking relationships, the use of each type depending on the location of open space, density, amenities, and view. These two relationships are garage-court entries and green-space entries. An important variation of either type would orient the entry and/or garage to the side of an individual unit. This would enhance a premium end location and is often a justification for buildings with fewer units.

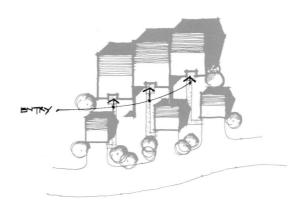

5-39 (above) and 5-40 (below) Typical garage-court entry buildings: guest entries face the court road/parking areas.

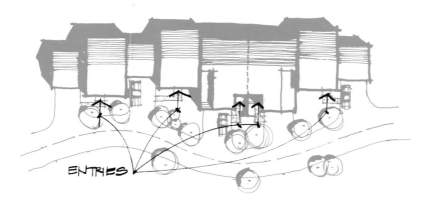

5-41 (top) Garage-court entry units with entries and deck space facing forward and attached drive-under garages. 5-42 (bottom) Garage-court entry units with detached two-car garages.

Home Entries

Garage-Court Entry Buildings. Garage-court entries have guest entries and garages or parking areas on the same side of the townhouse/condominium unit. This arrangement works well for the central units of a townhouse building. It also avoids having to bring a guest entry walk all the way around a building.

Workable densities for garage-court entries range from five to eight units per acre. If the garage is not built under the building or deck, the lower given density is recommended. In suburban locations or where a

90

more open feeling is desired, density should be limited to about six and a half units per acre or less. Lower densities are necessary for garage-court entry buildings with attached or nearby garages, because this garage/parking plan spreads the buildings further apart. Garage-court entry units with detached garages may have private entry courtyards with the addition of screen fencing or wall extensions. This type of orientation works well with a site that slopes away from the vehicular access courts, taking advantage of an amenity feature located away from the parking area. It also has the convenience of the garage and entrance on the same side.

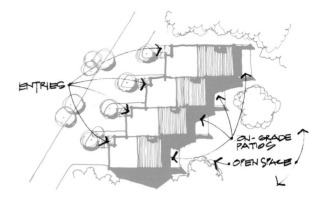

5-45 (left) and 5-46 (above) Garage-court entry condominiums with rear facing living areas and private patios.

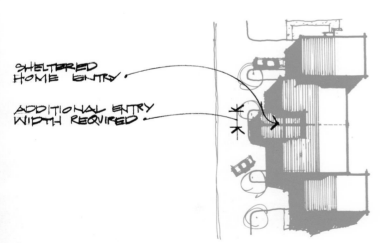

5-43 (above) Garage-court entry units usually require fewer units per acre, but offer convenient access and eliminate a walkaway around the building. 5-44 (right) Avoid narrow, unattractive guest entries to a garage-court entry townhouse.

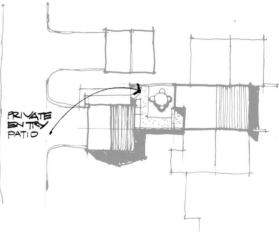

5-47 Create a private entry courtyard between a garage-court entry townhouse and the detached garage.

91

Green-Space Entry Buildings. Green-space entry refers to a townhouse/condominium unit type whose entry is at the side opposite from the garage, parking, or access court. Also called a green-belt entry, this building type may be used when open space and amenities are centrally located. A private entry space may be created with fencing adjacent to this open space, to buffer the front door from pathway traffic. Planning studies should determine the appropriate, livable density of units. Six to ten homes per acre is common for green-space entry homes.

A variation of the two above types is the side-entry unit. These units have corner entries or side entries in relation to the garage, parking, or access court. A particularly valuable design tool when used in conjunction with either green-space entry or garage-court entry buildings, this type takes advantage of the premium end locations in a typical townhouse configuration. The typical four-plex that has enjoyed popularity is essentially four, side-entry homes or a combination of garage-court entry, green-space entry, and side-entry units. Unit entry types will be discussed further in the home types section of the next chapter.

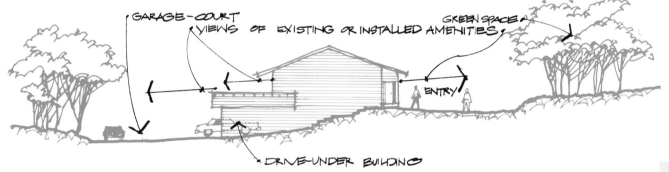

5-48 Green-space entry: main entry and open space are on side opposite drive-under garage.

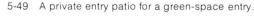

5-49 A private entry patio for a green-space entry.

92

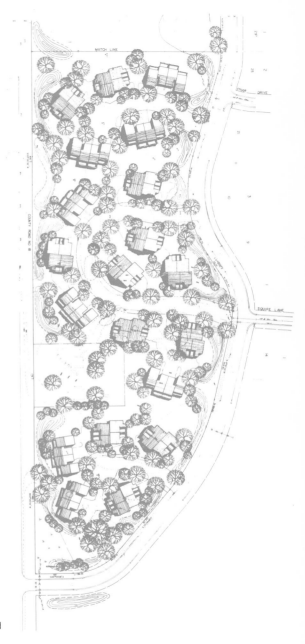

5-50 The garage-court entry side of a condominium with common service door and apron parking.

5-52 (top) and 5-53 (bottom) Side-entry units break the row house look.

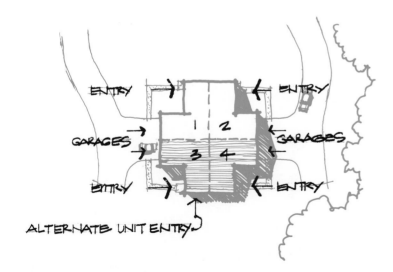

5-51 The four-plex is four side-entry units or "quads."

5-54 These "quads" are clustered and intermixed with standard townhouses.

5-55 Single-loaded drive-under courts, with decks over garages facing amenity space.

Building Arrangements

As buildings are first designed through a consideration of how they will ultimately fit into the site plan, site placement must be studied in detail. Some of the factors influencing the grouping of buildings are:

- the shape and slope of the buildable land areas;
- the location of views and amenities;
- the density to be achieved; and
- the character of the site's surroundings.

Buildings may be placed on one side (single-loaded) or both sides (double-loaded) of vehicular access courts. The coordination of buildings on a site may involve one or more of four basic configurations which will be discussed in the following sections. Depending on the site's locale, streets and alleys may determine the site plan. Or existing streets or city blocks may serve as a formal site perimeter for newly designed interior court roads. On less constrained (often suburban) sites, buildings located on linear courts or in clusters become the primary planning approach.

Single-Loaded Courts. The single-loaded court works well with garage-court entry buildings on a site with a narrow buildable area. However, a lower density of houses is the typical result. This is acceptable if housing prices are high enough to accommodate the increased raw land cost per unit and a large enough site development budget exists to properly improve or preserve the across-court views. In more dense construction with multi-story buildings, the single-loaded court road may be necessary to allow enough road frontage for adequate garage and/or parking. Where single-loaded courts are used with drive-under homes, homes may be designed with decks facing the green space beyond the pavement.

5-56 Earth berms screen garage entries to this single-loaded court. Decks over garages take advantage of view.

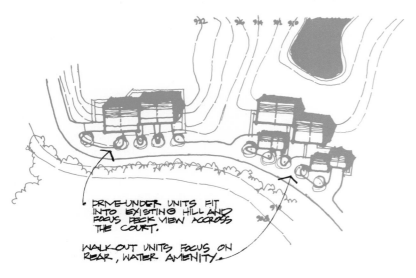

DRIVE-UNDER UNITS FIT INTO EXISTING HILL AND FOCUS DECK VIEW ACROSS THE COURT.

WALK-OUT UNITS FOCUS ON REAR, WATER AMENITY.

5-57 The single-loaded court road.

Double-Loaded Courts. A site planning technique to preserve open space and/or attain increased density will front buildings on both sides of a court road. Double-loaded courts concentrate buildings to disturb less of the site. The cross-court privacy problems make green-space entry drive-unders with decks built over the garages a less desirable solution. Moreover, double-loading drive-under homes on a site may result in canyon-like garage courts. Where this is necessary, focusing living spaces (and patios or decks) away from the paving area and other units is preferable.

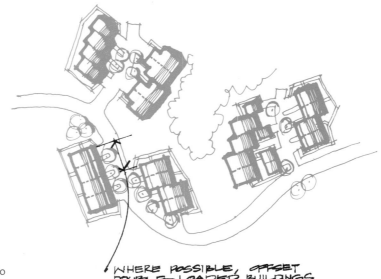

5-58 Double loading of the court roads, to preserve open space elsewhere and increase unit density.

WHERE POSSIBLE, OFFSET DOUBLE-LOADED BUILDINGS TO IMPROVE VIEWS AND REDUCE THE FEELING OF DENSITY.

5-59 (top) A double-loaded court of green-space entry, drive-under buildings may magnify the feeling of density. 5-60 (bottom) Just enough room for an infill townhouse.

Double-loaded courts permit densities in the upper ranges of six to eleven units per acre with green-space entry buildings. Garage-court entry buildings with entries facing the paving would yield a somewhat lower density because of the less regimented building configurations required for better livability. Buildable site area and site development economies are common reasons for double-loading roads.

However, improper or overuse of this planning method is a main source of the garage court syndrome. A land plan that places too many units off a given amount of court road magnifies the feeling of density. Even with an abundance of surrounding open space, the first visual impact of the homes may send away prospective homebuyers.

In urban infill areas, where the existing grid street pattern is fixed or inflexible ordinances force adherence to right-of-way and setback requirements, grid streets and alleys may be the only usable circulation system. Even with less restrictive controls on development, the orientation of adjacent structures will determine a building's appropriate positioning, setbacks, and street system, fitting it to the existing streetscape.

5-61 Increased density of 10.5 units per acre achieved by double-loaded courts and "T" turnarounds.

A somewhat larger infill site may provide enough interior open space for rear garages and parking courts. While street-sidewalk relationships would be maintained typical to other homes, the open space in the center of the block would give an interesting visual contrast. Parcels surrounding the open space could then be developed in individual phases. This could both break the linear alley feeling and provide some room for an intensive amenity, such as a tennis court or developed play area.

5-63 (above) This infill townhouse, designed to fit into a neighborhood of large, older homes, fronts three townhouses with entries off a city street. Garages and decks face an internal open space in the center of the block. 5-64 (below) A larger urban infill site: maintaining the existing sidewalk/building relationship but turning the alley into an open space and parking court area.

5-62 A small urban infill development maintaining setbacks and regular orientation to adjacent buildings.

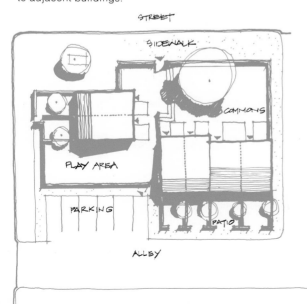

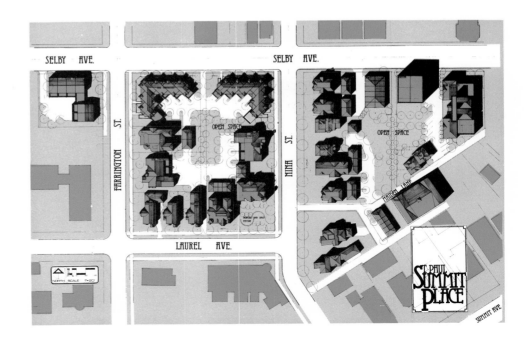

Linear Groups. Linear court roads are typically used on sloping sites and best adapt to a narrow buildable land area or to increased densities. With either a single-or double-loaded form, minimum excavation occurs if the proper home types are used. Again, the garage-court feeling may easily result if too high a density is used; building type variations may help to break this appearance.

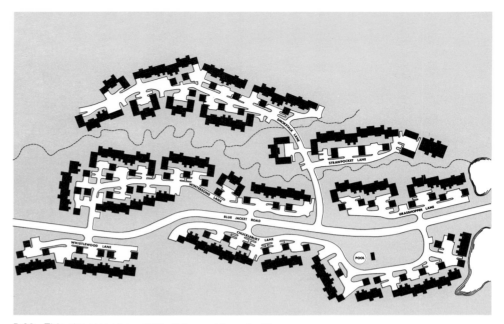

5-66   This site plan shows 27 buildings of three to 12 units placed off a major collector. Small parking bays or garages break the row house feel of this linear plan.

5-65   Detached garages on a linear court road. Even with vertical grade change, too much of the same kind of building creates a feeling of high density.

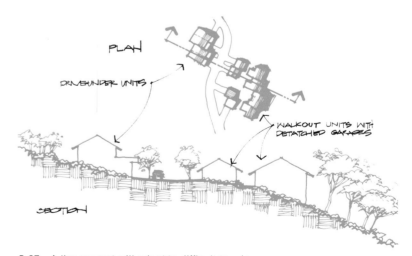

5-67   A linear court will adapt to difficult terrain.

98

Clusters. For sites with adequate buildable areas, clustering of townhouses or condominiums is a desirable planning approach. Assuming that design freedom exists with the absence of right-of-way requirements, side-, back-, and front-yard setback controls, an interesting, quiet, and safe site design may result.

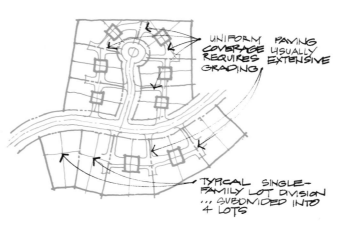

UNIFORM PAVING COVERAGE USUALLY REQUIRES EXTENSIVE GRADING

TYPICAL SINGLE-FAMILY LOT DIVISION ... SUBDIVIDED INTO 4 LOTS

5-68 (bottom) Single- and double-loaded courts with garage-court entry units. Rear patios face green space and path system. 5-69 (above) An individual building may be interesting. Repetition of a typical lot plan often results in a regimented appearance, requiring extensive paving coverage.

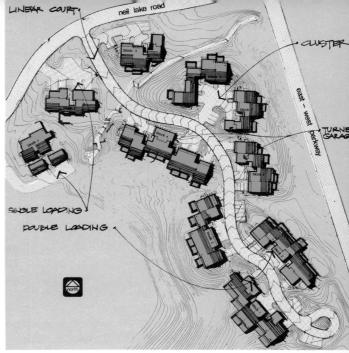

LINEAR COURT — neil lake road — CLUSTER — TURNE GARAG — SINGLE LOADING — DOUBLE LOADING — east-west parkway — north

5-70 (above) This linear plan combines walkout, garage-court entry buildings on some single-loaded courts, double-loading of the main cul-de-sac, and one cluster of seven townhouses. 5-71 (below) This townhouse cluster has some garages turned 90 degrees to the homes. Guest parking is provided by a combination of garage apron parking and designated guest parking spaces.

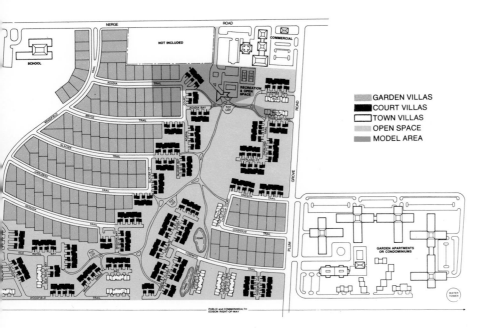

GARDEN VILLAS
COURT VILLAS
TOWN VILLAS
OPEN SPACE
MODEL AREA

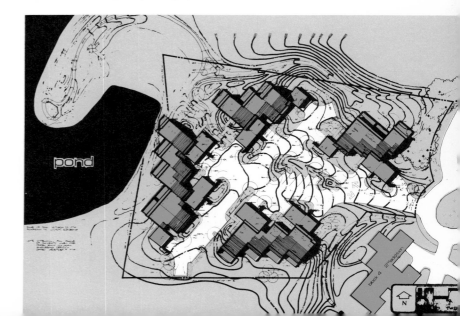

pond

There are basically two types of clusters: those that include cars and those that do not. Typically, the clusters that accommodate cars have some or all attached garages, with units and buildings that may be turned 90 degrees to adjacent units.

The other basic cluster type has homes grouped around a landscaped courtyard. Detached garages are grouped off to one side in small parking bays. In some markets acceptance for either of the two cluster types may run 50/50. Often a plan will include a mix of linear and cluster elements.

5-72 (top left) and 5-73 (top right) A cluster that includes cars, with attached garages and garage-court entry homes. 5-74 (bottom left) and 5-75 (bottom right) An intensively landscaped courtyard allows up to 25 feet of separation between the unit and main walkways.

100

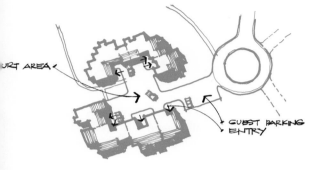

URT AREA

GUEST PARKING ENTRY

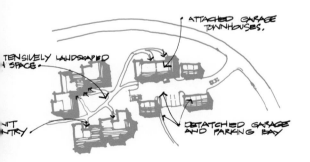

ATTACHED GARAGE TOWNHOUSES.

TENSIVELY LANDSCAPED SPACE.

NIT ENTRY

DETACHED GARAGE AND PARKING BAY

Regulation Effects

The typical garage court or parking lot image of some mid-density communities may be improved by design professionals who react to variations in the types of people, homes, and land that must be combined in a successful development. However, one of the largest obstacles to creating the quality townhouse/condominium environment illustrated by successful developments is the enforcement of inappropriate street and right-of-way widths, setback dimensions, and gradient requirements.

In a more standard townhouse configuration, where the common property area adjacent either to the garage or parking bay is deeded to and maintained by the homeowner, early design consideration is necessary. In most cases fencing of this space is inappropriate because it will yield a stockade-like feeling surrounding a parking or open space area, while normally creating a patio on the non-amenity side of the house.

In certain townhouse markets, front and rear yards result from adherence to subdivision regulations. In this case "front yards" should be of a size that a homeowner may extensively landscape, within the community association guidelines, with a moderate expenditure. The result is an interesting mix of groundcover, retaining walls, and plantings, offering a chance for individual expression. The community association should encourage improvement of individualized and personalized entry areas or "yard" landscaping through general guidelines established by the architectural control committee.

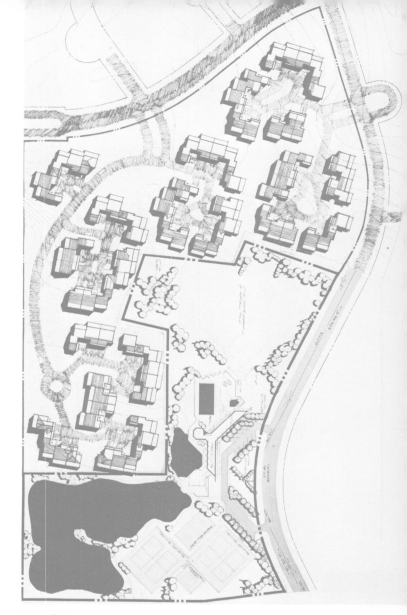

5-76 This development has all of the townhouses clustered off courts and turnarounds.

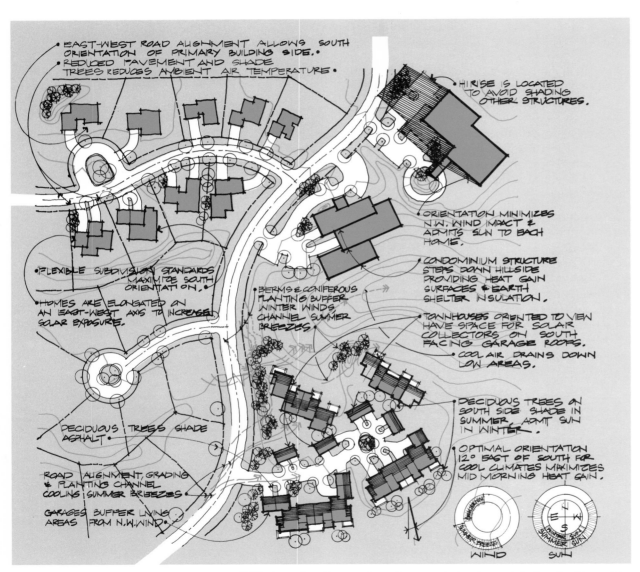

EAST-WEST ROAD ALIGNMENT ALLOWS SOUTH ORIENTATION OF PRIMARY BUILDING SIDE.
REDUCED PAVEMENT AND SHADE TREES REDUCES AMBIENT AIR TEMPERATURE.

HI RISE IS LOCATED TO AVOID SHADING OTHER STRUCTURES.

ORIENTATION MINIMIZES N.W. WIND IMPACT & ADMITS SUN TO EACH HOME.

CONDOMINIUM STRUCTURE STEPS DOWN HILLSIDE PROVIDING HEAT GAIN SURFACES & EARTH SHELTER INSULATION.

TOWNHOUSES ORIENTED TO VIEW HAVE SPACE FOR SOLAR COLLECTORS ON SOUTH FACING GARAGE ROOFS.

COOL AIR DRAINS DOWN LOW AREAS.

DECIDUOUS TREES ON SOUTH SIDE SHADE IN SUMMER, ADMIT SUN IN WINTER.

OPTIMAL ORIENTATION 12° EAST OF SOUTH FOR COOL CLIMATES MAXIMIZES MID MORNING HEAT GAIN.

FLEXIBLE SUBDIVISION STANDARDS MAXIMIZE SOUTH ORIENTATION.

HOMES ARE ELONGATED ON AN EAST-WEST AXIS TO INCREASE SOLAR EXPOSURE.

BERMS & CONIFEROUS PLANTING BUFFER WINTER WINDS CHANNEL SUMMER BREEZES.

DECIDUOUS TREES SHADE ASPHALT.

ROAD ALIGNMENT, GRADING & PLANTING CHANNEL COOLING SUMMER BREEZES.

GARAGES BUFFER LIVING AREAS FROM N.W. WIND.

WIND   SUN

5-77   In cool and temperate regions, good planning and design should consider the energy implications of the sun and wind.

Energy Considerations

Townhouses and condominiums have an advantage over other forms of housing when it comes to energy conservation—the attached unit(s) provide good insulation on one or more sides. With good climatic planning and design and flexible zoning and subdivision regulations, townhouse and condominium projects have a further advantage—entire buildings consisting of many homes may be oriented to incorporate passive solar energy conserving techniques. This is equally true of proper wind orientation to reduce the negative effects of cold winter winds and to take advantage of the cooling summer breezes.

However, for townhouses and condominiums climatic design considerations for passive energy conservation are complex, particularly in the more dense and site restrictive urban locations. The ideal of having maximum southern unit exposure cannot be fully achieved when the long axis of the unit (its common wall) faces east-west or when the southern facing wall is all or partly shaded by other buildings. Solutions to these problems, whether in low-, mid-, or high-rise projects, require careful consideration, particularly for the tradeoffs between passive energy conservation and other design criteria. For example, a creative solution to the problem of an adjacent building shading part of a high-rise condominium might be to zone non-residential uses to those floors most shaded.

Problems for active solar systems in town-houses and condominiums are similar to passive energy conservation problems. There are differences, however. For example in a passive solar design, deciduous trees would be located on the southern exposure to provide summer shade and winter sun, but for active solar design deciduous trees should be further away from the unit so that unit-mounted collectors will not be shaded to lose some efficiency.

One economical and operational advantage of townhouses and condominiums is that col-lection and storage facilities may readily be shared and need not be related to individual units. Community associations may be set up to operate common collector facilities that provide energy to a series of units or buildings. These collectors could be incor-porated unobstrusively in common areas (hillside, berm, or fence) or structures (park-ing garage).

For further information, other sources on the emerging and complex subject of energy conservation should be consulted.

5-79

Selected References for
Energy Design

The AIA Research Corporation (for U.S. Depart-ment of Housing and Urban Development—Contract IAA H-5574). *Solar Dwelling Design Concepts.* Washington, D.C.: U.S. Government Printing Office, May 1976.

The American Planning Association. *Site Plan-ning for Solar Access: A Guidebook for Develop-ers and Planners.* Chicago: APA, December 1978.

Jaffe, Martin, and Erley, Duncan. *Protecting Solar Access: A Guidebook for Planners.* Chicago: The American Planning Association, November 1978 (Final Draft).

National Association of Home Builders. *Cost Ef-fective Site Planning: Single Family Development.* Washington, D.C.: NAHB, 1976.

Robinette, Gary O., ed. *Landscape Planning for Energy Conservation.* Reston, Virginia: Environ-mental Design Press, 1978.

Wright, David, (AIA). *Natural Solar Archi-tecture—A Passive Primer.* New York: Van Nos-trand Reinhold Company, 1978.

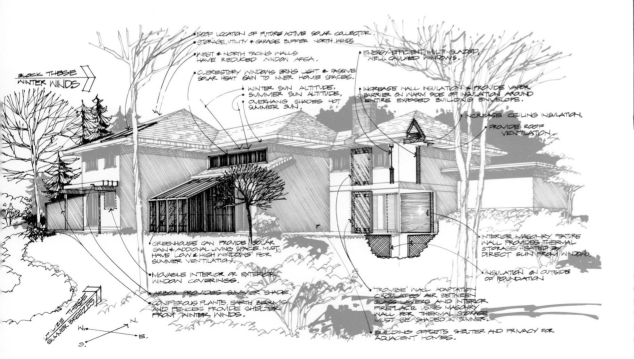

5-78   In this group of townhouses, numerous energy conservation ideas, suited mostly for temperate and northerly regions, are demonstrated. Reduction of air in-filtration increased insulation, and orientation for maxi-mum solar gain and winter wind protection are signifi-cant passive design features.

6 Building Design

Detailed building design involves considering various plan/cross-section types and integrating them with site characteristics and road patterns. The first part of this chapter isolates home design types and discusses methods for combining them into interesting buildings. Horizontal and vertical unit and building offsets as well as roof alignment details are considered. Private outdoor spaces and entry walkway areas are discussed as an important part of both unit and building design. Because extra attention to design details will enhance a townhouse/condominium living environment, construction detailing is also discussed. A latter section of this chapter, involving considerations for interior design, discusses factors that make a home's interior functional and interesting, livable and perhaps more marketable.

Martin Tornallyay

6-1 (left) Compared to other types, on-grade units may be built at a lower cost. 6-2 (right) The on-grade unit type provides an easy indoor-outdoor connection.

Home Types

There are several basic home plan/cross-section types that are typically used with different site conditions. The appropriate plan type is primarily determined by local market preferences and the topography of the site. On land that has a grade change of over 4 to 5 percent, use of more than one plan type is preferable. The utilization of two or more plan types enables the developer to adjust to grade conditions and provides architectural variety in the building massing and roof lines. The discussion of home types should be referenced to the previous chapter on garage and entry design options. From a marketing standpoint, when utilizing more than one plan type it is essential that the sales pace of the various plan types be monitored to insure that a development proceeds on a phased basis, rather than selling out one particular type at the start.

Slab-On-Grade

Most suited to relatively flat or "plateaued" sites, and frequently used in markets where basements are not standard, this home design's relationship to existing grade makes it the easiest type for indoor/outdoor connections. The on-grade construction reduces costs and is attractive to older buyers since it places the entry and living areas all on one level. This design type may consist of a one- or two-story form.

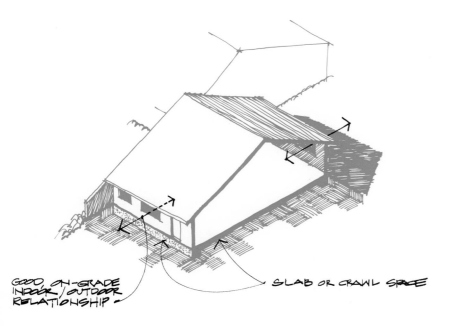

GOOD ON-GRADE INDOOR/OUTDOOR RELATIONSHIP

SLAB OR CRAWL SPACE

Basement

Most people are familiar with the type of home design that would include basements. This design type provides inexpensive lower-level living, storage, or expansion space. Constraints on the use of this type normally occur on sites with a high water table, a shallow bedrock condition, or, in warm, humid climates, where slab construction is common, because foundations and footings are shallower than in hard frost areas. If basements are typical of the surrounding single-family detached homes, they should also be included in the community's townhouses or condominiums.

Where possible, a full walkout basement provides a much more livable downstairs space than a partial or underground basement. The walkout basement area allows a home to adapt to existing or created hillside conditions, while providing energy-efficient living space and a convenient storage area—it turns an ordinarily dark basement into an economical expansion space. The full walkout form of basement permits dropping 8 feet of grade away from the entry side of the unit. This plan type is considered very desirable by most developers, primarily because it has been readily accepted by the marketplace.

In two-story adaptations of the basement design type, the use of a full walkout yields a three-story building on the low building side. Special care in planning should be given to this dominant facade to avoid too much repetition and to break up the three-story effect with decks and balconies. Also avoid the three-story facade in the entry area of what is really a low-scale project—buyers may perceive that the project contains a higher density than is actually the case.

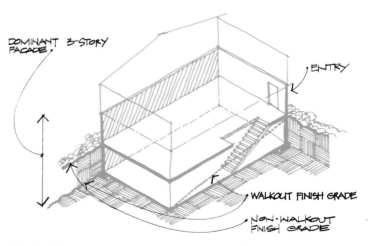

6-3 (left) Full walkout basement townhouses, with 8 feet of extra wall, window, and door space turn a basement into livable space.   6-4 (above) Build full walkout basement plan/section types where grade permits. This livable basement area is economical and energy efficient.

Split-Foyer

Besides adapting to flat sites, this design type has the capability of accommodating 4 feet of grade change falling along the length of a home and away from the entry. Improved interior function and the desirability of this home type are largely due to a perceived reduction in the number of stairs a person has to travel between floors and to the additional window area and living space on the lower level. A factor in this plan's marketability has been the economical lower level space and also the option to purchase unfinished space at a lower base price. In either case, the added space is accomplished by providing adequate lower level window area.

6-5 (left) The split-foyer plan type provides economical low-level space on a flat site or adjusts to a 4-foot grade change. 6-6 (above) These split-entry townhouses have their guest/front entries located on a heavily landscaped, green-space walkway. 6-7 (right) A townhouse block of drive-under homes. The two-story units in the middle of the block are green-space entry units with split-entry, side-entrance homes on the ends.

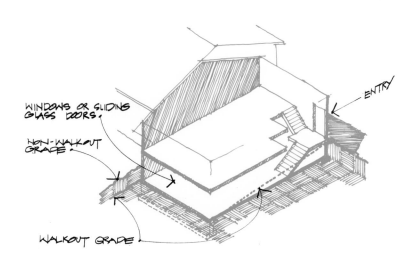

WINDOWS OR SLIDING GLASS DOORS.

NON-WALKOUT GRADE.

WALKOUT GRADE.

ENTRY

Drive-Under

This type of home design permits access from the lower, garage-court side of a townhouse or condominium building. The drive-under is the opposite site plan type from the walkout home and an extremely valuable site planning type for several reasons. Drive-unders will save cutting existing grade and, as a result, trees and plant material. Also the drive-under home with garage normally uses less land area than other townhouse/condominium plan types, permitting density increases of up to 25 percent or decreases in land coverage if the total unit count remains the same. Since, in many conditions, a road is cut into a townhouse site, the drive-under home is often used. Placing the court road at a lower elevation than the buildings will reduce the number of homes viewed from the road and help lower the feeling of density.

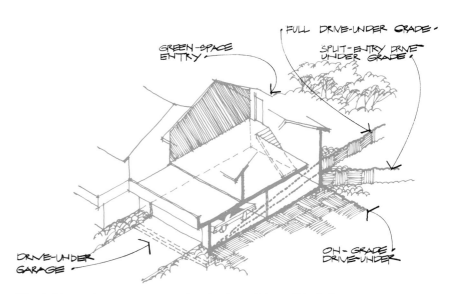

6-8   A drive-under, green-space entry plan type picks up 8 feet of grade. In single-loaded garage courts, good front and rear views may be possible.

The green-space entry variation of this home type provides an attached garage on the side opposite the home's front door. This garage is integral to the home and utilizes lower level floor space. Typically, this design will permit access from the lower garage court through a service entrance or the garage door itself. The green-space entry variation of the drive-under home may be narrower than the garage-court entry type because it does not require additional guest

(top) A drive-under with deck above the garage. Wood screens and arbor add privacy and a sense of outdoor enclosure.   6-10   (bottom left) A service access in the garage door provides convenience for this narrow, urban townhouse.   1   (bottom right) These narrow, urban drive-under townhouses have living levels above the garage. In addition to the guest entry, there is a service access in the garage door of each home.

entry width on the garage court. As a result, a land plan that partially uses this home plan type will cover less land and may require less paving frontage.

The garage-court entry variation of the drive-under type has the home's front door and garage on the same side. This plan type requires the narrowest site depth away from the parking or vehicular access court and can accept up to 8 feet of drop from the rear of the home to the paving.

As the drive-under plan may require a large number of stairs at the front of the unit for the guest entry, the on-grade or split-entry plan types, requiring few risers for access to the main level, are often preferred. Care should be given to the design of this plan type—avoiding the use of an unaccented two- to three-story facade. Without the use of decks, garage, or other wall projections, an uninteresting, canyon-like garage court may result.

6-12 This drive-under condominium with open parking bays has its guest entries facing the central open space and pathway system.

Martin Tornallyay

Because of the typically narrow spacing between garage doors for townhouses and condominiums, raising or dropping grade between units with vertical jogs may be difficult and may prevent buildings and courts from adapting to existing slopes.

The split-foyer or slab-on-grade plan types are typically usable where less than 4 feet of grade change from one side of a unit to the opposite side are required. The drive-under plan type may accommodate changes in grades of greater than 4 feet and up to one story.

VERTICAL JOG.

LARGER SPACES AND ISLANDS PERMIT GRADE CHANGE AND ACCEPT VERTICAL JOGS

VERTICAL JOG

NARROW DIMENSION MAKES IT DIFFICULT TO DROP GRADE.

6-14 With a block of narrow drive-under units, it is difficult both to offset the buildings vertically and to accept grade change along the court.

6-15 An uninterrupted three-story facade with drive-under garage may give a bleak appearance to a suburban setting.

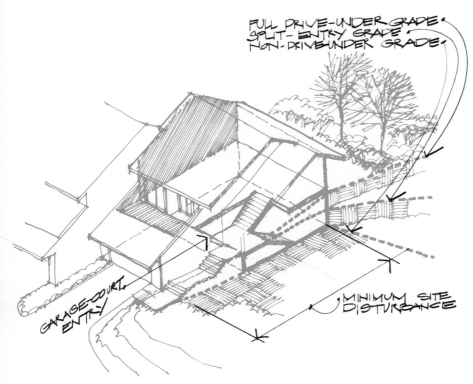

FULL DRIVE-UNDER GRADE.
SPLIT-ENTRY GRADE.
NON-DRIVE-UNDER GRADE.

MINIMUM SITE DISTURBANCE

GARAGE COURT ENTRY

6-13 A garage-court entry, drive-under townhouse requires a minimum cut into land sloping into the court.

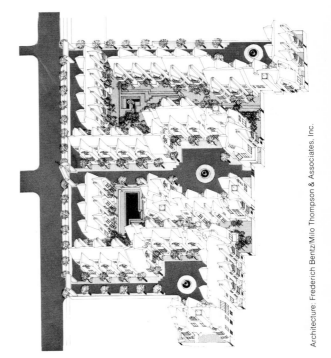

6-16 A 43-unit urban townhouse development completed in 1979, presold without a model. The three-story garage-court entry, drive-under home types conserved land, enabling a density of 17 units per acre.

111

Back-to-Back

In townhouse form, this plan may become a most cost-effective and energy-efficient alternative. It provides a personal, outside entry for each unit, without any wasted space or maintenance for common hallways. Another advantage is that this home type lends itself to either higher density or less land coverage. One disadvantage is that this home type does not have the benefit of front-to-back light or the ventilation of a typical townhouse—the floor plans may feel more appropriate for an apartment than a townhouse. Furthermore, the only private outdoor space is the front yard. Usually some or all of the garages and parking must be detached. In most climates, this plan type lends itself to a north-south building orientation with individual unit entries facing east or west, thereby giving all residents some sunlight during a portion of the day. This townhouse form is becoming increasingly popular as a lower cost ownership or rental alternative to the typical apartment building.

Variations

The use of the above basic townhouse plan types will vary to meet certain market or site requirements.

Duplex. Two-unit townhouse blocks referred to as duplexes or side-by-side units are often used with larger blocks as contrasting building masses. These two-unit buildings have the benefit of a premium end location for each unit. Additionally, they are more easily platted and allow many alternative site planning choices for turned garages, to break up a line of garage doors and the larger building masses. Because these units may be platted without common areas, similar to a typical subdivision, a community association is not always required.

The below-grade level of a one- or two-story townhouse may be designed for rental use if a separate entry is provided. This, too, is a townhouse variation that is appropriate to urban developments. An interesting feature of this variation is that it will provide potential expansion space for the owner. This type is frequently called a stacked townhouse.

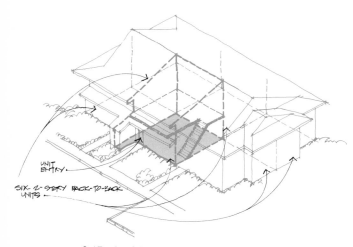

6-17 (top) A three-story, back-to-back townhouse represents a cost-effective plan type. 6-18 (bottom) and 6-19 (right) A six-unit townhouse building using back-to-back plan types is an economical site development and building solution where the cost is somewhere in between typical townhouses and garden apartments.

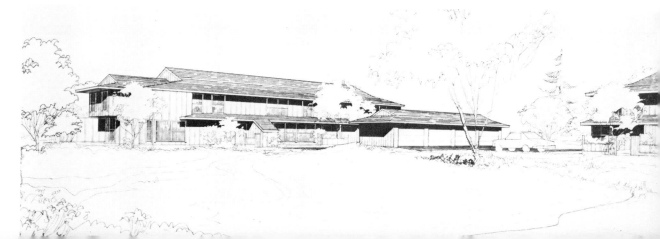

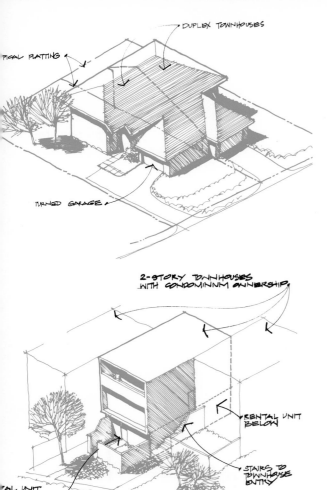

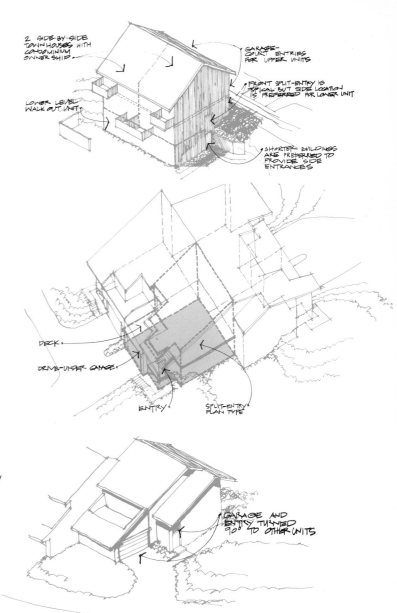

Triplex. A variation of a split-entry walkout, sometimes used in an urban setting, is a one-level plan with two townhouses above. These three townhouses must have a condominium form of ownership, since a lot footprint is not possible. The front entry for the lower split-entry unit is half a flight below the entry level of the upper units. This configuration results in less desirable lower level units in long buildings. A better solution would place lower level entrances in shorter buildings.

Quad. An adaptation of a back-to-back townhouse unit would be a "quad" building. As repetitious strings of uninteresting back-to-back units may result in a high perceived density and stereotyped project, building mass refinements may skillfully integrate smaller four-unit buildings with varied, interesting architectural character. The quad, however, can create difficult site planning situations, particularly in the large amounts of paving needed for unit access and parking.

Side Loading. A desirable variation for every plan type would place the guest entry/front door and/or garage door on a side wall. This configuration would allow a more private entry location on the valuable end walls. Interesting site planning variations as a result of this design do much to relieve the garage-court feeling.

6-20 (top) The duplex or side-by-side townhouse adaptation is an alternative that may provide a yard space similar to that of a single-family detached home. 6-21 (middle) A two-story townhouse above a single-story rental unit is popular in some urban markets.
6-22 (bottom) A rental unit below a townhouse unit at Walpole Point in Chicago.

6-23 (top) The lower level walkout unit and two above it comprise three units within the "footprint" of two side-by-side townhouses. 6-24 (middle) Numerous variations may be used with a four-unit building form offering attached garages and premium end/corner locations. 6-25 (bottom) Side entry/guest entry doors or garages improve the livability of the homes and introduce valuable site planning flexibility.

Plan Flexibility

A basic rule in combining homes into town-house or condominium building blocks is to have enough flexibility to be able to inter-change plans (or building blocks) that are not selling with those that are. This is complicated by the fact that marketable plans must adapt to different land forms. Fortunately, a wide number of plan type choices will adapt to the land with only a moderate amount of regrading. If a plat is filed in advance of construction or if units are presold, the width of the interior plans must remain the same. However, if the end lot is oversized, that unit may expand (or contract) to allow interchanges. When end lots are oversized but the unit does not cover the entire

lot, check with the tax assessor for possible inequitable taxes for the end units and make sure that the unbuilt area is maintained through the covenants and restrictions. Another approach to flexibility is to plat only the unit mix that is selling, but consideration should be given to possible delays in the platting process that will prohibit sales because finished units are not yet available.

One of the problems with interchanging units are the roofs. It is very difficult to have a continuous, integrated roof design that is adaptable to interchanging units. Jogging the different units horizontally and/or vertically often will permit only the use of gable, shed, or flat roofs. A careful study with cross-

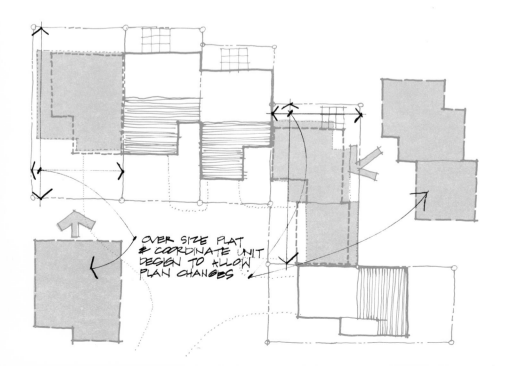

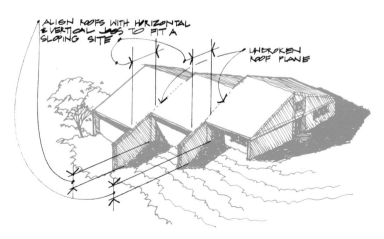

6-26 (left) Design plan types that are interchangeable within a platted building block envelope. This allows the developer to respond somewhat to the sales pace of different floor plans. 6-27 (above) Properly calculated horizontal and vertical offsets may produce unbroken roof planes. The result may individualize units and unify a building's overall architecture.

section overlays of each plan type may help to solve the problem. Horizontal or vertical shifts of similar or different floor plans will often allow continuous roof planes. A coordinated approach to foundation planning and roof design will help to avoid a uniform townhouse or condominium building block that looks like a series of attached boxes.

For all plan types, limiting the number of townhouse or condominium units to a building provides many advantages. For example, the use of four-unit buildings will yield 50 percent end units and sufficient site design flexibility to adapt to topography and plan constraints.

6-28 Coordinated roof planes will help avoid a uniform building block.

6-29 A combination of flat roofs on the garages and hip roofs on the townhouses helps make the garage court more pleasant by reducing the scale of the buildings.

Adding Interest to Building Form

Because people have different preferences, today's developer offers choices of various floor plans. In the past, strictly aligned townhouses yielded a rather monotonous environment without relief. Units were not accented or individualized except for surface treatments—like paint, masonry, or siding. Most designers and the consensus of today's marketplace would agree that there are better ways of achieving a visually exciting home environment. Tacking on different surface treatments over long rows of houses seems a last ditch effort to add on character that could have been integrated throughout planning and architectural design. This kind of superficial treatment may be viewed as a holdover from the original townhouses; reminiscent of the time when this type of housing conformed to regimented city blocks and setbacks, a time when higher density living really looked it!

By combining various plans into a building block, today's designer creates natural building offsets or recesses. This is the first step in overcoming the barracks stigma of early townhouse/condominium developments and rental projects.

6-30 Horizontal building jogs lend interest and privacy and eliminate the need for repetitious privacy fences.

Horizontal Offsets

Today's developer finds that it is ordinarily more effective and economical to have fewer large offsets than a series of small jogs. In a large building, a 2-foot jog is barely noticeable; 4 feet is better; 6 to 12 feet cast a recognizable shadow and have definite visual impact.

Horizontal offsets accomplish a number of things at once. They emphasize the individuality of the homes composing a building block. In fact, it is appropriate in many situations to accentuate this individuality by extending wing walls, party walls, or privacy fences from the offsets. There is no question that this adds some construction expense to the homes. However, the added character and additional window orientation results in a much more saleable, interesting interior home environment. Economies of construction may also result from using building offsets. For instance, sheltered recesses for both entries and patios are naturally created, which in turn usually reduce the need for privacy fences and wall extensions to isolate home entries and patios.

A careful mixing of floor plan types may create interest by turning several units at an angle to the other homes within a block. The

6-31 (left) and 6-32 (above) Each building cluster in this project has a unit that turns a corner, creating a horizontal offset.

116

interior spaces of individual homes will then orient in two different directions. Combined with architectural massing, good roof lines, and offsets, a very interesting building form may result.

Horizontal offsets should be coordinated with the home types and roof pitches of the encompassing block. For instance, a townhouse block composed of different unit types will have various roof pitches and wall heights which should determine the offset dimensions. These horizontal building offsets may be accentuated with garages, carports, or parking facilities.

6-33 The barracks stigma: overcome it with offsets.

ROOF PITCH

HORIZONTAL OFFSETS / VERTICAL OFFSETS		3:12	4:12	5:12	6:12	8:12	12:12
1 COURSE	STD.	34"/32"	25.5"/24"	20.4"/19.2"	17"/16"	12.75"/12"	8.5"/8"
	MOD.						
	STD 8½"						
	MOD 8"						
2 COURSES	STD.	68"/64"	51"/48"	40.8"/38.4"	34"/32"	25.5"/24"	17"/16"
	MOD.						
	STD. 17"						
	MOD 16"						
3 COURSES	STD.	102"/96"	76.5"/72"	61.2"/57.6"	51"/48"	38.25"/36"	25.5"/24"
	MOD.						
	STD. 25.5"						
	MOD 24"						
4 COURSES	STD.	136"/128"	102"/96"	81.6"/76.8"	68"/64"	51"/48"	34"/32"
	MOD.						
	STD. 34"						
	MOD 32"						
5 COURSES	STD.	170"/160"	127.5"/120"	102"/96"	85"/80"	63.75"/60"	42.5"/40"
	MOD.						
	STD 42.5"						
	MOD 40"						
6 COURSES	STD.	204"/192"	156"/144"	122.4"/115.2"	102"/96"	76.5"/72"	51"/48"
	MOD.						
	STD. 51"						
	MOD 48"						

(Left column label: CONCRETE BLOCK HEIGHTS OR 8" MODULES FOR POURED WALLS)

6-34 This table provides the horizontal and vertical offset dimensions that allow roof plane alignments of units with equal plate heights. For instance, to find the horizontal offset between units that are separated vertically by four courses of standard concrete block, with a 6:12 pitch roof: find **four** courses on the left column (4 or standard block = 34"). Read horizontally to the 6:12 roof pitch column and obtain the standard block horizontal offset dimension (68").

Vertical Interest

The mixing of unit types is not only important in site planning flexibility, it also helps introduce vertical changes to the mass of the building. Interesting roof lines and connections are possible if vertical offsets are calculated correctly. Repetitive use of a single building configuration, however, should be avoided. Identity and character normally result from variations, not repetitions.

Properly fitted to the landscape, the stepping down of roof lines from middle interior homes to exterior one-story plans helps buildings to blend with the land. It may visually put large buildings on a more human scale. A side benefit of vertical staggering is the opening up of side walls for window placement. Care must be given to insure that additional windows located on side walls do not infringe on the privacy of adjacent decks, patios, or balconies.

A fringe benefit of vertical building offsets is that, while being an architectural aid to the composition and massing of the overall building block, they are also viewed by owners as a unique distinction, setting individual homes apart from others. Thus, vertical offsetting may add to the marketing impact of a development.

In some sections of the country, a fear of the complexity of jogged buildings and resultant concern over increased costs leads back to the traditional plateauing of townhouse/condominium building sites—standardized blocks of homes built at the same grade. Many projects within the last decade, however, have shown that design in the vertical dimension is economically competitive and holds as much potential for interest and variety as the horizontal offsetting of homes.

6-37 (top) Brick wall with raked joints and wood detailing gives a simple contrast to a visually prominent wall. 6-38 (bottom) The end wall of this garage has special brick-surfaced treatment. Note the extra guest parking provided in addition to the space in front of the garage.

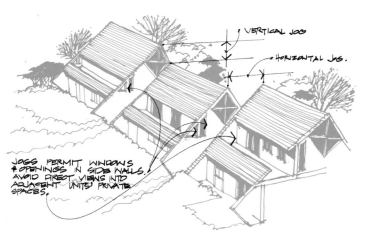

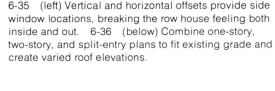

6-35 (left) Vertical and horizontal offsets provide side window locations, breaking the row house feeling both inside and out. 6-36 (below) Combine one-story, two-story, and split-entry plans to fit existing grade and create varied roof elevations.

Exterior Material Selection and Detailing

As townhouse and condominium buildings are larger in scale than most detached homes, the selection of exterior details and surface materials is more important and complex. For example, a 1-inch by 8-inch facia board may be adequate for a 45-foot long single-family home, but for a 120-foot long townhouse block, a 2-inch by 10-inch is more appropriate to be compatible with the scale of the larger building. In developments where construction efficiencies limit variations between buildings, or when economic factors or site conditions limit the use of jogs or offsets, it is usually best to emphasize the horizontal lines of a building.

Selection of the color and texture of the exterior materials is integral to the architectural character of a development. Errors in material choices affect large surface areas. Before committing to entire buildings or clusters, it is worth the extra time and effort to see samples of the stain and paint selections on the actual building materials.

Brick selections using subtle color blends are desirable. Mixing brick with strong color contrasts to produce the "salt and pepper look" should be avoided. Colored mortar should be investigated as a refinement in color coordination between siding and trim. Mortar joints in masonry walls may be made more interesting through the use of untroweled, flush, or raked joints. Where stucco exteriors are used, seeing an actual application that has aged will give a better indication of the true color than a small sample.

Budget allocations usually restrict the use of high cost surface materials. Thus, any contrasting, higher cost materials used should be grouped in the most visually prominent locations rather than divided into small surface areas among units. Typically, these visually prominent areas would include end walls of units and garages, exposed walls at points where a building jogs, or areas around unit or building entries.

The architect will usually unify a development by using a consistent system of surface materials, trim design, and color selection. For instance, in a townhouse development of numerous buildings, he might maintain similar siding materials between buildings while creating contrasts with different trim detailing and color changes. An alternative would be to use contrasting siding materials—such as vertical siding on one building and horizontal on another—and unify them with similar facia, window and door detailing, and feature wall materials. Generally speaking,

Martin Tornallyay

6-39 Strong roof design and consistent use of siding materials are reflected in fence extensions.

the architect will limit the number of siding materials used on a single building to one or two types and unify the various buildings with repeated feature wall materials and trim details.

Typically, the pitch of the roofs is determined early in the design process. This may influence the selection of roof materials in that the steeper the roofs, the more important it is to provide materials that have a coordinated color and appealing texture.

6-40 (below) A subtle texture change may be provided by brick walls with flush or raked joints. 6-41 (right) Horizontal siding with spaces to create stronger shadows. Balcony detailing has a contrasting vertical emphasis.

Entry and Walkways

Walkways leading from parking lots, garage areas, bays, or apron parking in front of a person's garage must receive special attention. They serve a function similar to the court drives of the road system, funneling larger volumes of outdoor area into smaller home entry spaces. Warmth and livability of these spaces is achieved through a combination of careful architectural massing, detailing of buildings, and landscape treatment. The landscape architecture of home walkway spaces may include: surfacing, retaining walls, benches, planters, fountains, arbors, and roof extensions, as well as lighting, handrails, and steps, which are functionally necessary for grade changes.

As they walk through the walkway/home entry space, the first reaction of potential home-buyers may determine their entire attitude about the desirability of the home and environment. Since the entry approach to the front door is an identity marker, it should be a semi-private space, partially screened or sheltered from view and inclement weather. A wide, good-quality single or double door with side and/or overhead glass may help make the home entry a distinctive space.

Generally, the spacing/building scale bordering entry/walkway areas is determined in the preliminary design stage. The proportion of building height to horizontal spacing

6-42 A restored townhouse entry with identity.

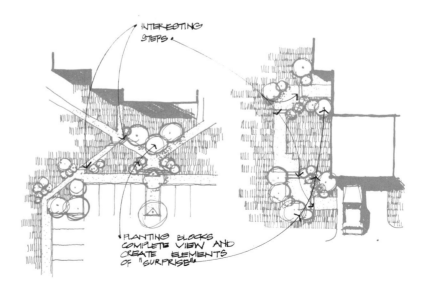

6-43 (left) Create interest for the front-entry space. This photograph shows two model homes in the Terrace neighborhood of Irvine, California. 6-44 (above) Make the walk from the parking or garage to the home as interesting as possible.

should be studied in an enlarged scale. The final locations of windows, entries, and decks, the horizontal positioning of one townhouse block relative to another should also be carefully studied with reference to the entry spaces. Whenever possible, orient any opening out of the home toward an open space view, and if possible away from any windows and doors of neighboring units.

In urban infill sites smaller dimensions than otherwise are acceptable for walkways. For instance, the Greenway Gables, an urban infill townhouse in Minneapolis, has open space widths of 9 feet between two-story homes. Ordinarily, entrance walkways should not be less than 2- to 6-feet wide. Usually, a subtle improvement in the image of the home occurs when the pavement widths are at least 4 feet. This enables two people to walk side-by-side to the front door.

Concrete, a standard paving material, is rather drab in ordinary application. However, it is a permanent surface that is resistant to weather extremes, and there is much that may be done to improve the design and character of concrete. Expansion joints may be added in interesting patterns with redwood, cedar, or treated wood, replacing the more common fiber or break joints. Textures may be added by using special brooms or even patterned stamps. These metal stamps, normally used in pairs by the concrete finisher, come in a variety of forms and create very interesting surfaces, such as the brick-paving look. The grooves may then be grouted to make the finished surface look like hand-placed stone. An economical alternative is a concrete surface washed to expose a special aggregate added to the concrete mix. Any of the above treatments will work well in conjunction with the use of a coloring agent mixed with the concrete or applied to its surface.

Other masonry materials should not be overlooked. Brick pavers or cut stone are excel-

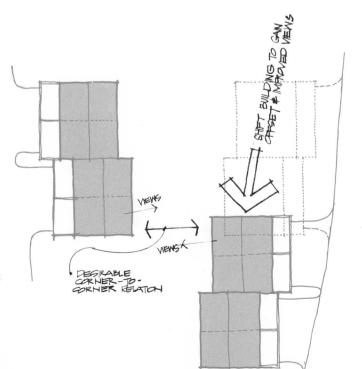

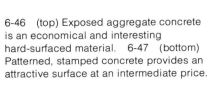

6-45 (left) Where two buildings have parallel faces, it is best to offset them to gain a corner-to-corner relationship as much as possible.

6-46 (top) Exposed aggregate concrete is an economical and interesting hard-surfaced material. 6-47 (bottom) Patterned, stamped concrete provides an attractive surface at an intermediate price.

121

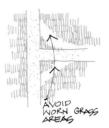   

AVOID WORN GRASS AREAS

STEP STONES

MAJOR WALKWAY INTERSECTION

ANGLED CORNER

6-48 Design sidewalks and pathways that anticipate walking patterns.

lent materials for adding elegance to a paved surface. Depending on the architectural style and design theme, wood entry decking or steps, having a warm character, may be used. Where walks fall under roof overhangs, place them either at least 2 feet beyond or well underneath the overhang. Wider overhangs and water diversion strips are usually a better solution than gutters and down-spouts.

Many detailed site development features may contribute to the livability of home entrance spaces. Although pathway materials and design are certainly important, the unpaved areas are equally significant. Sod is usually the first groundcover material that comes to mind, largely because after installation it has a finished look—an instant visual impact. Sod is a frequently used

groundcover, even though when used in tight spaces it is difficult to maintain, may be shaded out, or may die from excessive moisture.

In warmer climates, groundcover plants may quickly spread to provide a hardy green mat, although an inert material must be used initially to cover the soil. Redwood bark chips, normally a rich, natural red-brown color, blend well with plant material and most siding colors. Wood shavings or chips are also utilized as an economical soil covering, often produced by chipping trees felled during on-site clearing operations. Crushed rock in a wide variety of sizes, textures, and colors is commonly a very stable, economical material to use as a cover.

Color and texture selections should be made

to complement the style and colors of the buildings. For instance, if a trim, smooth-finish, painted exterior siding is used for the buildings, small-grained, colored stones may be appropriate. On the other hand, if a more rustic, natural appearance is desired, a more coarse earth-tone rock or bark chips/wood shavings may be selected.

The use of these inert materials in conjunction with groundcover planting will save the developer and community association continued lawn mowing maintenance expenses. Further maintenance cost reductions may result if residents are individually encouraged to landscape home entry areas within the guidelines set by the community association. Maturing groundcover plants may eventually eliminate the need to mow these individually-maintained areas.

6-49 (left) The owner of this townhouse added timber-edged planting, improving the overall court appearance and reducing community association maintenance responsibilities. 6-50 (right) The sodded area adjacent to the pathway provides a trim appearance and an edge for the low-maintenance groundcover of ivy.

Interior Character and Function

While building codes and practices have long established minimum interior standards, successful townhouse or condominium homes must be an affordable balance of privacy, function, and character to be marketable. Inside the home, the views from the entry foyer should be directed at strong interior design elements, strategically placed windows, and/or sliding glass doors. An open stairway may be a strong, interesting design element. Floor covering in the entry area is an important consideration. A durable, higher quality material such as brick pavers or tile is preferred. The impact of the material is strengthened if the ceiling can be lowered (or floor raised) in this area to accentuate the entrance leading to the living areas of the home. Interior excitement may be added by vaulted ceilings, exposed rafters, clerestory windows or skylights, accented with strong masses like fireplaces or overhanging loft spaces.

6-51   Exposed roof structure for interior character.

6-52   Something special: a kitchen greenhouse to accentuate the effect of natural lighting on a townhouse or condominium's interior.

Natural Light Orientation

Within a townhouse/condominium unit, the number of rooms that open to natural light and outdoor views is dependent on the width of the unit and number of levels within the building. Typical condominium design is limited because the homes are normally served off a corridor with units on either side. Townhouses, normally opening in at least two directions, permit greater interior floor planning flexibility. While having windows on only two or at most three sides of a home does reduce heat loss, it also emphasizes the need for well-placed or larger windows to open up more interior spaces to the cheerful, room-enlarging impact of natural light.

GREENHOUSE WINDOW BOXES

Zoning Interior Uses

Protection of privacy through zoning conflicting uses is a basic consideration of any home design. Necessary acoustic and visual buffering between active and passive areas is best provided by using closets, hallways, or stairways. Townhouse/condominium family profiles indicate, however, that there is not an extreme need for strict zoning within a home due to children's noises—there are fewer families with children.

Buffering the noisemaking kitchen appliances from the dining and living spaces is desirable. Because much of a family's time is spent in the kitchen, open planning and the use of "shared space" require that movable partitions, raised counters, or overhead cabinets be used as partial buffers. A completely enclosed kitchen space, normally located within the interior of a townhouse or condominium, may make it a disagreeable place and the most difficult part of a floor plan to market.

The best use of available interior area puts additional floor space in rooms that will receive the most "living." For example, an expansion of the typically small kitchen into a "country kitchen" makes it a much more practical and functional part of the home for many families. Another good use of interior area with strong marketing appeal puts the additional space in the master bedroom. Similarly, the master bath should receive special design attention—it should be large enough for two people and have strong vi-

6-53 Zone a floor plan to separate active areas from passive . . . avoid direct sight lines into passive areas.

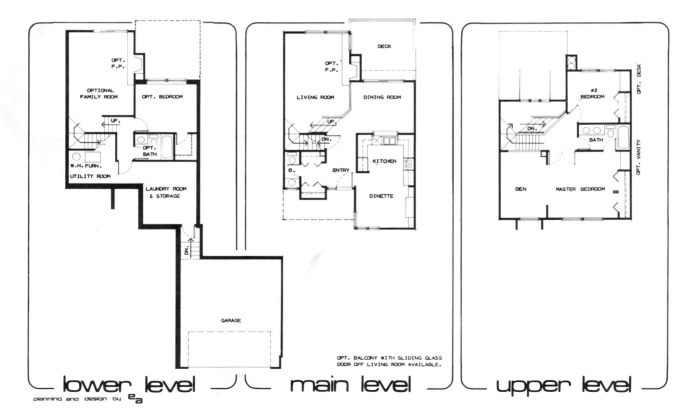

lower level

planning and design by ea

main level

upper level

sual appeal. Special bathroom fixtures, such as oversized vanities with two basins, large mirrors, and interesting lighting and plumbing fixtures, are especially important to the townhouse/condominium buyer.

When possible, bedrooms should be separated from the more active areas of a home by hallways, closets, or baths. Particular segments of the market require particular bedroom configurations. Townhouse/condominium homes intended for purchase by older couples are most marketable when active areas and passive living areas, like bedrooms, are on one level. Two master bedrooms, each with a private bath, may have great appeal to certain older couples or single buyers. On the other hand, markets anticipating larger families should design children's bedrooms and play areas, but separate them from the master bedroom and study spaces of the home.

Market experience indicates that, in contrast with single-family detached homes, two-bedroom townhouse or condominium homes are more acceptable and often more desirable than three- or four-bedroom options within the same amount of space. The additional space is typically added to the master bedroom suite. Because the floor area need not be divided into additional bedrooms with closets and doors, there is greater design flexibility, with the option of providing special use areas such as studies, loft spaces over living areas, or dens.

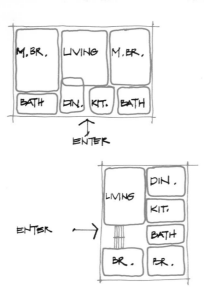

6-54 (top) A condominium plan with two master bedrooms and private bath appeals to single buyers and some retired buyers. 6-55 (bottom) A side-entry townhouse reduces the long hallway inherent in front/rear-entry townhouses.

6-56 A trend in townhouse/condominium design is to use the extra bedroom space for a library, loft, or den.

125

Martin Tornallyay

6-57 (left) A kitchen/patio pass-through is a popular feature. It enhances the indoor-outdoor relationship. 6-58 (right) A private outdoor space is desired by all homebuyers.

Private Outdoor Spaces

Extending a home's interior to a private outdoor area is perhaps the most important use of open space made by the developer. It is this space within which owners have the most freedom and spend much of their time. Private outdoor living areas buffer the home from non-private outdoor spaces. Acting as outside extensions of a home's interior, carefully placed windows, doors, and roof treatments adjacent to private outdoor space may visually expand inside rooms out to the edges of decks or patios.

Patios

On-grade, hard-surface patios are the most common type. From a marketing standpoint, having no patio would be better than building an inadequately sized standard 6-foot by 8-foot patio. In this way, homebuyers themselves may provide what they want and need within community association guidelines. If a standard patio is offered, an allowance should be made for people who want to build their own patios or add on custom features to the standard patio. In this latter case it is helpful for the architect or landscape architect to prepare alternative designs that are approved by the developer. The use of building wall extensions, overhead arbors, or trellises will enhance the indoor-outdoor relationship of inside room to patio. Privacy fences, earth berms, or plant material should be used where the privacy of a person's patio would otherwise not be assured. A building offset, however, would provide the greatest degree of privacy.

The interior dimensions of patio space depend upon the type of enclosure required. Many developments have made the error of providing too much security, too much en-

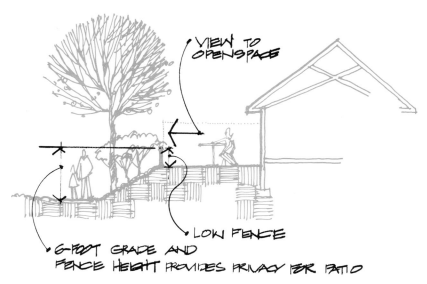

6-59 Privacy, yet openness—a low fence, planter, bench, or hedge give privacy while not obstructing the view.

closure. For most site conditions, a 6- to 8-foot-high fence blocking the view of well-landscaped open space may be a marketing disadvantage affecting livability. There are circumstances, however, that may warrant a high, solid partition. University Park townhouses at Irvine Ranch, California offered options of 3- or 6-foot fences around individual patios. About half of the buyers chose the higher fence for privacy, the other half chose the 3-foot dividers to preserve the view. Without options to accommodate different buyer preferences, the sales pace of University Park would have suffered—a family who had wanted a view might have been offered a solid wall instead. Thus, providing various options may prove cost-effective.

The detailing of private open space enclosures may permit views through to adjacent open space. If security is a buyer concern, on-grade patios require higher fences. In setting the final grades for a townhouse block, a developer should remember that a low fence permitting a seated person to look through or over, coupled with a 3- to 5-foot grade change, will achieve the same secure results.

Because those elements that most frequently and directly affect residents should receive the greatest design and budgetary consideration, the design treatment of the open space adjacent to private decks and patios is very important.

6-60 (above) A larger, more unified appearance results from privacy fences that are covered with the siding material used elsewhere on the building. 6-61 (left) The recessed open space pathway enables homeowner privacy without a 6-foot fence.

Decks

Decks are a vital part of townhouse and condominium living. For some homes, they represent the only private outdoor space, extending interior function. An on- or above-grade wood deck is a popular solution, becoming an "outdoor room" that may improve the architectural appearance of the home.

Different unit types and buyers require various deck sizes and locations. In fact, it is good practice to incorporate design flexibility in the positioning of decks. For instance,

it may be desirable to locate a deck either off a family room or a dining room, depending upon buyer preference.

The most ideal location, however, is not always possible. The size and location of the deck affects not only the upper level but also the light admitted to the lower levels of the home—underneath or beside the deck. Sun angles should be considered before locating deep, second-level decks that overlap bedrooms or living areas below. In multi-level buildings where the depth of the decks or balconies will affect views out of and sun-

6-62   (top) Decks may extend the interiors of homes by becoming outdoor rooms.   6-63   (bottom) Private outdoor space: a deck over a drive-under garage. The arbor may be a buyer-selected option, as part of the initial purchase, or may be added later.

6-64   Decks: the private outdoor spaces for many townhouses. This deck built over a drive-under garage has a privacy fence and a beam as standard features, while the arbor canopy provides added enclosure and individuality.

light admitted into lower level balcony windows, reduced-depth structures may be warranted. Decks may be cantilevered by beams or joist extensions, or supported with posts or wall extensions extending to the lower levels. If this latter method is utilized, care should be given to avoid obscuring windows.

Security and privacy are two important aspects of deck design. Screens and fences should assure visual privacy and give a small degree of acoustical separation from adjacent decks, windows, and walkways.

6-66   Reduce the upper deck depth to improve natural lighting for lower decks or patios.

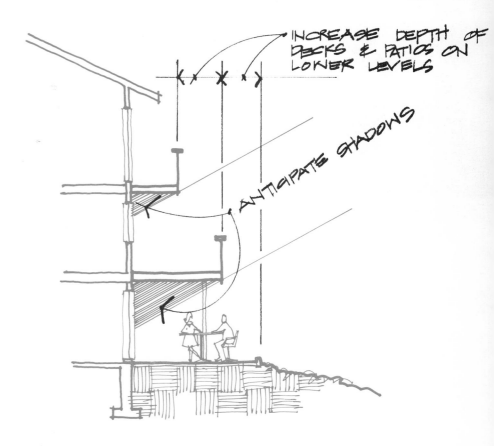

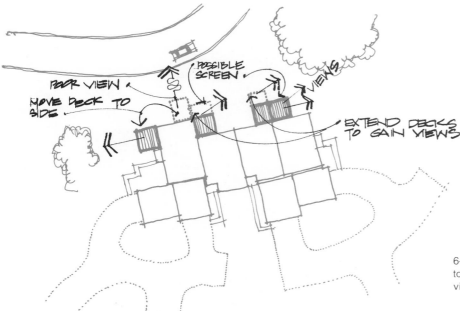

6-65   Optional deck placement allows buyers to select their floor plan, deck placement, and views.

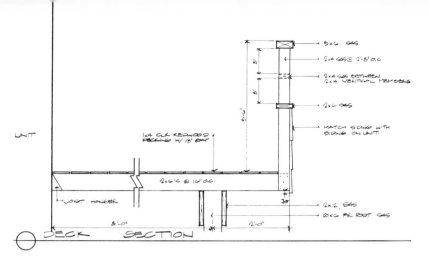

DECK SECTION

6-67 (above left) and 6-68 (above right) This semi-open rail design provides a view of the surrounding open space while using the siding material for enclosure. The decks and privacy walls then appear as extensions of the buildings. 6-69 (right) Two types of deck structural supports: one for a more massive look, one for a less obstructed view from below.

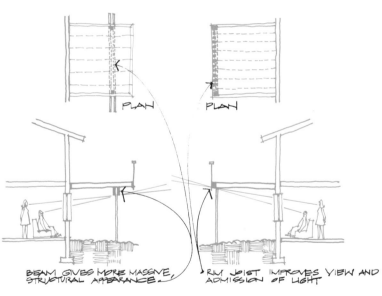

PLAN   PLAN

BEAM GIVES MORE MASSIVE STRUCTURAL APPEARANCE.

RIM JOIST IMPROVES VIEW AND ADMISSION OF LIGHT

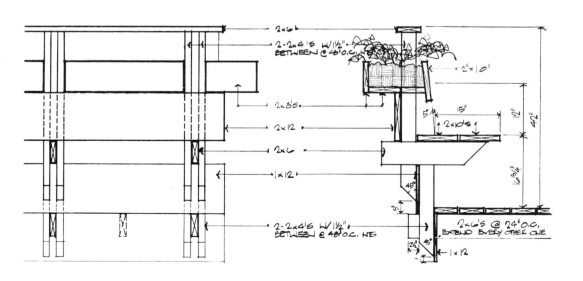

6-70 This more complex deck railing provides a framework for outdoor planters and an integral bench.

Deck railings play an important part in a resident's ability to visually enjoy the open space surrounding his home. Various open rail designs will allow a clear view of a vista or open space. Other designs will enhance a deck's privacy, screening out a disagreeable view by extending siding materials, privacy fences, and walls around the deck.

In areas of harsh winter climates, it is good practice to drop a deck at least 4 inches below the finished floor level to avoid snow and ice interfering with door operation. To enhance a view out of a door overlooking the railing, it may be desirable to further lower the deck.

Where access off the deck to open space or other features is desired, stairs leading to the lower level are an option. The stairs should be designed into the deck rather than added on as an afterthought. A different, accented home exterior may be created or enhanced by wrapping decks around corners of homes. This makes the deck a more integral part of the home—avoiding the "tacked on" look.

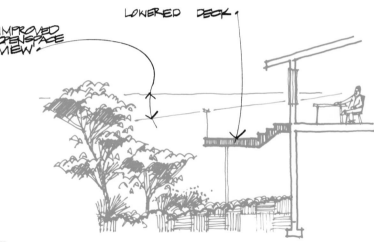

6-71   Lower a deck to improve the view from inside.

6-72   This deck reflects architectural detailing found elsewhere on the buildings and integrates a stairway to the existing grade of this side-entry townhouse.

131

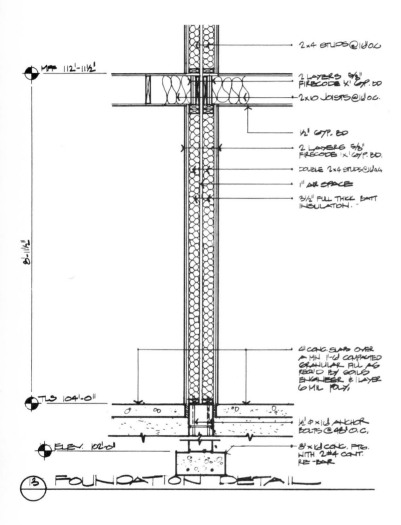

2×4 STUDS @ 16" O.C.

2 LAYERS 5/8" FIRECODE X' GYP. BD.

2×10 JOISTS @ 16" O.C.

1/2" GYP. BD

2 LAYERS 5/8" FIRECODE X GYP. BD.

DOUBLE 2×4 STUDS @ 16" O.C.

1" AIR SPACE

3 1/2" FULL THICK BATT INSULATION.

4" CONC. SLAB OVER A MIN. 4"-0 COMPACTED GRANULAR FILL AS REQ'D BY SOILS ENGINEER & 1 LAYER 6 MIL POLY.

1/2" Ø × 16 ANCHOR BOLTS @ 48" O.C.

8" × 16 CONC. FTG. WITH 2 #4 CONT. RE-BAR

FOUNDATION DETAIL

6-73 Common wall construction details are no place to economize.

Construction Details

Many of the same design qualities common to single-family detached homes also apply to townhouses and condominiums. In fact, salespeople like to refer to a well-designed townhouse/condominium as "homelike." They especially like to point out the livability details and features built into a condominium as contrasted with a rental apartment. Properly designed townhouse/condominium architectural details, like the common wall, improve livability and are a vital marketing feature.

Common Walls

No other architectural construction detail plays as significant a role in assuring the livability of a townhouse/condominium community as effective common wall design—prohibiting sound transmission. The common wall is no place to economize; it has such a profound effect on the homebuyer's feeling of privacy, perception of density, and general attitude about the quality of construction that went into the home.

As contrasted with rental apartments, continuous frame floors and common plates are unacceptable for long-term townhouse/condominium buyer satisfaction. While numerous party wall designs are available for frame construction, the assembly of two frame walls separated by a dead air space has one of the best sound transmission ratings in light construction. With this type of design the only linkage between two homes is a common foundation wall and continuous roofing and siding. Homes are totally isolated from each other from a structural standpoint. With the use of two layers of 5/8-inch fire code gypsum board on the interior walls of each home, it is generally recognized that a two-hour fire rating results. In addition to the sound-resistant qualities, another advantage of this type of wall detail is that the gypsum material may be applied under controlled weather conditions after the framing is completed. Also, this detail permits easy access by workmen between unfinished units.

Unfortunately, some communities arbitrarily require masonry parapet walls. A preferred alternative detail returns gypsum board 5 feet into the home from the fire wall on top of the trusses or rafters. This solution, accepted as an equivalent by most codes, is an aesthetic improvement because the repetitious use of extended masonry walls constrains architectural design alternatives and may make a townhouse building look like a row of boxes.

Generally, waste pipes, water pipes, and noisy appliances should not be placed in or against the common wall. Where this is unavoidable, added sound conditioning is required. A minimum number of electrical outlets should be placed on common walls. Code required outlets should be staggered, caulked, and insulated.

Foundations and Footings

The greater foundation lengths covered by townhouse/condominium buildings often require increased footing sizes or reinforcement to adjust to soil changes. To insure accuracy, the surveyor must field stake the excavation and footing locations. Naturally, this is an important consideration where a plat must be filed in advance of building construction and the lot line must fall on the common wall. After the footings are installed, the surveyor then places a metal marker at all individual unit corners. If it is possible, a better procedure would be to file the plat after the foundations are installed, thereby reducing the possibility of construction errors. An improved city filing procedure grants building permits based on final plans with subsequent plat completion.

Where concrete block is to be used, before the foundation and construction working drawings are started the architect should determine the use of either modular or non-modular block. If modular block was anticipated in design but non-modular block is used, the additional ½ inch per block vertical differential will lead to dimensional problems in the field.

Plumbing

Early in the planning process, the placement of the various pipes and vents that penetrate the roof should be considered. It is preferable for the majority to fall on the roof plane least visible from the court. Another solution would be to combine the vent stacks and flues in the attic area and place them within a common enclosure above the roof.

Plumbing fixtures that function more quietly and use less water are available at competitive prices and should be specified. The sound rating of the dishwasher and the

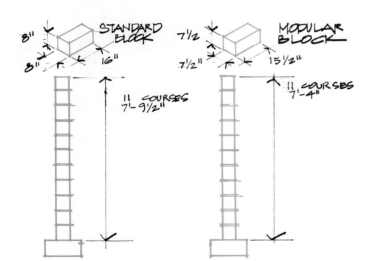

6-74 Specify modular or standard non-modular block: the one-half inch difference may cause difficulties.

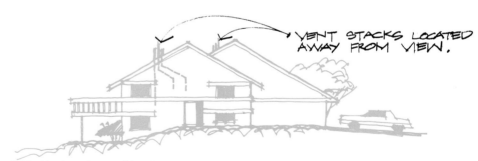

6-75 Vent stacks: combine them in the attic space when possible. Where practical, place stacks on the roof away from the side of greatest visibility.

133

energy efficiency of the hot water heater should be evaluated as part of product selection.

It is preferable for each townhouse to have a sillcock on both the front and rear for private use. The problem of watering community-owned/private lawns and plant material needs special attention. One solution is to have the community association pay the entire water bill and divide the total expense equally among homeowners. A more common, preferred method is for each owner to have his own water meter and for the community association to have separately metered sillcocks at the ends of each building for use in watering common area lawns and plant material. An alternative to this system would be to have the community association reimburse homeowners for the water used from their sillcocks that is above the average usage. For townhouse/condominium developments in arid climates or communities requiring a high level of maintenance for intensively developed open space, an underground irrigation system would be more appropriate than the use of sillcocks.

Electrical

If left to the imagination of the installer, the thermostat often ends up in the center of a feature wall. Therefore, switches, fixtures, and thermostat locations should be shown on the final working drawings.

As fluorescent lighting produces more light for less energy than incandescent bulbs, it is particularly appropriate for indirect and soffit lighting. Luminous ceilings are especially effective for townhouse/condominium designs that include buried interior kitchens.

Exterior outlets on the patios or decks are convenient. However, in some code areas they are expensive because of new code requirements for ground fault interrupters. The placement of utility meters is probably the most important feature in exterior detail utility design. If possible, the electric and gas meters should be grouped together and screened. For townhouses, the exterior location of an air conditioner unit should be predetermined. Since the noise will be objectionable to the owner and neighbors, its location should be away from outdoor living areas. Location on the entry side is usually preferable.

6-76 (top) Utility meters are virtually hidden in this recessed service area of two drive-under garages. The overhang of the deck above provides a shadow line that eliminates screening requirements. The trash containers are accessible at all times, thereby eliminating the need to set the containers out on collection day. 6-77 (middle) Addition of this wood frame is an economical method of subduing the visual impact of the air-conditioning unit. 6-78 (bottom) Proper plants finish the screening job.

HVAC

To properly size the heating, ventilating, and air conditioning (HVAC) equipment for a home, heat loss calculations should be done for each home unless identical repetitions occur within the development. In hot climates the greatest complaints have related to the inability of the system to cool the unit adequately, particularly the upstairs areas. Conversely, in colder climates purchasers often complain that the furnace just doesn't heat the rooms farthest from the air handling equipment. Proper balancing of the HVAC equipment and distribution system is important, keeping in mind that while detached homes may often depend on cross-ventilation, townhouses, because of reduced exterior exposure, may not contain the same natural ventilation effect.

In principle, heat loss from a home varies through different cross sections of building materials. In this light, townhouses are unique because of their ability to shift vertically and horizontally in relation to grade and adjacent units, which introduces numerous areas of different material combinations.

For this reason, townhouse energy calculations are more involved than for detached homes and perhaps even mid-rise condominiums.

The energy efficiency of townhouse/condominium common wall construction has become a marketing advantage. The Dallas builder who offered an energy conservation package including such fundamental items as double-glazed windows and thicker insulation provides an example of the desirability of other energy conservation features. Nineteen of 20 pending buyers purchased this $600 energy conservation optional package.

Both architect and builder may have a significant impact on future energy uses by implementing both passive and active energy conservation features. Passive features would include orientation to sun and wind, as well as the use of cost-effective materials and technology.

The first priority and most cost-effective practice in energy conservation is the use of insulation and the reduction of air infiltration. Improved on-site quality control should see that special care is taken in placing insulation around window jams and framing. If spaces are too narrow for proper insulation placement, these areas should be caulked. The use of triple-glazed casement or awning windows in addition to insulated, all-weather stripped doors are other positive energy conservation details. Industry sources indicate that air infiltration accounts for up to 40 percent of the total energy required for residential heating and cooling, causing energy loss that insulation alone cannot prevent. One critical location of leakage is the area beneath the base plates. It is estimated that 25 percent of all air leakage occurs between the base plate and slab or the foundation and the perimeter joists. Other leakage points causing a high percentage of loss are around electrical wall outlets, exterior windows and doors, and duct systems.

Growing energy conservation awareness in the marketplace makes it prudent for the architect and developer to design attainable energy conserving features for the homes. The complex and specialized subject of energy conservation is further discussed in numerous technical publications.

7 Amenities

Amenities are the comforts and conveniences designed into a residential development. For townhouses and condominiums, the term most often refers to those man-made recreational facilities that add to the quality of the environment. However, amenities also include things like a site's preserved natural features and other aspects of the built environment that add to the physical landscape and to the livability a project—like man-made sculpture, fountains, lighting, security, and so on.

The following are some broad developer guidelines for programming the development of townhouse/condominium amenities features:

- Design and develop the attainable.
- Buyers believe what they can see and are unlikely to purchase based solely on exotic future plans.
- Early installation and completion of amenities features are a definite marketing asset.
- Features that are to be built in later stages of a development should be

7-1 Some of the highest valued amenities don't have to be installed . . . just preserved.

specifically tied to the total number of homes sold. A clear understanding of the timing of these facilities will greatly aid builder/buyer relations.

- The least expensive amenities, like natural features, may have a higher perceived buyer value than expensive elements like a clubhouse.
- An elaborate recreational amenity package should not be viewed as a substitute for good land planning and design.
- When the merits of various amenity features are evaluated, long-term maintenance costs should be an important consideration.

As townhouse/condominium living is by its very nature conducive to community interaction, recreational amenities which provide built-in social opportunities are a vital development feature—and may very well spell the success or failure of a project. Recreational amenities enhance the livability of the townhouse/condominium environment; often minimizing the maintenance responsibilities of individual homebuyers by their jointly sharing the maintenance costs of these features.

In deciding what amenities to install and when, the developer must familiarize himself with the facilities offered within the immediate market area—not just those provided by competitive residential projects, but also by private recreational clubs and local government. The developer must have a fairly firm grasp of the expected market and the portion of the home price that may be allocated to amenities. A preliminary but cautious amenity selection and budget should be made early so that the design team may show desired amenity features graphically on preliminary plans. This allows the developer to make accurate representations during the public approval process.

7-2   A pathway at Walden, a 100-acre PUD in a Minneapolis suburb.

Natural Features

Some of the highest valued amenities are the ones costing the least—in marketing surveys, homebuyers have indicated that the amenity for which they would be most willing to pay would be a preserved, natural site, containing interesting land forms, trees, natural water bodies, and other natural environment features. People so highly value these features in today's townhouse/condominium living that their preservation should be assured. Even such man-made amenities as pools or community buildings are secondary in value to the preservation of natural site features.

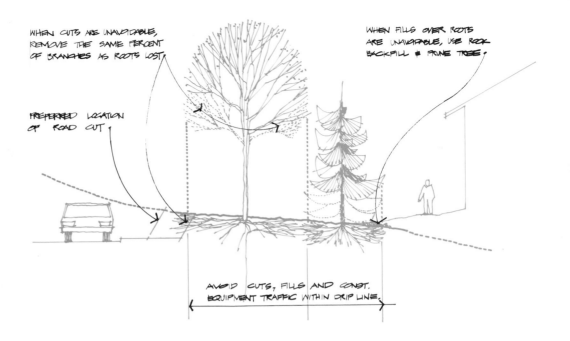

7-3   To save trees, balance water and air intake and evaporation.

Preserving Existing Vegetation

The marketing success of recently developed townhouses and condominiums which have preserved natural land forms and features seems to indicate that natural features have both environmental and economic advantages. In many cases, saving trees and existing grade may prove economically advantageous by reducing the developer's earth moving budget. Although the cost of building around trees may be initially more than construction on open land, most developers have found that lot premiums that accrue to homes beside a stand of existing vegetation more than offset the initial planning and construction expense. Replacing vegetation on a site that has been leveled would be far too costly and never quite the same—planting even half as many trees and shrubs would prove expensive. When there is a good supply of quality trees with a less than 4-inch trunk diameter either on the site or nearby, the use of a hydraulic tree spade could make a massive tree replanting cost effective; increased marketability and sales prices would more than offset the cost incurred in moving large numbers of trees on the site.

If a tree is to survive, its roots, bark, and leaves must remain largely undamaged. Preserving trees necessitates preserving existing grade—road plans, unit types, and building configurations shown on site grading plans should minimize cutting within the drip lines of existing trees. When it is necessary to lower the grade adjacent to an existing tree or group of trees, this cut should occur outside the drip line of the vegetation. If this is not possible, and a foundation, retaining wall, or back slope must be placed within this drip line, the amount of roots removed should be reflected in upper branch pruning—this will increase the survival chances of trees tolerant to "root pruning."

Roots usually grow within 4 feet of the existing grade around a tree. The larger roots, quite close to the surface, are involved in anchoring and providing structural support. Fibrous roots, normally growing most dense at the leaf perimeter or drip line, where water is most prevalent, are the primary moisture absorbers. The vital process of water intake and transpiration (involving roots and leaves) must be kept in balance. Certain trees are able to tolerate up to 50 percent loss in the number of roots as long as an equivalent of leaf area is removed. As a general rule, designers and construction personnel should remember that the amount of water evaporation through the leaves should never exceed the amount taken in by the roots.* As some trees may evaporate up to 3,000 gallons of water per day, the importance of proper moisture and maintaining the delicate root to leaf balance cannot be overstated.

7-4 (left) Preserving natural features, even a small line of trees, make a more livable and marketable environment. 7-5 (right) Existing grade and vegetation create an interesting entry image that may increase marketability.

*Robert L. Zion, *Trees for Architecture and the Landscape* (New York: Van Nostrand, Reinhold Co., 1968), p. 111.

7-6 (top) The value of preserving existing trees (background) and creating land forms and water retention areas far exceeds the cost. 7-7 (bottom) This existing tree line is the primary focus for views. Preservation of the tree line required a building form that stepped down an existing slope.

Where it is necessary to raise the grade around an existing tree, it is desirable to prevent soil from coming in contact with the bark. Where filling within the tree's drip line is required, rock or drywall welling should be installed adjacent to the tree trunk. Additional vertically placed drain tiles or stacks of rock extending to the final grade for approximately ⅔ of the diameter drip line should be installed to permit the roots to "breathe." A tree's bark is the protective layer over the vessels that conduct water to the leaves. Narrow vertical wounds heal rapidly; lateral gashes, the type made by construction equipment, heal very slowly and, if left untreated, endanger the survival of the tree.

Protection of existing trees and vegetation requires diligent and almost unrelenting attention by the developer and members of the development team. In the past, some owners mistakenly assumed that the land's potential for development would be enhanced by clearing trees—an impatient developer mistakenly began preliminary site preparation based upon early designs; surveyors were a little too diligent in clearing survey lines; and utility contractors have cleared excessively wide permanent and even temporary utility easements. Preservation begins when the property is acquired.

At the preliminary design stage, if not earlier, an accurate inventory and evaluation locating all trees and shrub masses by size,

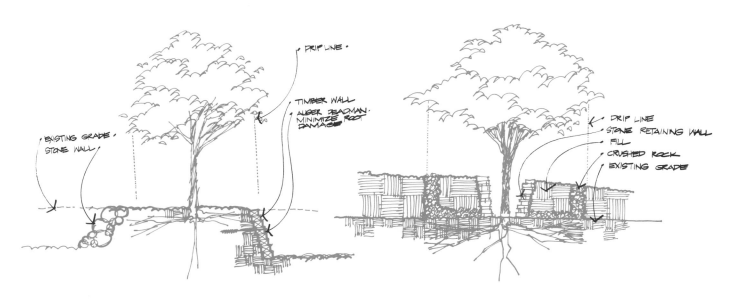

7-8   Cuts or fills within a tree's dripline: take precautions to help insure survival.

species, and quality should be made on the site plan showing topography. The inventory requires a physical examination of a site's trees and shrubs so that priority trees may be selected for preservation. A decision as final as the destruction of valuable existing vegetation should not be made until final design construction documents are completed and approved and bids are let. At that time, special attention must be given to avoid damaging or removing the growth that should remain and which has been carefully integrated into the design.

Because tree survival is influenced by conditions beyond the control of the designer/developer, using specific trees as central design features is an inviting but risky practice. However, once significant trees are identified and the final site plans show those that must be saved, immediate action should be taken to insure their survival through treating scars, pruning, removing dead wood, and fertilizing. Before construction begins, the contractor should be appraised of his responsibilities to protect trees and vegetation that are to be retained and to bear the cost of replacement should his construction activities result in loss of vegetation. Specifications should be prepared for protecting the trees during construction: where heavy construction activity is anticipated over tree roots, boards should be placed temporarily over the roots to prevent soil compaction; where construction machinery will be working close to existing trees, they should be protected by spaced boards fastened to the trunk with wire. Existing undergrowth, including shrubs and low trees, should be protected with temporary fencing.

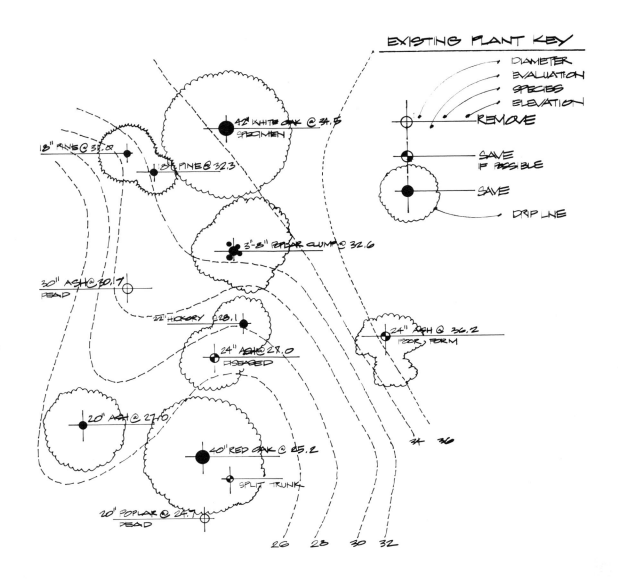

7-9 Inventory and evaluate existing vegetation for preservation, repair, or removal.

141

Planting New Vegetation

To complement the existing plants selected for preservation, new plants added to a townhouse/condominium site may provide a desirable amenity and functional engineering element. New plantings for this kind of development need to be carefully introduced into the site plan. The added plants may serve such engineering uses as control of soil erosion and drainage. They may also provide the "finishing touch" and promise of a continually changing townhouse/condominium environment. Planting can also reduce glare at the same time it removes pollutants from the air. Properly placed coniferous trees and shrubs can channel or decrease winter winds, preventing snow drifts over roadways and walkways. This can both reduce maintenance expenses and improve

vehicular pedestrian safety. Properly placed deciduous trees can provide passive solar energy conservation by screening the hot summer sun and admitting the warming winter sun. Plant material may also serve the architectural function of acoustic screening as well as create and define spaces, walls, roof and floor plans. Vegetation can screen, soften, or hide less attractive elements of the project. It can also partially reveal or extend building forms, or provide a smooth blend of buildings to land forms.

A landscape architect begins preparing a preliminary planting plan with an approximate estimate of the planting budget. Based upon a budget, from a low of $200 to several thousand dollars per dwelling unit, the landscape architect prepares a plant "massing" plan. The preliminary budget must be known

because approved schematic planting plans for the first phase of the project are often used by the approval authorities and the community association to evaluate final construction drawings for consistency throughout the project. From a rough sketch that represents what is appropriate regardless of budget restraints, the early plant massing plan is brought within budget by removal of least important trees and shrubs.

There are many different ways of designing new plantings for a residential project. The decision where to spend money should be based on a rather simple concept—the places that receive the greatest visual contact should have top priority. Even under the most strict budget limitations, several trees of 4 inches or more in caliper should be placed in the highest visual impact areas to gain promotional value. Evergreens are especially good in creating immediate impact; they can be the backbone of a planting plan, particularly for developments in areas that experience seasonal changes. Individual building entries should receive first attention, as well as the development's entry zone and, if there is such a place, the point at which entry roads split into collectors (see Chapter 4, p.49). Other areas around the periphery of the site that either need screening or enhancement should be high on the list of planting priorities.

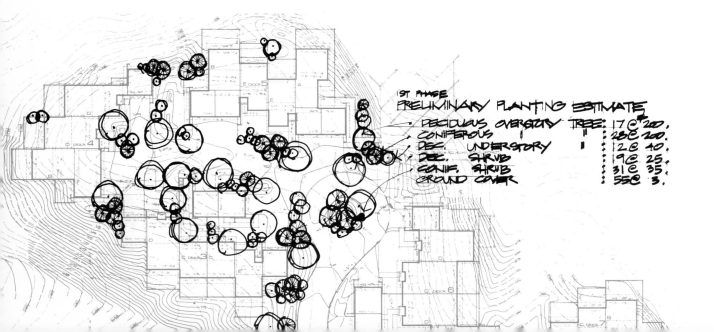

7-10 Schematic planting plans show repetitive unit design, plant massing, and initial budget estimates.

The loose preliminary plant massing plan should indicate the anticipated use of various classifications of plants. Normally these would include:

- deciduous overstory trees, such as oaks or maples;
- coniferous overstory trees, such as pines, firs, or spruce;
- deciduous understory trees that normally form a canopy below the larger trees, such as ornamental flowering fruit trees;
- coniferous and deciduous shrubs: upright, tall, or low;
- ivy, groundcovers, and flowers;
- sodded and seeded areas; and
- rock and wood chip areas.

The proper selection and placement of the new plant material is a complex task. At the preliminary design stage, approximate sizing according to the available budget should be noted on the plan, although careful study of plant sizes, textures, and shapes is not warranted at this stage. For detail design, a knowledge of plant types, growth habits and rates, hardiness, tolerance to transplanting, disease resistance, moisture and soil requirements, shade tolerance, urban conditions of pollution and salt is required. More importantly, even though at this point the creative landscape exists only on paper, "A skillful designer must have a highly developed visual imagination, an ability to see each tree in its maturity, to see its changing colors in each season and its changing form over the years."*

---

*Zion, *Trees for Architecture and the Landscape*, p. 155.

7-11 Install largest trees and shrubs in the most visually prominent places.

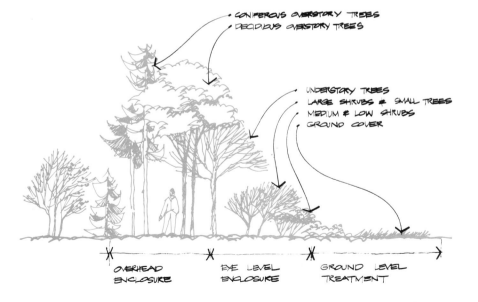

7-12 Typical plant types called for on a preliminary planting plan.

143

Design for Maintenance

One of the main reasons people prefer townhouse/condominium living is its maintenance-free aspect. Of course, residents must pay for someone else to maintain a site's landscape. With this in mind, the landscape designer should avoid a costly maintenance-intensive plan by remembering certain facts:

- Plants of hardy species requiring little or no winter protection should be selected.
- Along roadways and parking bays, avoid plantings that secrete sap, shed sewer-clogging seed pods, or that are short-lived or brittle by nature.
- Trees that have the desirable aspect of attracting birds should not be planted so that their branches overhang parking areas.
- To avoid unrelenting lawncare expenses, natural grasses or low-maintenance groundcover should be installed where appropriate.
- To avoid repeated pruning, slower growing shrubs should be used for hedges.
- To speed lawn maintenance, rock, wood chip, or paved strips should be used instead of sod or turf adjacent to buildings

and around other plantings.
- Turf or sodded area clearances between tree or shrub masses should be spaced according to the sizes and clearances of maintenance equipment.
- Growth retardants to help lower lawn mowing costs are becoming available.
- Mulches help to reduce the handwork necessary to maintain a neat appearance.
- In winter climates where salt is used to keep streets clear of ice, the salt usually collects adjacent to pavement, sometimes killing grass, shrubs, or even trees. Mixing gypsum into the soil at runoff points allows the salt to leech through and beneath the lawn root zone before it can damage vegetation. This can greatly reduce the need to re-sod or re-seed.

Selecting the best plants for a site means understanding soil types and choosing accordingly. An informal planting plan might augment existing trees and shrubs with new plantings, repeating certain combinations throughout the development site—this creates a pleasing but low-maintenance residential environment. Successful town-

house/condominium landscapes do *not* require an artificial, sculptured look. However, in some projects, building pathways or open space layout may dictate a more formalized plan, calling for architectural plants—such as the little leaf linden tree. In any case, the repeated use of the same plant or plant combinations throughout the development makes a plan cohesive and cost effective. Grouping a number of plants of the same type in one tightly spaced location may provide a very strong visual accent. This also makes the use of smaller plants possible.

In making preliminary and final planting plans, plants should be drawn to scale at ⅔ to ¾ of their ultimate mature size. This kind of preliminary diagraming helps both the developer and the design team to anticipate the impact of the plan, enabling early modifications and explanations to prospective homebuyers. Quite often, plans which anticipate eventual plant growth help to justify budget modifications.

7-13 Showing mature sizes on a planting plan helps the design team and buyers visualize the plants' impact.

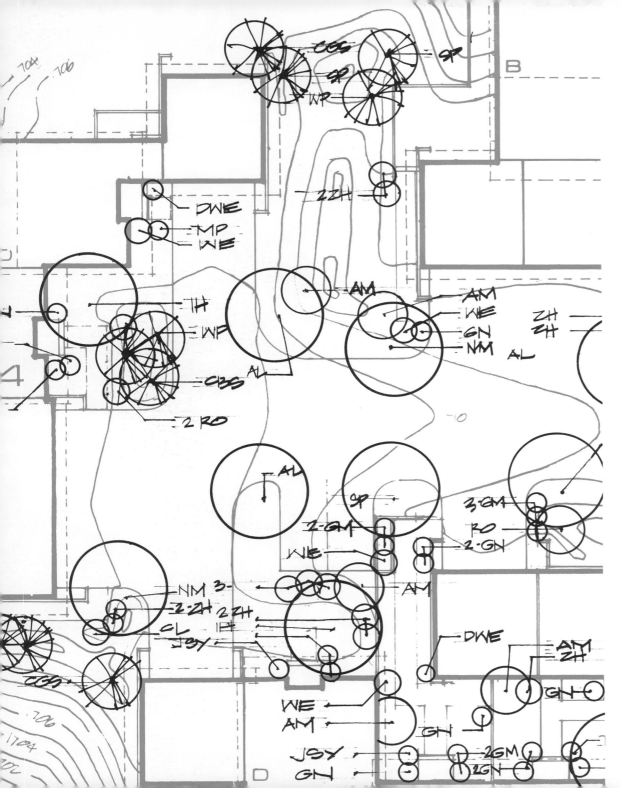

Just before landscaping begins, the landscape architect or contractor should stake various plant locations as illustrated on the plan. The landscape architect should then go to the nursery and tag the stock that is to be planted. Stock is then brought to the site and placed at approximate locations. Before actually planting, the landscape architect should take time to decide whether to shift or rotate certain plants to achieve the best orientation and relationship to buildings. After shrubs, groundcover plants, grass, and trees are planted, inert wood chips, rock, shavings, or other materials should be spread over backfill areas to hold soil moisture and to provide a trim appearance.

Many developers seemingly assume that plants are like streets or buildings—once they are installed, one can leave them alone. Plants, however, must be maintained in a regular and continuing maintenance program. This facet of land development is often overlooked and has cost builders many dollars in plant replacement. Contracting with the installing nursery or a competent maintenance organization is a good solution to the problem.

145

Water Features

Any discussion of natural site feature amenities for townhouses and condominiums would be incomplete without mentioning the impact of water. Marketing benefits from the inclusion of water on a site may very well outdistance the functional reasons for deliberate water ponding. While stormwater detention and storage may not be economically beneficial, real estate has long established the high value and desirability of a site with water. Even small, man-made ponds or lakes can greatly offset a feeling of high density and provide an aesthetic, pleasing amenity.

The ease or difficulty of creating a pond, lake, or linear water body is dependent upon a site's soil type. If a clay-based impermeable soil exists, sealing an existing or created low area for ponding should not be a problem. Common granular (buildable soils) do require a seal of some sort, such as ben-

tonite clay, a processed expansive material that, once worked into the upper layer of soil, will provide a water-retaining liner.

The shoreline of a created water body must be protected from wave action or rain erosion. A 25 percent slope will typically be suitable to prevent erosion of granular soils. Steeper slopes require protective vegetation and very steep slopes require a filter blanket cover of crushed rock. Embankment slopes of 50 percent require the addition of rip rap to prevent erosion if much wave action is present.*

---

*For more information about lakes and pond management see Joachim Tourbier and Richard Westmacott, *Lakes and Ponds* (Washington, D.C.: Urban Land Institute, 1976).
William A. Hanson and Frans Bigelow, *Lake Management Case Study: Westlake Village, California* (Washington, D.C.: Urban Land Institute, 1977).

7-15 (top) By maintaining the flexibility of having no required setback, these townhouses are able to gain maximum amenity value from this man-made lake. 7-16 (middle) Water features reduce the feeling of density. 7-17 (bottom) An interconnected water feature including water falls provides the central amenity for this townhouse and garden apartment community.

7-14 (left) This permanent pond which acts as a stormwater retention basin provides an attractive entry setting for these three-story condominiums.

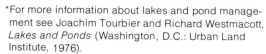

Recreational Amenities

Swimming Pools

An outdoor swimming pool is one of the most desired amenities for townhouses and condominiums. Even in areas with a short summer season, a swimming pool is important—it establishes a townhouse/condominium's image, projecting a maintenance-free/leisure-oriented lifestyle and a certain prestige. It also serves as a place to socialize with neighbors, a focus for open space and a meeting ground for the community as a whole. After a project is completed and the community association takes authority, the swimming pool takes on another important function—it becomes the key feature of the community association's recreation facilities and a mainstay of association vitality. All of the above are central reasons for a developer's decision to install this rather costly amenity.

In *Townhouses and Condominiums: Residents' Likes and Dislikes,* Carl Norcross states that recreation facilities are of special importance to townhouse and condominium families, and when swimming pools as well as other recreation facilities are provided, many people use them.* However, the decision to build a pool within a development should consider whether similar facilities are available close to the site.

*Carl Norcross, *Townhouses & Condominiums: Residents' Likes and Dislikes* (Washington, D.C.: Urban Land Institute, 1973), p. 70.

In the process of site planning for a swimming pool, a balance is necessary. A pool should be within walking distance of the dwelling units and the open space system of the development. At the same time, pools should be properly buffered and separated from homes—they are not the quietest of amenities. It is normally good marketing practice to place the pool in a prominent location relative to the flow of homeowners. This consideration must, of course, be balanced with other planning considerations.

7-19 Pools are a focus for "neighboring."

7-18 The pool expresses a townhouse/condominium lifestyle. Note the tot lot in foreground.

At the preliminary stage of swimming pool design, the drawing scale is usually too small to consider detail dimensions. Generally, a 20-foot by 40-foot or 20-foot by 50-foot rectangle, L- or T-shape pool is sufficient design specification. Several decisions, primarily governed by economics, may be made at this stage:

- the placement of the pool and/or distribution of pools throughout the development;
- the placement of deck areas accompanying the pools;
- whether toilet and/or changing facilities are to be provided; and
- the need for a children's splash pool.

At the detail design stage, final amenity budgets should temper the pool facility designs. The final pool program is determined according to the functional sizes necessary for anticipated resident uses and the image afforded by various pool sizes and facilities. The developer must construct a pool that, in the eyes of homebuyers, is not too large (perceived as too expensive) or too small (perceived as a token or half effort).

7-20   Save dollars and improve the pool's appearance by including some lawn within the fenced deck area.

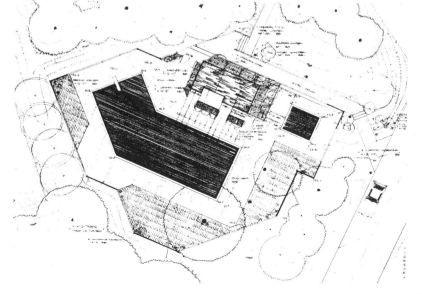

7-21   A wading pool and large sitting area are provided in this pool complex serving over 300 homes. The National Swimming Pool Institute (2000 K Street, N.W., Washington, D.C. 20006) has published detailed suggested minimum standards for private and public swimming pools. These standards are updated periodically, and they can be obtained for a nominal charge.

Some rough guidelines for pool size follow:

Number of Homes	Pool Size in Sq. Ft.
Under 50	800–1,000
50–100	1,000–1,300
100–150	1,200–1,500
150–200	1,400–1,800
Over 200	1,800 up

These are at best only loose general standards. A safe diving area may be at a minimum approximately 16 feet by 24 feet given a deck-level board. Usually the ratio of swimmers to non-swimmers is 1 to 2 or 1 to 3, yielding a minimum size pool with diving of just under 800 square feet. In large developments, a series of smaller pools relating to individual housing groups is a planning option instead of a centrally located, large pool.

If the projected market includes children and competitive swimming is popular in the area, a regulation 25-meter pool should be considered for larger developments. On the other hand, if buyer profiles predict few families with children, the wading pool and/or diving section may be omitted. This omission may also be appropriate in the design of smaller pools for particular housing groups, rather than one central pool facility. In all cases, user enjoyment will be enhanced if the deck or patio area is three to four times the pool area. Part of the patio area may be well-drained lawn. The pool should be oriented so that the diving board does not face the sun during normal hours of use and so that the main deck area is normally the long axis of the pool.

Wading pools should be provided where the anticipated child population indicates that they will be used. Because these pools often serve as substitute bathrooms, the filtration equipment must cycle water at least once every four hours. The installation of a spray pool with little or no standing water is an alternative to providing a child's wading pool.

A pool's filter-bathhouse structure, fencing, benches, and lighting provide the architect and landscape architect with an opportunity to complement strongly and interestingly the architecture of the homes. Pool area structures can utilize similar materials and the style of the homes but in a more playful or uncompromising way. Typically, filtration pump and heating equipment require a space approximately 6 feet by 12 feet, which is adequate for all but the largest pools. In the same instance, each bath/dressing facility should have toilets, and can include showers, lavatories, mirror, seating or bench area, and several storage lockers. From a practical standpoint, a pool facility immediately adjacent to the homes it serves may not include toilet/shower facilities. Local health ordinances should determine these requirements.

For safety, access to the swimming pool facility is usually limited by perimeter fencing. In most situations, a well-placed swimming pool complex provides general good views of open space and screens out undesirable views. It is best to have two fence details or sections—one visually open, with vertical, diagonal, or horizontal slats and

7-22 This wrought iron fencing provides safety yet does not obstruct the view.

another that blocks both the view and the noise. The solid sections can also be used as a wind barrier. In any case, the swimming pool design should include a fence that is 4 to 6 feet tall, difficult to climb, and impossible to slip through.

Many building codes require that a reverse sloping perimeter of concrete be installed adjacent to the pool coping so that contaminated surface water cannot re-enter the pool. This prohibits the interesting alternative of using a blend of both concrete and wood decking immediately adjacent to the pool. Treated wood, cedar, or heart redwood, however, have held up well under wet conditions. An often overlooked detail is the provision for a backup valve to relieve hydrostatic pressure which, under high groundwater conditions, can actually lift the shell of an empty pool.

Tennis Courts

By all present indications, tennis will be one of the major family sports of the future. Statistically, the typical American tennis player aligns well with today's townhouse/condominium buyer profiles. A casual observation of people waiting to use municipal courts should lead developers to conclude that tennis courts are a very desirable townhouse/condominium amenity.

The area requirements of a tennis court are not that demanding. A double court is typically 120 feet by 120 feet, and the width can be decreased to 110 feet by reducing the center space between the courts. There is disagreement as to an appropriate ratio of players to courts. On the average, the ratio should be one court per 20 to 35 players, without a reservation system.

Depending on soil conditions and the type of court surfacing, two completed courts, including surface treatment and fencing, should cost between $15,000 and $25,000. Lighting can add as much as $15,000 to the cost of two courts, but in a townhouse/condominium development can effectively double the available hours of prime time.

Generally, building one or two courts does not significantly affect the per unit amenity cost, and the addition of the second court does not double the cost of tennis facilities. Another reason for building two courts even for a smaller size project is the method by which people waiting to play tennis gain access to the court. Having two tennis courts permits the gradual *phasing in* of new players and *phasing out* of those people who were there previously. A more congenial at-

7-23 (top) Tennis, a low cost-per-unit amenity with growing value for low-maintenance, recreation-oriented communities.   7-24 (bottom) For most developments, two courts are preferable to one.

7-25 A community may be designed around a theme tennis facility. (Westlake Village, California)

mosphere exists between the players waiting to play, largely because their wait is cut in half. There is less animosity between those people playing and those waiting to use the courts, contributing to interaction on and around the tennis courts.

If budget constraints are a consideration, perhaps the best route to take is to build one court, saving on amenity dollars by partial fencing. If only one court is built, providing additional space for more courts allows the community association or homeowners groups to install additional tennis facilities if desired later on.

Once a tennis court's general location has been chosen, it must be oriented properly relative to the sun's movement. Several factors should influence this decision: (1) buyer profiles should suggest the normal hours of play for the proposed tennis courts (generally, tennis court facilities for townhouse/ condominium communities receive the greatest use in afternoon and evening hours); (2) sun angle information for the site's latitude should be researched; (3) the months of play, coupled with the anticipated normal hours of play, should give optimum orientation; and (4) the azimuth of the sun during the most popular hour of play should lie 90 degrees to the direction of play, minimizing the impact of sun in the players' eyes.

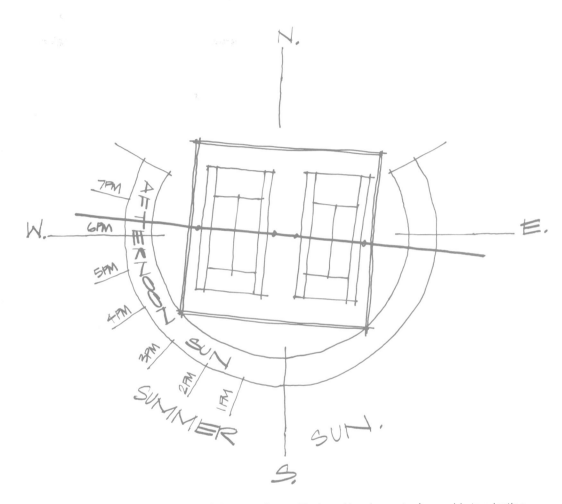

7-26 Sun orientation is one factor that influences the positioning of tennis courts. As a guide to orienting a tennis court, a line extending parallel to the nets should point in the approximate direction of the sun during the most popular hours of play. This plan shows a tennis court position favoring late afternoon/early evening play. Much information on the physical characteristics of tennis courts—construction, maintenance, and equipment—can be obtained from Tennis Courts (United States Tennis Association, 71 University Place, Princeton, New Jersey 08540).

7-27 (top) The Wilderness in Naples, Florida. 7-28 (bottom) A golf course is high value, easily understood central open space.

Golf Courses

A townhouse/condominium developer's decision to build a golf course must be based primarily on the anticipation of increased land value over the cost of construction. The cost of installing and maintaining a golf course must be offset by financial gains through increased lot or unit premiums, reduced carrying costs resulting from an increased sales pace, and perhaps an increase in marketable density. While on the surface a golf course may appear as an instantly saleable townhouse/condominium amenity, there are a number of negative aspects that must be considered: (1) full-size, 18-hole championship golf courses take up to 150 acres of a project's most developable land (as the land must be relatively flat, golf courses are often located in the valleys of a rolling project); (2) to establish their value to prospective buyers, golf courses must be built before any sales begin. There is nothing attractive about 100 acres or more of bare dirt.*

Golf courses can extend the typical geographic areas that will accept townhouses and condominiums. As sub-tropical areas may allow year-round use of golf courses, this amenity is particularly desirable in such places. At the Wilderness Country Club in Naples, Florida, the developers skillfully combined natural and man-made amenities to create a townhouse/condominium market away from the Gulf shoreline. The combina-

tion of a preserved tropical forest and a man-made golf course provided condominium sales outside the traditional prestige area within Naples.

Golf course construction will generally take a minimum of a year and frequently 18 months for completion—6 to 9 months for construction and an additional 6 to 9 months of time to establish the greens, turf, and fairway planting, all of which constitute *front end money*. In addition, the construction of a golf course will normally put a developer in the business of managing the course for several years. Other management alternatives exist, however, such as hiring a management company or selling to a golf course operator.

As evidenced by the number of golf courses that have been constructed in conjunction with townhouses and condominiums, there are definite gains that can accrue:

- In government review sessions of modern, open space, moderate density development, government officials frequently have difficulty visualizing the open space part of the plan. When a golf course replaces the label of "Open Space" on a plan, even the most skeptical or naive officials can understand and visualize that use.
- For the prospective homeowner, golf courses place an established value on open space.
- Obviously, a developer can establish an increased value for homes abutting a golf course over internally-sited townhouses or condominiums.

*For more information about golf courses see Rees L. Jones and Guy L. Rando, *Golf Course Developments* (Washington, D.C.: Urban Land Institute, 1974).

152

The developer's decision to design a golf course, like so many things in land development, involves rather complex value judgements. Generally, a developer may decide to develop a golf course within his project if among other things:

- the land is reasonably low priced;
- it has the right natural features;
- there are overcrowded courses within the market area; and
- the development is being built for upper income homes.*

To discern the demand for golf courses within his market area and to accurately estimate the probability of success in utilizing a golf course as a marketing tool, the de-

---

*Carl Norcross, *Open Space Communities in the Market Place,* Technical Bulletin No. 57 (Washington, D.C.: Urban Land Institute, 1966), pp. 51–52.

veloper must analyze the market for this kind of recreation facility and research buyer profiles. A careful analysis of the proximity to other courses, the successes and failures of particular course types, and various other considerations should provide the necessary information to determine the demand in a market area.

There are a number of specific design and construction considerations for golf course development:

- Minimizing earth moving expenses is central to economical golf course construction. On the average, a golf course requires excavation of 250,000 cubic yards of dirt.
- Adequate surface and sub-surface drainage must be assured. If not, additional tiling and regrading expenses will have to be borne by either the de-

veloper or the community association at a later date.

- A large quantity of landscape material must be either saved, moved and planted, or brought in, to distinguish the fairways.
- Fairways may be strung out in a single consecutive width or doubled up as two side-by-side widths. Where land is plentiful, the single width fairway configuration provides the greatest lineal frontage from which lot premiums may be gained.
- A close examination of the soil is necessary to assure proper turf growth. High clay or organic content soil warrants additional expense, earthwork, and topsoil replacement.
- A high capacity irrigation system, providing from 1.5 to 3.5 million gallons per week and costing from $100,000 to $300,000 must be installed.

There are a number of alternatives to constructing a full, *championship-size* golf course. While the par 70 to 73, 7,000-yard course is desirable, if dollars or land are limited, a 9-hole regulation course, a 9-hole with a choice of various tees, an executive course (18 holes that can be played in half the normal time), or a par 3 course should be considered.

Due to the complexity of golf course design and construction, professional input by those experienced in golf course architecture and contractors skilled in grading according to topography plans should be gathered early.

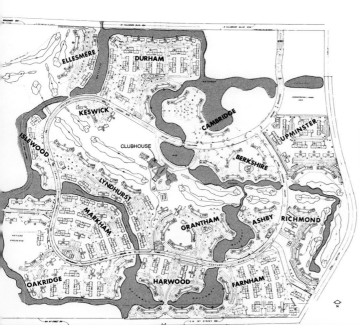

7-29   A golf course is easily visualized by both government officials and buyers. The National Golf Foundation (200 Castlewood Drive, North Palm Beach, Florida 33408) provides information sheets pertaining to various phases of golf course planning, financing, and operation.

153

7-30 (above) The developer's architect may make a strong visual statement with the architecture of a community building.

Carmichael-Lynch Adv., Inc.

Community Buildings

Depending on the development size, budget restraints, and people that will buy in a particular townhouse or condominium project, a central recreation center/community building may be a beneficial amenity for a developer to include. In developments with a swimming pool, the requirement of a place to put the pool filtration and heating equipment can justify connecting it with an adjoining community building. A community multi-purpose room of moderate size can be included at a relatively low additional cost and can serve as a meeting room and office for the community association. This would be a more economical approach than going to a full-scale clubhouse facility.

Development trends seem to indicate that several smaller, decentralized recreational facilities within walking or easy biking distance, will have a high perceived value to the residents. The day of the big clubhouse is over. Again, the total size of a townhouse/condominium development is a central factor in the decision to provide a large facility or any building at all, although even a small development requires storage space for maintenance equipment, tools, and vehicles. Access to any such storage area should always be separated from the general entry to a community building. One hundred units is the approximate minimum for a community meeting space. Indoor pools/clubhouses usually require 200 units and up.

7-31 (left) A well-designed, modest structure for pool equipment and open shelter.

154

Today's buyers are quite critical of the scope of a community facility. If, for instance, a facility is large enough to require extensive maintenance personnel, this would place a large financial burden on the community association long after the developer has completed the project.

As a general rule, it is not practical to support community building maintenance personnel with less than 150 dwelling units. In fact, in most price classes, it requires a minimum of 300 dwelling units to support the cost of maintenance and operation at a reasonable annual fee. A properly-scaled community building can act as a year-round focus for neighborhood activity and is the logical place for the community association office and meeting room.

When front-end capital and construction phasing permits, it is most beneficial to utilize the community building as the model center and sales area for the community. The fact that the open space plan may not permit the prominent location required of a home sales area should be given consideration in the early concept stage of site planning.

Because the physical form of a community building is not bound by the rather tight functional constraints of the housing units, the developer's architect may make a strong visual impact with building architecture. Care should be given to using a scale and materials that complement the rest of the project's architecture, but the design should be somewhat freer. Sited in a proper location, a building of this type can create a very positive community image, more or less setting the trend for the rest of the project's architecture, despite the fact that the community building usually is designed after the architecture of the housing units has been determined.

7-32 (left) For very large developments, a community building provides an amenity focus for the residents. 7-33 (above) This small, interesting clubhouse is an extension of the pool deck, serving as community association meeting space, small party room, bath, and filter enclosure.

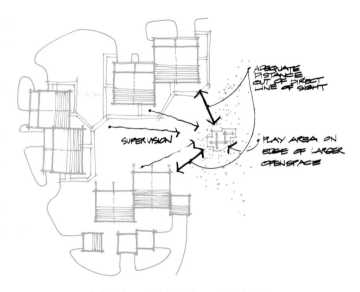

Labels in figure:
ADEQUATE DISTANCE OUT OF DIRECT LINE OF SIGHT

SUPERVISION

PLAY AREA ON EDGE OF LARGER OPEN SPACE

7-34   Locate tot lots to avoid infringing on adjacent homes' privacy and near larger open spaces. Several small ones are usually better than one big one.

Play Areas and Tot Lots

If the market for a townhouse or condominium development will include children, play areas should be provided but located away from the direct view of private outdoor spaces. An observation of children's play habits seems to indicate that this recreational amenity should be located reasonably close to home if it is to be actively used. Homebuyers with children or who are planning to have children will consider play areas a desirable amenity. However, the construction of a tot lot very close to a home unit is almost always perceived as a real or imagined threat to privacy. Careful design consideration given to this problem will stem conflicts and disagreements between homeowners, the developer, and, ultimately, the community association.

In the design of play areas/tot lots, the following rules should be applied:

- A tot lot/play area should be placed adjacent to the zone surrounding the townhouse blocks—close to the larger open space or in the large open space area.
- Unless a site contains a highly visible location, there should be a number of small, well-dispersed play areas instead of a few major ones.
- A skillfully designed tot lot/play area can take on a sculptural and color accent role when placed in a prominent location.

Generally speaking, tot lot/play areas should be integrated with natural land forms, making the architectural construction blend with the landscape rather than defying it. Of course, play areas should be separated by distance or grade change from streets, collectors, subcollectors and looped streets. The small traffic volume handled by courts and cul-de-sacs serving townhouse units does not pose as much of a danger as major roads, but there should still be some natural or architectural separation between pavement and play areas.

A townhouse/condominium pathway system should be a link from homes and streets to open space, tot lots, and play areas. However, if the paths are to act as bikeways, this relatively fast moving traffic should be separated from play areas by short pathway offsets.

Although there should not be a direct view of a play area from the deck or front door of a unit, supervision of the play area is desirable from a kitchen window. Again, a certain distance separation from the home unit is important.

Once general locations for play areas have been identified on the detailed site plans, early market data, kept up-to-date as the design progresses, should indicate the expected population of children by various age groups. This information should be considered in the design of play areas and in the inclusion of particular facilities. A tot lot should be both a functional and sculptural landscape accent with marketing value.

Generally speaking, materials that go into making a tot lot or play area should complement those found in the rest of the project. Almost any groundcover is better for play areas than asphalt and concrete. Sand, bark chips, gravel, and even earth is safer and more "play inducing."

As with any equipment that will be owned and maintained by the community association, upkeep expense must be considered. Unfortunately the materials and designs that are characteristically low in maintenance create a rather harsh environment that is hostile to children's play. Ironically, cold, anti-play materials, such as the ready-made tubular assemblies purchased at the local hardware store, may actually incite vandalism and other destructive acts toward the play equipment. Children may try to test the limits of such equipment. On the other hand, play areas that are visually interesting, durable, and challenging may well develop a built-in "maintenance crew"—a group of youngsters taking pride in ownership and patrolling their use and upkeep.

A casual observation of children's play will demonstrate that if an area does not present a certain degree of challenge, children will soon grow disinterested and seek more exciting territory. A balance, therefore, must be achieved between safety and challenge, much as there should be between maintenance, budget, and aesthetics.

7-35 (left) A tot lot should be both functional and a sculptural landscape accent with marketing value.

Les Turnau

7-36 (left) Keep play areas within sight of the homes but not close enough to infringe on unit privacy. 7-37 (above, left) Tot lots should be accessible by pathways. 7-38 (above, right) Tot lots need not be complicated.

157

Jogging Trails and Exercise Areas

When a townhouse/condominium project will
be catering to adults, or as an adjunct to a
child-oriented project, the provision of a jogging path with occasional exercise areas
can be an attractive amenity. Jogging has
become a national exercise/pastime. A suitable circuit would be a half mile or longer.
The number of exercise stations will be determined by the length of the pathway. These
stations would include some simple pieces
of outdoor exercise equipment, such as a
chinning bar, a slant board for sit-ups, etc.
This amenity can be provided at little cost
and will be an attractive marketing feature in
a physical fitness-conscious society.

7-39   This sitting area takes advantage of the
quiet woods.

Other Amenities

Sitting Areas

Benches and sitting areas, while being a relatively easy, uncomplicated amenity addition, are an intangible element that add to the way homebuyers and homeowners perceive a development. They can be a subtle indication of the lifestyle that a homeowner can expect. In this light, benches and sitting areas should be visible from the model center area and entry zone to the community. An observation of resident behavior indicates that if benches are located at the end of a dead-end pathway, they are less likely to be used. The authors' experience indicates the popularity of walking paths and leads to the conclusion that people will use benches if they are properly placed along these paths rather than at created destinations.

While a bench may be all the sitting area that is necessary, there may be certain areas within a development that warrant a more elaborately designed sitting area. This could incorporate a special landscape feature, a spectacular view or vista, a rock outcropping, or a stand of mature trees with a combination of benches, planters, or perhaps a small water feature.

7-40 (above left) Locate and design a sitting area in a special location. This cantilevered bench and deck overlook a water feature. 7-41 (above right) Benches: a relatively uncomplicated amenity accent. 7-42 (left) A well-designed bus stop with a sitting area is both functional and an attractive part of the streetscape.

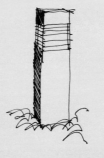

7-43 Selection of light fixtures to blend with the architectural style of the surrounding landscape should consider the many alternative styles and types available.

Site Lighting

There are five basic areas within most townhouse/condominium developments that require lighting attention:

(1) streets;
(2) courts or clusters;
(3) open space;
(4) unit entries; and
(5) unit entry walks.

If a street system is to be dedicated to a municipality, designers should familiarize themselves with the standard light fixtures installed on other municipal streets, although the architectural or landscape character of a new community may warrant different fixtures from the standard utility lights used in many parts of the United States. Many communities may have several standard fixtures that are approved for use. A local utility company or engineering department should respond to a new community's varying needs by aiding and researching improved quality lighting standards. When non-standard fixtures are selected, the utility company can require the community association to be responsible for maintenance and upkeep. Normally, there is an additional expense for fixtures which vary from the standard. This additional cost can simply be reflected in higher fees, normally part of the city's assessment. If the street system is to be entirely private, the lighting selection and cost allocations simply become part of the amenity budget.

With either a linear or cluster road scheme, general illumination that utilizes the same type of fixture placed along collector and subcollector routes is frequently necessary. This is typically required of developments having a density below seven units per acre, where the unit or garage/wall mounted lights do not adequately illuminate courts or parking bays. The same type of fixture found on the major streets or a fixture with similar appearance mounted at a lower height may be used adjoining the housing units. An alternative would be to use the light fixture style of the open space pathway system, if lighting of the pathway system is planned.

Townhouses/condominiums should provide lighting for open space systems in order to gain the maximum benefit from them. Even marginal illuminations of the pedestrian walkway system will be an approved resident amenity investment due to the resultant added hours of use for these areas. Lighting should give special emphasis to natural features or accent points of a pathway or open space. Unless very large areas must be illuminated, fixtures no higher than 10 feet may be placed on center at intervals of up to 100 feet. Typically, amenity budgets are inadequate for including even one foot-candle uniformly along a pathway, but a spacing of typical landscape lights 40 to 75 feet on center makes pathways much more usable and secure. Greater security may even require

more, brighter, and/or additional light fixtures.

Light fixtures mounted at home entry doors are necessary for townhouses and condominiums and are the lowest cost site lighting fixtures. Quite often, with proper architectural detail, a low-cost incandescent fixture can lend a custom-design appearance. Of course, the decision to adapt low-cost lights must consider initial and long-term cost; short-term, low fixture installation cost versus maintenance expense due to bulb life; fixture deterioration; and vandalism.

To eliminate shadow areas or other conditions that would pose a security threat, care should be given in locating these fixtures, particularly where separate or combined parking bays or garage units require the homeowner to walk past fences or building recesses.

For green space entry townhouses or condominiums, unit entry lights may provide most of the open space lighting, particularly in higher density conditions. Similarly, in more tightly clustered court conditions, unit or garage-mounted lights may cast enough illumination into the paved area to eliminate a need for additional street lighting.

Under tight budgets, additional lighting expenditures (beyond home entry, garage, and street lighting) should be directed at lighting

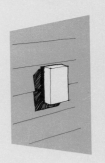

7-44 Examples of two basic entry fixtures with inexpensive wood detailing.

the walkways that lead from homes to garages, parking bays, or lots. In some situations, adequate walkway illumination levels and surprising visual impact can be gained by use of ground-mounted spotlights, angled or shooting straight up. These are particularly effective for up-lighting large trees or illuminating feature walls of buildings or garages.

On a plan utilizing a rectilinear design theme it is typically good design practice to consistently locate open space/landscape lighting fixtures on only one side of a given pathway. For an irregular or curvilinear site plan type, alternating or irregular placement of fixtures is preferable. In any case, the offset distance from paving should be the same.

Consideration should also be given to selecting the type of lighting element. Sodium bulbs give a warmer shade of light than the bluish light normally emitted by mercury vapor elements. While incandescent and sodium vapor lights emit a warmer color than mercury vapor lights, they are more costly, but do much to create a warm, welcome feeling for the community's night landscape. Remember that the character, identity, and image of a community are largely set through viewing it from the street. The more hospitable the impression gained, the more welcome homebuyers feel. Both mercury vapor and sodium light sources are approximately twice as efficient in light production as the

incandescent bulb—initial expenditures must be balanced with amortization and long-term cost. One must also consider that 20 percent of a light's efficiency is lost at night because of glare. The use of a defuser, refractor, or reflector is preferable and can eliminate this problem.

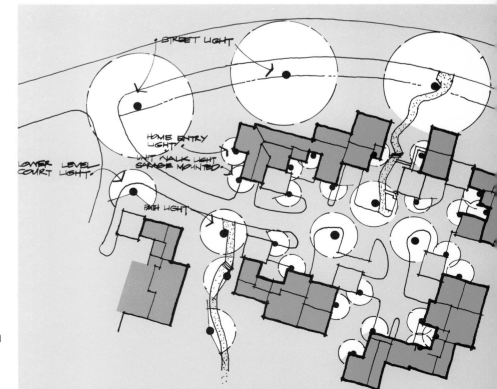

7-45 Exterior lighting: function and safety, identity and character.

Signs, Names, and Graphics

Although the signage system normally will not make or break a project's success, signs constitute one of the many small amenities that produce community character and help to set developments apart from one another. Well-executed and placed signs create an image of attention to detail. More importantly, they give a sense of order to what may be a rather complex site plan. One of the few drawbacks of a curvilinear road plan is that it can be difficult to get one's bearings within a community. A well-designed signage system will visually organize a community, enabling people to know where they are. It can also greatly enhance the identity of the various separate housing clusters. Lost drivers who are trying to read small, inadequate street signs or home numbers may pose a hazard to community safety; thus well-designed signage makes the community a safer place.

At the preliminary design stage, site graphics and signage requirements should be analyzed and added to the list of amenities that should be budgeted. At this stage it is not necessary to develop specific designs or signage standards. However, the specific naming of collector and subcollector routes within the development must be made at this stage. Street names on the site

7-46 (above) Home number grouping signs are important for townhouses with green space entries, because guests normally can't see the individual unit doors from the road or parking areas. 7-47 (right) Signs can take on a sculptural appearance.

development preliminary plans as early as possible aid in the many communications that must take place among the design team, government agencies, utilities companies, and others involved in development. The creative or imaginative selection of a project's street names should not be overlooked for image/identity value—a design aspect of a townhouse/condominium community often overlooked. There is a distinctly different psychological impact between buying a home on "Smith Street" versus one on "Berkshire Trail" or "Island View Drive."

The signage graphics system for townhouses and condominiums should be located and identified on preliminary site plans. This will allow a budgeting inventory of necessary quantities and will indicate the comprehensiveness of a developer's planning approach. Most of the successful, award-winning projects have paid close attention to the design and placement of informational signs, including entry markers, home number grouping signs at the junction of entry courts and loop roads, home or garage entry numbers, notations of guest parking, and open space signage.

Signs at an entry may provide a new development's "first impression." While their detail design should be delayed until final contract documents, establishing their locations early on the site plan is necessary. Discussions with local street department officials for county and state highway agencies may be necessary to secure these locations. Safe sight distances must also be considered in the placement of signs. A location close to the arterial roadway, which exists within the government right-of-way, may be gained by review and making an agreement with involved government officials to assure that the sign will have a low enough profile and an adequate pavement setback within the right-of-way to assure safe sight distance.

In a cluster community utilizing a number of streets that terminate in turnarounds, it is important to provide visitors, delivery trucks, and particularly emergency vehicles with a means to avoid wasting unnecessary time and gas, as well as house-hunting trips. Street name or number markers should be placed in the area most visible from the prevalent traffic flow direction. In cluster design where parking bays are located away from home entries, it is desirable to install home group number arrows. This signage helps designate where a visitor should park to minimize the walk to a home entry. In other cases, properly located individual home numbers attached to the home entries will suffice.

7-49 (top) A routed wood sign with quality typestyle is simple, durable community identification.
7-50 (bottom) This entry marker, built on a center island of a divided entry road, has lettering and project logo cut from corten steel.

7-48 This economical townhouse directional sign uses silk-screen lettering on reflectorized background material.

163

7-51 (above) Identifying a home with signage on the garage as well as on the home entry improves visitor orientation. 7-52 (right) Pathway signage expressing a more natural design theme. 7-53 (below) An architecturally sensitive traffic control sign.

In green-space entry and some garage-court entry (attached garage) cluster housing design, the view of home entries is obscured from the entry court or parking area. From the standpoint of the homeowner, this is a very desirable feature, enhancing privacy. From a visitor's standpoint, however, it makes locating a specific home difficult. For this reason, individual residence numbers can be placed nearest the entry walkway leading to the home if the garage is attached or detached adjacent to the entry door. Sometimes it is desirable to mount home numbers on garages visible from the court road in addition to locations at home entries.

In more extensive open space systems, where separate pedestrian walks and bikeways or trails are provided, it may be desirable to mark these routes. An interesting open space adaptation is provision of a running course with exercise stations. Obvi-

ously, any such precise course will require adequate signage. In more wooded open space systems, the interest of residents in the natural environment can be reflected with signs identifying plant names and other natural features.

Normally, it is best to differentiate the two major categories of signage—informational and traffic control signs. Specifically, the informational signs should not detract from or interfere with the visibility and prominence of traffic control signs. It is best to either maintain the standard shape of the traffic control signs, i.e., stop—octagonal, yield—triangular, or to silhouette signs or overlay them with a standardized framing system. Informational signage need not be governed by the same constraints, but should be integrated with standardized materials and frame structures. Both sign types should complement materials used in the architecture and other site amenities.

Standardized die-stamp metal signs bolted to metal posts are the most familiar signage for most municipalities and have several advantages for townhouse/condominium use. They are normally low in cost, vandalism resistant, easily installed, replaceable, and relatively maintenance free. Another standard municipal sign type uses a metal sheet with reflective material applied to its surface. The use of either standard sign type may be desirable for speed limits, pedestrian crossings, and parking control within the community. Additionally, familiar signs may be more readily identified by drivers than more unusual traffic control signage. The metal/reflective material combination is also durable and moderate in cost, coming in a number of different colors. However, if the developer and his design team desire a fresh, unique image, standard signage types may be replaced by more distinctive signage. (See Figure 7-53)

The importance of utilizing a uniform, crisp, and well-proportioned lettering style for a development's literature and stationery is a part of signage that cannot be overemphasized. As the American consumer is constantly presented with high-quality graphic material in every medium, the developer hurts his image in a subtle way if he fails to recognize the importance of quality printed materials. Once a lettering style and logo design have been prepared, they should be used consistently—for letters, labels, numbers, advertising graphics—in all communications with a prospective homebuyer. If those individuals doing the planning have graphic design capabilities, occasionally the design of a project logo and a style of lettering can be made a part of the planning and design contract.

7-54 Select a clear, simple logo, name, and type face, and then use it consistently and repeatedly.

Mailboxes

In many cases, the townhouse or multi-family condominium is required to place centralized mailboxes so that they are convenient for the mailman to operate. Custom-designed mailboxes have occasionally met with resistance by the local postmaster. In some cases, the post office has begun furnishing a standardized banked unit of individual mailboxes, located along a community's residential street or mounted within the entry foyer of a multi-story condominium.

Generally speaking, the idea of individual home delivery to townhouses and condominiums has met with resistance from the postal service. There appear to be inequities in this attitude toward mail delivery—if one compares the delivery time and dollars required for house-to-house delivery of mail to single-family detached homes, one would appreciate that this would be far more costly

and time consuming than individual delivery to townhouses and condominiums. As townhouses are closer together, mail may be delivered much more efficiently. Mail delivery to a mid- or high-rise condominium development is even more efficient. These homeowners, therefore, are unfairly not receiving the same benefits that single-family detached homes enjoy. Townhouse/condominium owners pay the same price for mail delivery, but are required to retrieve their mail from mailboxes some distance from their homes. If everyone must pay the same for mail service, an equitable delivery system should grant equal benefits to all types of homeowners. Steve Chamberlin of Wilmington, Delaware, conducted a study in the large cluster community of Wilton, Delaware, of the time taken to hand deliver mail versus the use of a separate, centralized mailbox system. He found that even in winter, due to the cluster site plan, the mailman would de-

7-55 through 57   Centralized mailboxes.

Les Turnau

liver to individual homes in less time than he could stuff the large storage box.

A designer should research the best achievable delivery system solution and design facilities accordingly. Mailbox locations should be noted on the site plan, and an approximate cost per unit should be incorporated into the amenity budget. Generally, a cluster of mailboxes should vary in number but be limited to less than five or six mailboxes per cluster. Mailbox clusters, located within a cluster of townhouses or condominiums, may accent the landscape. Commonly, a mailbox with door and flag is coupled with an open tube for newspapers. Clustered mailboxes may modify the standard mailbox, being an interesting, combined structure, or may consist of a number of individual boxes. Numbers or lettering on the boxes should be in the same style as the other project graphics.

7-58 (above) These custom-designed mailboxes add interest to the streetscape.
7-59 (right) An attractive mailbox structure becomes part of the streetscape.

Retaining Walls

Townhouse or condominium construction usually creates elevation differences that cannot be handled by sloping grades alone—a maintainable slope grade of 1 foot of rise to 3 feet of run will not save very many trees or much vegetation; thus, a retaining wall can be a functional and attractive alternative. In many cases it is desirable to shift grade steeply between units or buildings. In site development work, steep grades often necessitate retaining walls at stairways or at the ends of drive-under courts.

In some applications, handrails may be required for walls of over 30 inches in height.

In areas receiving much pedestrian traffic, handrails would be appropriate. However, in untravelled or more natural settings, they can represent an unnecessary expense and can be aesthetically detracting. If strict code adherence becomes an issue, handling a 6-foot grade change in two 30-inch terraces with a moderate slope between the walls is a workable solution.

Concrete walls are usually neither economically feasible nor aesthetically desirable for townhouse/condominium developments. The use of wood or rock materials, more appropriate to residential environments, eliminates the cold feeling fostered by concrete.

In the construction of retaining walls, the strength of the materials to be used and soil type should be considered. No matter what materials are used (except for boulders), reinforcing members, commonly called deadmen, should be installed as shown in Figure 7-60. Walls in widespread use, built of 4 by 4 or 6 by 6 treated timbers laid either horizontally, placed in a shallow trench, or tied together vertically, require no foundation. Masonry walls may be appropriate to carry an architectural theme, or where structural conditions require the strength, a steel-reinforced wall may be necessary. For unusual or extensive installations, a structural engineer should be consulted. It is important to assure positive drainage away from the soil immediately adjacent to a retaining wall.

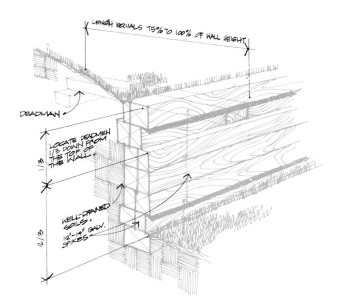

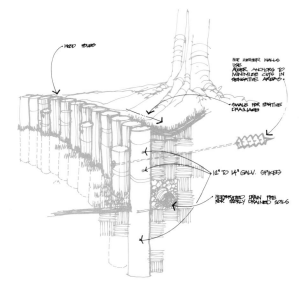

7-60 Design considerations for retaining walls. Dimensions and specific details should be determined by local site conditions.

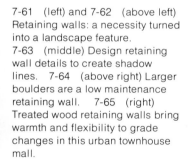

7-61 (left) and 7-62 (above left) Retaining walls: a necessity turned into a landscape feature.
7-63 (middle) Design retaining wall details to create shadow lines. 7-64 (above right) Larger boulders are a low maintenance retaining wall. 7-65 (right) Treated wood retaining walls bring warmth and flexibility to grade changes in this urban townhouse mall.

Fountains and Sculpture

Fountains can have a positive environmental and marketing impact, particularly for townhouse/condominium developments in urban areas. Because of their high initial cost and maintenance requirements, fountains should be centrally located and adjacent to as large a number of homes as possible.

Several functional and aesthetic rules should be incorporated in fountain design:

- To avoid pipe breakage in winter, a fountain should be self-draining.
- Even if full-time maintenance people are anticipated, an automatic water level valve and feeder line should be used. Rather than running a separate metered water line, a stub off a sprinkler system line can be an economical supply source.

- The fountain should serve as both a visual and audible feature. A resident of the Cedarview development in Minneapolis reported that even on hot days homeowners left their windows open to hear the water falling in the open space court fountain.

Whether planning for urban or suburban development, another potential use for open space would incorporate sculpture. The selection or design of an appropriate piece of sculpture should be guided by the architectural theme of the development and buyer profiles. For instance, a contemporary development would accept a more contemporary sculpture. As with fountains, the location of sculpture should be in a visually prominent area—placement along an entry road or in a central open space would be possibilities.

7-66 (top) A fountain in each court of this urban townhouse development is visible to the majority of home entries. 7-67 (bottom) This fountain was placed in pedestrian traffic patterns so homeowners could walk through it. The water falls from sculptural elements so that, in winter months, the fountain retains visual interest.

7-68 Sculpture: an open space accent.

Security

Designers of a residential community must provide for security against crime. At least one police department's statistics indicate that roadway access design, limiting the number of potential "escape routes," deters crime.* Furthermore, the trend toward cluster housing or "mini-neighborhoods" fosters "neighboring"—an informal but effective surveillance system formed of residents. By all indications, crime rates in suburban locations will continue to move upward. This will then demand greater anti-crime design attention by all land developers and homebuilders.

A number of townhouse and condominium developments across the country have chosen to make security a central aspect of their marketing program. In urban areas, the most visible security provision is the doorman. In a suburban setting, a development which utilizes a number of different accesses and

*New Brighton, Mn Police Department (Windsor Green Municipality, 1976).

7-69   A full-time functioning gate house: a strong, though costly statement about security.

7-70 (top) Security is important for all developments, and vital for infill townhouses or condominiums.
7-71 (bottom) The long-term maintenance costs should be analyzed before committing to a marketing program that includes a staffed gate house.

building clusters makes the doorman concept economically unfeasible. However, access to such a site from a single entry is possible through the installation of a gatehouse. The decision to install a gatehouse must be based on a very careful analysis of the prospective homebuyers' attitudes and financial capabilities. The developer should explain the full cost of operating a 24-hour, staffed gatehouse to the buyer at the time of purchase. To install a gatehouse during the selling period, which will be abandoned after the homeowners realize the full impact of the operating cost, is a foolish waste of amenity dollars.

Normally, a centralized electronic security system, like those found in many high-rise buildings, permits the monitoring of fire, smoke, forced entry, or even movement. This may be part of the staffed security system, or decentralized with each homeowner having his individual home's system linked to an automatic police- or fire-signaling device.

One of the few drawbacks of an interconnecting open space area is that it can often provide entry to a project from its periphery, which may not be easily patrolled. Well-designed open space should provide some access control to private open space through fencing and gates.

In the planning of closely defined pedestrian walkways, care should be given to avoid creating hiding places behind obstructions or plant material. Where this cannot be avoided, good lighting is a necessity. A well-lit common ground encourages resident surveillance.

Buyer attitudes on crime and the types of security provisions that should be designed into a new community may be quite difficult to derive. Once a development is completed, the community association may assume the job of raising funds for installing and managing security elements as they become necessary.

This discussion of amenities clearly illustrates the wide variety and cost of the amenities that may be included in a townhouse/condominium development. Each new project must be addressed with a fresh outlook when selecting those elements that will make up the amenity package. Further, the developer should always keep an eye out for new amenity possibilities. However, a new recreational feature should not be used just to enhance marketing, and "fadish" amenities should be avoided. Again, it is appropriate to emphasize that a good amenity package will begin with the preservation and enhancement of natural site features, followed by the careful addition of man-made features and recreational facilities.

7-72   In every case, plan and design amenities for homeowner enjoyment.

173

8 Mid-Rise and High-Rise Design

Martin Tornallyay

As contrasted with townhouses and garden apartments, mid-rise structures consist of four to eight stories. High-rise structures are buildings of nine stories or more. Both of these building types use the condominium form of ownership. Although this ownership form owes its heritage to its first codification in Roman law, today's application of that law permits an individual or family to own a specific part of a building with common ownership of all the spaces beyond the home unit. Today's mid-/high-rise condominiums are viewed as affordable, livable home environments.

There are important differences between townhouse design and mid-rise/high-rise design. Perhaps the most significant difference is the separation of mid- and high-rise units from the ground level. Since each individual uses it for access to and from his unit, the mid-/high-rise hallway or corridor space must receive special design attention. By contrast, townhouses have immediate access from the out-of-doors, assuring a greater measure of identity and a greater similarity to single-family detached homes.

8-1 (left) and 8-2 (right) Mid-rise structures consist of four to eight stories.

Shipp Corporation Ltd.

Furthermore, because mid-rise and high-rise homes are normally bounded on two sides by adjacent units and hallway or landing on a third side, the amount of exterior wall that may be utilized for windows and ventilation is reduced. This places great importance on open floor planning and carefully positioned windows and balconies. Mid- and high-rise condominium living offers the benefits of a maintenance-free lifestyle, the potential of increased security relative to other forms of housing, and the advantages of living on a single floor. The "closer-in" locations normally chosen for mid- and high-rise structures attract a greater percentage of individuals and couples over the age of 40.

8-3   This high rise in suburban Toronto provides homes for many people in a convenient location.

Development Decisions

Most purchasers of mid- and high-rise condominiums move out of single-family homes. More than likely, they have come to enjoy and expect a certain level of livability. To improve the chances of sales success, designers and builders should provide as many similarities to the single-family detached home as possible. In this higher density lifestyle, people are even more sensitive to their genuine need for privacy and security than in single-family homes. They require surroundings that satisfy a desire for identity and character.

It is both an important design reminder and, ultimately, a marketing advantage to remember that whatever the type of homebuyer, he will be a "buyer" not a "tenant," purchasing a "home," not a "rental unit." This viewpoint should compel careful attention to detail, from a careful evaluation of the image created at the community entry to the selection of a quiet exhaust fan in the kitchen.

The Development Team

The design and development of the larger and generally more complicated mid- and high-rise building calls for a greater use of professionals throughout the project. Because this kind of development normally involves more inflexible building types requiring a greater commitment of front-end expenditures, a thorough design program assembled by a development team is even more important than for low-rise townhouse/condominium design. It is best to assemble the development team early because of the complexity and commitment of time and effort necessary to generate a completed set of construction documents, taking into account delays for approvals and internal refinements.

Early in the design process, initial design concepts should be discussed in the light of construction feasibility and current costs, at a joint meeting of the developer, architect, structural engineers, and a selected experienced contractor. This early incorporation of construction and cost expertise may seem inconsistent with conventional bidding procedures but is an invaluable aid to minimizing revisions. The design input may be purchased on an hourly basis, or a representative of the selected general contractor could be enlisted. A maintenance company representative is also an invaluable aid in programming and in the later design stages of detailing and specifications.

Choosing a Site

High-rise condominium development allows efficient placement of a large number of homes on a relatively small land area. Thus, after adequate research into parking requirements, the developer and his design team may seek out sites that might otherwise be thought unsuitable for development, due, for instance, to difficult terrain or soil conditions.

For a luxury mid- or high-rise condominium, select a site that is considered a convenient, prestigious location, with pleasant views and a natural setting or a distinctive urban environment. View and proximity to amenities are primary considerations for luxury developments.

Knowing the Market

Before detailed designs may be started, a careful market analysis of potential buyers should be made. As contrasted to townhouses, an alternative plan is usually not available once construction begins. Therefore, the market analysis should reaffirm the locational desirability and provide special design guidelines for unit size, unit mix, special features, and amenities. Much of this information may be projected from a careful and complete study of existing competition. By ascertaining the current buyer profiles of existing properties, a fairly safe assumption may be made about new buyers. A close look at similar condominium unit types offered, the relative mix of the various unit types, the effort put forth in sales promotion, and the rate at which units have been sold will permit an understanding of the expected absorption rate. In the absence of prior market examples, the void in the market (the absence of one form of housing for a certain market group) may justify a development attempt.

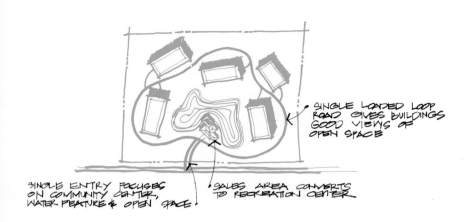

SINGLE LOADED LOOP ROAD GIVES BUILDINGS GOOD VIEWS OF OPEN SPACE

SINGLE ENTRY FOCUSES ON COMMUNITY CENTER, WATER FEATURE & OPEN SPACE

SALES AREA CONVERTS TO RECREATION CENTER

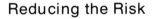

8-4   This plan shows a model center that converts to a recreation/community center after sales are completed.

Reducing the Risk

To partially reduce the risk of committing so many front-end dollars to the construction of what could turn out to be an improper model mix or unsaleable floor plan, a separate pre-sale model center may be constructed, displaying the home floor plans that will be available. This facility may be of a temporary nature, or it could be the shell of the recreation building to be repartitioned once sales are completed.

Additionally, legal documentation must be completed and an attorney should prepare clearly defined guidelines regarding minimum sales requirements necessary to commence construction. Because of the high pre-sale percent requirements that may be imposed by financial institutions, developers should attempt to segment the project into manageable sections. For instance, three, 100-unit buildings completed in three phases are far more achievable than one, 300-unit building.

Phasing

If, under good market conditions, the single-family home is the ideal form of speculative residential development because of its small equity requirement and simple platting requirements, then mid-/high-rise condominium construction represents the other end of the risk scale. While both single-family detached and low-rise townhouse/condominium development may shift model lines to meet changing market demands, the mid- or high-rise development cannot easily do so and therefore must rely on specific market research. With so many homes constructed at once, only small changes may be made, but the unit perimeter, ventilation, and plumbing stacks are determined once and for all, making subsequent plan mix changes extremely difficult.

8-5   (top) The problem of phasing is illustrated at Harbor Point, a 740-unit condominium in one tower, built near downtown Chicago. The adjacent building was built as a rental and converted to a condominium.
8-6   (bottom) A Naples, Florida developer obtained a 70 percent pre-sale at this stage of construction from this modest sales center.

177

Planning and Design Considerations

As the developer and his design team research, evaluate, and combine diverse factors in the design of mid-/high-rise condominiums, they must always remember the vantage point of the individual homebuyer. The homebuyer's overall impression of the building, units, and site will ultimately test the marketability of the development team's designs and construction. In pleasing the homebuyer, where then must the developer start? How do individual kitchens, living rooms, and bedrooms fit into an efficient structural system, combining with other floor plans in a total building that will blend with the land and fit surrounding roads, parking, and other buildings?

Planning and design for mid-/high-rise structures should begin with individual home units. Homes should then be integrated into buildings that are both functional and interesting inside and adaptable to the overall site. Lastly, buildings should be balanced with open space, roads, and parking.

The Home

The challenge in designing homes is to find the balance between an efficient floor plan/structural system with low exterior wall frontage, on the one hand, and open, natural sunlit rooms on the other. Illustrated in Figure 8-8 is a unit floor plan that shows a moderate exterior dimension yet minimizes the impact of a "buried" kitchen. The plan avoids dividing the home space into too many small rooms and thereby gains multiple use from available space.

Buyer profiles, cost parameters, and market input should indirectly give the unit mix and square footage limitations for the homes. Four unit types with options are normally adequate to provide a range of bedroom and cost choices. Again, planning and design become a balancing act. Construction efficiencies and dollar savings are achieved by repetition within each building level and from floor to floor. On the other hand, an-

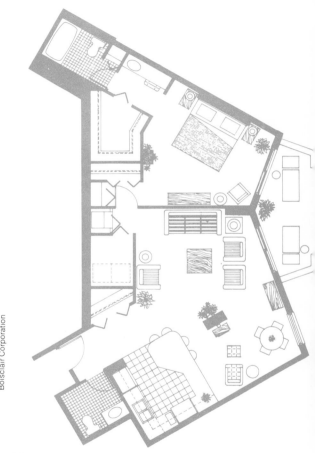

Boisclair Corporation

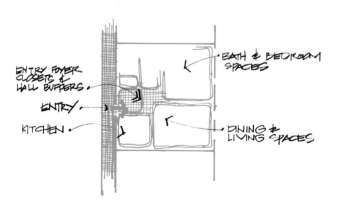

8-7   An interior room buffers and blocks sound as well as provides a transition space between outside and the private interior spaces of the home.

8-8   (above) An open kitchen and flexibility to use the available space in more than one way.   8-9   (right) An open area adjacent to the living room may be sold as either a den or, with an enclosed wall, as a bedroom.

ticipating what homebuyers will like or dislike is anything but an exact science. For this reason, the flexibility of inserting various floor plans within a module or home perimeter offers a developer a certain amount of security against building a series of homes for which there will be no buyers. Constraints on this flexibility include utilities, plumbing cores, and structural members. In reality a shift from two, two-bedroom units to one, three-bedroom and one, one-bedroom unit may be all that is possible. One of the simplest options is an open area adjacent to the living room that may be sold as either a den or with an enclosing wall as a bedroom.

Angled interior and structural exterior walls offer another possibility for breaking the regularity and repetitive similarity of mid- and high-rise condominium homes. Figure 8-10 shows a utilization of angled interior and exterior walls to achieve more interesting homes. The use of one unique corner unit with angled exterior walls may prove economical, adding interior and exterior visual interest as well as site flexibility. Maintaining a 90 degree relationship on structural walls with angled infill, non-load bearing walls is an effective, lower cost option.

Because economics usually dictate that most units connect directly to a single semi-public

Boisclair Corporation

8-10 Angled interior and exterior walls create interesting homes.

179

hallway space, design for privacy calls for foyers, closets, and short hall sections near entrances to buffer the interior private spaces from this exterior semi-public area.

Typically, vaults, beamed ceilings, or clerestory lighting are difficult to incorporate into any but the top floor units of mid-/high-rise condominium structures. Certain market conditions, however, may warrant putting high ceilings throughout a building and/or dropped ceilings in some areas or exposed ceiling structural elements.

As discussed in Chapter 6, perhaps the most common method of breaking the regularity of a large building is the use of offsets. If budget permits, it is a good practice to incorporate a jog into a larger unit of the model mix. This breaks the interior boxlike charac-

ter of many mid-/high-rise condominium buildings, dramatically differentiates one unit from another, justifies price differences, and should result in greater interior interest and saleable value. If at least 4 feet in size, these jogs will create strong shadow lines and visual breaks on the exterior of a building, serving as integrated accents or decorations.

Furthermore, jogs do much to break the potential homebuyer's perception of being "sandwiched" between other homes, an attitude which accounts for some of the hesitation about buying in mid-/high-rise condominiums. A building floor plan alternative that would also minimize the sandwiched in feeling is shown in Figure 8-12. While this would be a middle or upper price alternative, the isolation of each unit from others by use of different hallways creates the impression

that these are freestanding, individual homes, quite similar to single-family detached dwellings.

Another structural, justified offset might utilize vertical grade changes between floors within one building—this may be in response to existing or created land forms. Moreover, floor level changes may be created within individual homes; the unusual surprise of a split-level condominium home or a sunken living room area within what is expected to be the typical, predictable building unit could mean the difference between rapid market acceptance or a more staid sales pace. Certainly offsets complicate the task of unit design, reducing the possibility of repetitive floor plans, interior flexibility, and a flexible overall structural system, but, on the other hand, may lend a unique marketing advantage.

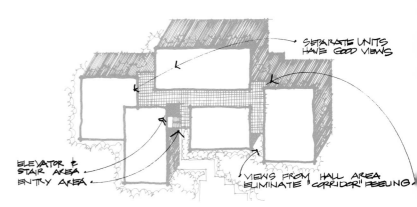

8-11 Integrate "jogs" into the buildings. They create exterior interest and saleable interior character.

8-12 This floor plan of separate units along hall spaces minimizes the feeling of units being sandwiched together.

Decks and Balconies

The great majority of condominium buyers have never before lived above ground level. To do so, initially requires a marked and difficult change in lifestyle. Thus, to maintain some of the direct access indoor-outdoor lifestyle that many people are accustomed to and most require and to ease the transition to above ground living, a relatively private, specifically designed area for outdoor activity and relaxation must be added to the living unit. Important for visual accent and shadow line creation on a building, the deck or balcony is an identifying element of the residential mid- or high-rise condominium structure. From a functional standpoint, it may serve as an outdoor storage area. However, each home should have some type of private exterior space for more than this functional reason.

The use of hinged or sliding screen panels across all or part of a deck enables residents to leave sliding doors open in warm weather, enlarging the interior floor spaces of their homes. When provision is made to screen in all or part of the balcony, this should be integral to the basic design, not impairing the visual impact of the building exterior. The enclosed porch or solarium is a great place for plants and provides an indoor-outdoor atmosphere.

The use of building offsets may better integrate decks and balconies with buildings. The typical three-sided balcony often appears to be tacked on as an afterthought. A building offset would eliminate this feeling. A two-sided deck tucked into an offset enjoys more privacy, as well as being better sheltered from wind. A third, more subtle consideration is that a deck anchored in a corner of

8-13   Decks and patios are a primary marketing feature for mid- and high-rise condominiums. They expand a home's usable floor space and enhance the building's exterior.

a building's structural members is perceived as being more secure. This is an important aspect for high-rise balconies. Figures 8-14 through 8-16 show the benefit of careful balcony placement. By staggering or offsetting decks above part of the living areas of the units below, natural light and views are not obstructed.

Semi-Public Areas

The front entry walk and approach to a home's front door constitute the semi-public areas of a mid-/high-rise condominium building. Since these areas are widely used by all residents on a regular basis, it is important that they be both functional and pleasing.

Entries. Many times an entry that has received little design attention, such as a stairway at the end of a building or a service entry, will receive the majority of resident use because building design is not coordinated with site planning. In an attempt to create a more pleasant front entry, designers may sometimes move parking away, thereby making the most direct access to secured interior areas through secondary doors. Both horizontal distance and stairs act as obstacles to the use of any entry. No matter how well-designed or plush a main entry, it will not be used if it is harder to reach than secondary entries. It is a questionable allocation of decorating or amenity budgets to intensively develop an entry foyer/office area to be used only by prospective homebuyers. Moreover, elevators located away from most of the parking will be a continual source of inconvenience and perhaps aggravation. If, due to site constraints parking must be distributed near several entries instead of concentrated near the main entry, additional budget and design attention should be given to the various entry areas.

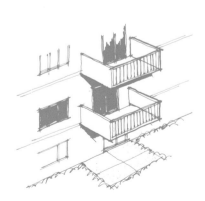

8-14 (left) and 8-15 (right) Three-sided deck may appear "tacked on." Decks built into jogs appear more integral to the building.

8-16 Use of alternating decks improves natural light admission to living areas of homes.

8-17 (top) and 8-18 (bottom) The semi-public spaces of a condominium must receive special design attention: they are the front entry walks to many families' homes.

Hallways. One of the most dramatic ways to increase the value of a mid-/high-rise condominium home is to *reduce the number of homes perceived as being served by a given section of hall, stairway, or landing.* This may be accomplished by reducing the number of homes on each floor. An extreme example would be the construction of a tower structure with only four homes on each floor, each being a corner unit. While giving a great measure of privacy and security, two-directional orientation, and many interior floor plan options, this plan would be too costly for all but the most high-priced condominiums.

A more practical method of achieving interior interest and a feeling of lower density is to introduce angled walls, varied widths, or enlarged foyer or atrium areas at points where the building jogs or where laundry or stair towers occur. Level changes may carry into the hallways or utilize the wall variations of individual unit designs. For instance, a recessed entry or "popped out" entry closet will break the linear quality of a hall into smaller, more private spaces.

Detailed design selections for hallways will also aid the battle against institutional appearances. Carpets with no pattern or with non-linear patterns, paint color or texture changes at different points along a stretch of hallway are effective.

As the exterior identity of an individual home is all but lost in some typical mid-/high-rise structures, character may be added to a hallway or landing in a number of ways besides recessing an entry door. Individual home front doors may be highlighted by painting or paneling. Further impact may be gained by locating the primary hallway lighting at doorways. Dropped ceilings, the use of wood on the ceilings or walls, or a ceiling

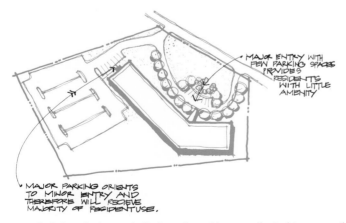

8-19 Building design and site layout must be coordinated to assure that the main entry is not the one that is least accessible from the primary parking area. Unfortunately this plan forces the residents to approach their homes through a secondary entrance.

MAJOR ENTRY WITH FEW PARKING SPACES PROVIDES RESIDENTS WITH LITTLE AMENITY

MAJOR PARKING ORIENTS TO MINOR ENTRY AND THEREFORE WILL RECIEVE MAJORITY OF RESIDENT USE.

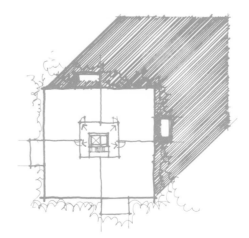

8-20 A condominium building plan with maximum unit exposure and entry identity.

183

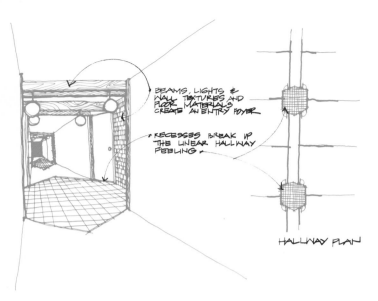

BEAMS, LIGHTS & WALL TEXTURES AND FLOOR MATERIALS CREATE AN ENTRY FOYER

RECESSES BREAK UP THE LINEAR HALLWAY FEELING

HALLWAY PLAN

8-21 (top) and 8-22 (bottom) Design hallways as entry spaces for homes, not as corridors. For instance, vary the widths, accent with raised or dropped ceilings, arbors, or built-in lights.

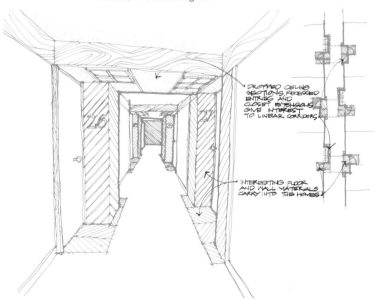

DROPPED CEILING SECTIONS, RECESSED ENTRIES AND CLOSET EXTENSIONS GIVE INTEREST TO LINEAR CORRIDORS

INTERESTING FLOOR AND WALL MATERIALS CARRY INTO THE HOMES

arbor will create a unique home entry space. If masonry material is used on the interior of the home, carrying it into the hallway both breaks the linear appearance of the hall and enhances the home entry.

Depending on the type of building constructed, individual units may be located off stair landings, single-loaded, or double-loaded hallways. In many moderate and warm weather locations, a fresh air walkway access like a protected atrium is more pleasant and energy efficient than a double-loaded corridor.

Details

Storage. Adequate storage room must be provided on each floor of a mid-/high-rise structure and in the basement, where it is possible to provide additional rooms for storage that may also be rented for shop or recreational use.

Barbeques. The permitting of outdoor charcoaling with gas or charcoal grills on exterior patios or decks is a desirable condominium feature. Thus, decks should be safely constructed to allow this feature. Requiring that all grills be of a covered type goes a long way toward eliminating fire problems, although there still may be the problem of the smoke drifting to balconies above. The new self-venting grills as a standard kitchen feature are a solution to the problem.

8-23 The space on top of a building, if developed for use, may yield an excellent common area, such as the sun deck shown here.

Roofs. The ordinarily highly dense land use patterns of mid-/high-rise condominiums mean that after the buildings are constructed there is often little extra space, other than for parking, sidewalks, access roads, and rights-of-way. The space on top of a building, if developed for use, will yield an excellent common area with unusually good views. With proper fencing and landscaping, it may serve as a sun deck area or swimming pool site. Additionally, parking structure roofs may make excellent locations for tennis courts.

Amenities

Much of the open space in mid-/high-rise condominium design is the result of setback requirements. Without screening or buffering, it serves little usable purpose and may become a maintenance liability. With proper earth forms, fencing, or low level landscape architecture and plant material additions, the space becomes pleasing as well as usable. A distinction between usable mowed and unmowed or heavily planted areas may be made. Pathways, gas grills, sitting areas, and other passive amenity features could be included in this open space area.

Relatively inexpensive natural site features, such as rock compositions, timber walls, and plantings, or more expensive features such as fountains or sculpture, may be used to accent frequently viewed building entry points. These features should be placed along major pathways and adjacent to parking entries.

In high-rise structures, the view from above may be as important as the view across the landscape. Amenities on the ground will be viewed at a distance from a birds-eye perspective. Therefore, location, form, massing, and color consideration should be given to this point of view. Paving, for example, may have bold geometric patterns and colors, to create an interesting view for the high-rise unit owner.

Blue Ridge Aerial Surveys (Photograph courtesy of International Developers, Inc.)

8-24 (top) By the geometric forms of parking, buildings, and landscaping, the site plan of the Rotonda near Washington, D.C. has considered the view of the owners from their units. 8-25 (bottom left) and 8-26 (bottom right) Whether with an expensive fountain or less expensive landscaping, the walk to the buildings should be made as pleasant as possible.

185

For both traffic control and general information purposes, well-designed graphics provide the opportunity to carry the theme and accent colors of building materials to the building entry areas and other places throughout the site. The attention to graphics details will yield the impression of coordinated design attention throughout the entire site.

Site Planning

Some program determinants for mid-/high-rise condominium site planning are:

- the buildable zone—gained from site analysis and an understanding of government restrictions;
- the building "footprint"—gained from the preliminary building designs (If more than one building is planned, the proper relationship between structures must also be studied); and
- access points, road widths, and parking requirements—based on market demands and local government ordinances.

Building Placement/Orientation. For any given parcel of land, there are a number of different building placement alternatives, each resulting in a markedly different community image. The grid or rectilinear plan, where the building or buildings are placed at a 90 degree relationship to the roads and normally fall on due east-west or north-south lines is one planning approach. A more visually irregular plan is one where several angles are used to determine the relationships of buildings to one another. These angles often set buildings at roughly a 45 degree angle to the typical north-south or east-west building lines. If executed correctly, this planning approach may minimize direct northerly exposure.

Each of the approaches mentioned will yield a stiff, formal appearance which may be preferred in an urban setting—the newly constructed buildings will thus better relate to existing development, reflecting a similar type of plan regularity. Use of these plan alternatives should not rule out the importance of proper interior building orientation.

A less formal building site plan lets existing topography determine the placement of buildings. This normally results in a more irregular, free-form appearance at ground level.

Because of the often rigid space requirements for parking and road circulation, building placement will often be restricted by parking. Although this happens more often than it should, there must still be some site

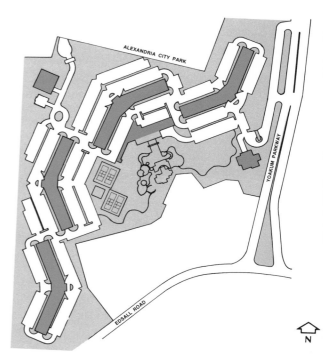

8-27 One site plan method orients buildings, streets, and parking to repeated angles or parallel lines.

planning flexibility in orienting buildings according to views, sun, and wind factors. Consideration should also be given to the outdoor privacy of low-rise units which may be nearby. While an error in site placement for a typical townhouse or low-rise building will affect only a small percentage of homes, an orientation error in a mid-/high-rise building will affect a greater number of people. Thus, proper building orientation is important for these structures, particularly where smaller, more regular unit floor plans are used.

In northern and midwestern climates, the best building orientation admits sunlight to all homes for at least a part of the day. Developers should strive for the middle ground—rather than having 50 percent of units with great views and good light and 50 percent with poor views and light, buildings should be oriented so that each home has some sun or a partially satisfying view. Where it is difficult to provide ample sun orientation for all sides of a building, the presence of natural feature views may offset the lack of adequate sunlight.

In regions experiencing harsh winter seasons, the prevailing wind should be considered as a negative element. Avoid orienting the largest walls into the prevailing winter winds (usually from the northwest). The main

building access should face in the direction opposite these winds, both to shelter this pedestrian entry and to expose it to the sun for a longer period of the day. As a general rule, developers should first consider the impact of a building's placement on views and light admission to each home unit before deciding exterior geometrics or alternative site planning/building relationships.

Roads and Parking. Roads and parking devour large amounts of land in virtually every residential project, and particularly so in mid-/high-rise condominium projects. Prior to beginning a site plan, specific parking requirements by spaces per unit along with the dimensional specifications for parking bays and roads must be known. In early planning, it is helpful to draw out these areas to the same scale as the property boundary survey and topography, using approximately 300 square feet per car including circulation. This gives a visual image of how much of the total site area will be used for parking. A parking structure or enclosed parking underneath the buildings may become a consideration, if not a necessity.

If the building or buildings will have separate service accesses, attention should be given to separating resident and visitor traffic from service vehicle traffic. Service accesses should anticipate maneuvering

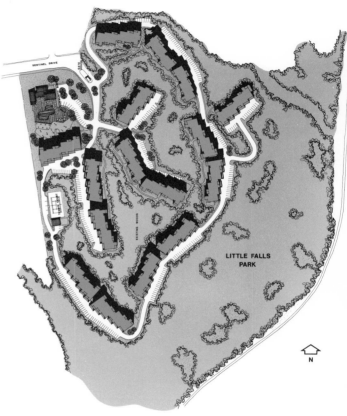

8-28 Four-story condominiums located on curving, single-loaded drives, oriented to fit existing topography. By preserving the majority of dense tree cover, the community "feels" about one-third as dense as it is.

space for medium-sized trucks and parking of short duration. In medium- or upper-price condominium units, more frequent service deliveries may be expected. The placement of the service drive entry point must therefore be direct, although not visually prominent to the residential access routes. It should also be outside the security zone of the building and within view of the office.

Placing exterior parking close to the main or secondary entry foyer is convenient and reduces the amount of time a person must spend moving outside the building security zone, a significant buyer consideration. Moreover, the walkway from the parking area to this entry should be as direct and pleasant as possible. Care must be taken in placing the walkway so that users do not infringe upon the visual or acoustic privacy of the patios or decks of the first floor units. A grade change relationship will often alleviate this intrusion problem.

Because of their constant use, parking areas should receive amenity design attention with higher quality, warmer appearing surface materials such as colored, pattern-stamped or exposed aggregate concrete, or brick pavers accented by improved lighting. In addition, parking areas should be planted, but not to the point where mature trees or shrubs will provide potential hiding places.

8-29 Visually hidden but within view of the building manager's office, this service entry does not conflict with resident activity.

Condominium Conversions

A national trend has been emerging—the conversion of mid- and high-rise rental property to condominiums. The condominium conversion is already claiming wide acceptance and is helping to fill the demand for the ownership of housing. Some factors stimulating demands for condominium conversions are:

- Rising costs of virtually every element in the operating budget for an apartment structure led by increasing energy costs. This may also turn developers away from future rental construction.

- Increasing construction costs and high construction loans and mortgage interest rates are likely to continue making new rental construction uncompetitive with existing rental properties.

- The potential of tenant political pressure and the latent threats of rent control are powerful forces pressuring increased condominium conversion and reduced rental construction.

- In established cities and maturing suburban communities, new mid- and high-rise condominium conversions offer older residents the opportunity of owning a permanent residence within the same neighborhood while renewing a municipality by freeing up underutilized housing for younger families.

- Furthermore, families are electing to

have fewer children as more women enter the labor force and people are increasingly aware of the population growth pressure on economic resources. As single-family detached homes prove too large for smaller families or empty nesters, condominium conversions serve their housing needs by furnishing the privately-owned homes they still desire.

A successful condominium conversion, however, is not easy to achieve. Rental construction of earlier years was not designed with ownership conversion in mind. As a result, uninteresting interior and exterior design, inadequate storage, and poor quality materials may lead to initial sales resistance and owner dissatisfaction. Unfortunately, some conversions of badly designed rental properties cast a poor reflection on new condominium construction.

In design for rental conversion to condominiums, special attention should be given to injecting character and identity into the ownership property. Improving the interior character, quality of materials, and appliances in addition to the exterior landscape, plantings, and other exterior amenities is important. Most important of all, careful redesign should consider the future resident's demand for security and privacy by checking and possibly improving the quality of sound deadening in common walls and hallways.

8-30 Condominium conversion of older, in-town buildings requires special attention to residents' needs for security and interior, "homelike" quality.

9 The Community Association

In the first chapter, Boston's Louisburg Square was identified as the first townhouse development in the United States, with common open space designed as a part of the project. In order for this common open space to be held jointly and maintained by Louisburg Square property owners, the first community association was created, the Committee of the Proprietors of Louisburg Square. Since that first effort in 1844, design concepts and the nature of commonly held or shared facilities for townhouse and condominium development have gone through a tremendous amount of change. In actuality, the nature, character, and design of community associations have a much more contemporary focus.

In 1964, when the *Homes Association Handbook,* ULI Technical Bulletin 50, was first published there were only approximately 500 automatic-membership community associations in the United States. Rather than townhouse projects, the majority of these were associations related to single-family development projects with common open space. At that point, the condominium form of ownership was not even considered as a viable concept for residential development in the United States. By 1978 there were an estimated 30,000 associations, with new as-

9-1 The community association landscape management is important to the marketing success of this North Carolina townhome project.

sociations being formed at the rate of 3,000 to 4,000 each year. In recent times, a significant portion of the associations being created have been in conjunction with townhouse or condominium developments.

The community association is an institutional cornerstone of townhouse or condominium development. A condominium project simply cannot be created without a condominium association or a council of co-owners. Further, it would be the rare townhouse project that would not contain some common area requiring the creation of a community association for the purpose of ownership, maintenance, and management.

So important is the creation and ongoing effective operation of community associations to the support of townhouse and condominium developments that ULI—the Urban Land Institute in conjunction with the National Association of Home Builders assisted in the creation of CAI—the Community Association Institute in 1974. Since that time, ULI and CAI have jointly published four publications dealing with various aspects of community associations' design and operation.*

In a single chapter of this book it would be presumptuous to try to capsulize all of the information contained in these publications.

On the other hand, it would be insufficient merely to provide a recommended reading list.

The design, legal structure, and delineation of community association responsibilities must begin simultaneously with the earliest of townhouse/condominium design considerations. All too often it has been the lack of attention to this important aspect of townhouse and condominium development that has ultimately led to residents' dissatisfaction with the completed project. Where the legal foundation is inadequate to the nature of the project or ill-conceived, where the provisions for organizational structure and self-regulation have not been properly tailored to the particular characteristics of the community, and where the financial structure of the association is insufficient for its role in ownership, operation, and maintenance responsibilities, an otherwise well-conceived project will become burdened with management problems. Such circumstances may lead communities to reject the idea of further townhouse or condominium development; create negative reactions in the future market, thus diverting potential buyers to other housing forms; and, of course, threaten the future appreciation of existing developments, an important factor in the ownership of any home.

As an appropriate community association is so important to the long-term value of a townhouse/condominium development, the design team should include a person not only knowledgable in the legal aspects of community association creation but in the ongoing functioning of the association from the first sale to well after the developer has relinquished any participation or responsibility for the governance of the community via the association. The following discussion is intended to focus on the relationship of various aspects of community associations to the design and planning process.

---

*The following publications will be of great assistance in understanding the design, maintenance, and operation of various community association types:

Managing a Successful Community Association (2nd ed., 1976).

Financial Management of Condominium and Homeowners' Associations (2nd ed., 1976).

Creating a Community Association: The Developer's Role in Condominium and Homeowner Associations (1977).

Condominium and Homeowner Associations That Work: On Paper and in Action (1978).

Homes Association Handbook, Technical Bulletin 50 (rev. ed., 1966).

Types of Community Associations*

In order to define the various types of community associations for townhouse and condominium developments it is first necessary to define the form of ownership which leads to the legal form of the association. As mentioned in Chapter 1, a *townhouse* is a physical design form in which each dwelling unit has a direct point of access to the ground. It is quite possible for a development which includes only townhouses to be sold under a condominium form of ownership. As a matter of fact, the condominium form of ownership has also been used for single-family detached housing. Thus, by definition, a *condominium* is purely a form of ownership—the condominium concept may be applied to any physical form and to nonresidential as well as to residential uses. For example, there are now numerous office and industrial condominiums. The following definitions are offered as a basis for the further discussion of community associations.

Community association is used generically to refer to all automatic-membership associations for real estate developments. Inasmuch as all automatic-membership associations are organized and operated in a similar fashion and perform the same basic functions,

*See ULI's *Residential Development Handbook* (Washington, D.C.: author, 1977), pp. 282-284 for community association types other than the basic types described in this section.

this single term may be applied to all such associations.

Townhouse developments are housing projects with units grouped in attached clusters and each housing unit sited on a defined parcel of land. The ownership form of the unit and parcel of ground on which it is located is fee simple. The parcel of land may be limited to as small an area as the precise footprint of the individual unit's foundation or may include a larger *lot* which would constitute a front and/or rear yard or patio area for the unit.

Within the context of this book, where such units and their lots comprise *in toto* 100 percent of the development's site and where each lot fronts on a public street, this form of development could more logically be referred to as *row housing,* and a community association would not be required since there would be no common interest ownership or maintenance responsibilities. However, even in such a situation, a community association may be desirable, particularly where covenants related to standards of exterior maintenance, architectural control, and/or use of premises suggest the need for an organization to assure orderly and effective enforcement.

Townhouse development as discussed in this publication is different from the row

housing mentioned above. In addition to fee simple ownership of the townhouse dwelling unit and its lot parcel, a townhouse development owner would be a member of a community association with ownership, maintenance, and operating responsibilities for all of the land held in common with other development owners.

A *condominium* is a legal form of ownership whereby an owner gains title to an interior space within a building. The building structures and all the land around and under them are co-owned by all inhabitants on a proportional, undivided basis, except where modified by a specific state law. In addition, each individual owner has an undivided percentage ownership in the entire condominium estate. Each state in the United States and its possessions has enacted specific enabling legislation which sets forth the precise parameters of condominiums in that jurisdiction. As by definition a condominium development will contain common areas and facilities, there must be an association of owners for the purposes of maintaining and operating these areas and facilities. It is important to remember that it is possible to have a condominium townhouse development; that is, a development where the physical configuration is as described for townhouses but where the conveyance is via the condominium form of ownership.

9-2 Although patios and balconies are defined as limited common areas in this project, they still fall under the project's architectural controls.

Homeowners' Association (HOA)

The HOA is the specific community association type used in conjunction with a townhouse development. It holds title to common property, manages and maintains that property, and enforces the covenants and restrictions set forth for the development. Through the purchase of real estate and an individual townhouse unit, an owner becomes an automatic member of the community association and assumes certain rights and obligations. Each person owns a unit and the land beneath it, whereas the association owns and maintains the common property to which each owner has access under the provisions of the deed. In townhouse developments it is possible that the common area will be divided into general common and limited common areas. In the instance where the townhouse parcel is the precise footprint of the unit's foundation, the front and rear yard or patio area for such a unit might be classified as limited common area, meaning that the particular dwelling unit has exclusive use of this area even though ownership rests with the community association.

Condominium Association

The condominium association or Council of Co-owners describes the community association type that administers and maintains the common property and other common elements of the condominium development. The condominium association itself does not normally hold title to the common property; instead, each unit owner has title to his own unit and an undivided, proportionate ownership interest in the common areas.

9-3 The limited common space adjacent to and between these condominium units is used by the owner for a flower bed and vegetable garden.

Choosing the Association Form

As the definitions indicate, the condominium association may be used for any type of residential development, whereas the homes association may only be used for a subdivision of real estate where individual unit owners acquire fee simple title to a unit (and its lot parcel) with the remainder of the development parcel held in common. Therefore, the design of the residential community will, in large measure, dictate the choice of association form. It is very important to assess the acceptance of either form in the market. For example, it is quite possible that the typical condominium project may be less marketable because of a condominium ownership and association form. Thus, the option for ownership and association form must be made simultaneous with the selection of a physical design form for the project.

Association Legal Structure

The creation of a homeowners' association or condominium association is a complex legal undertaking. While the net results of either association are similar, the particulars of their legal structure are significantly different. Much has been written about how to develop a proper legal foundation for a common interest community such as a townhouse or condominium development. The list of ULI/CAI publications referred to earlier will provide detailed insights into the development of appropriate legal documentation. What is important to recognize is that in townhouse and condominium development, the design and plan for the community association, which will have ultimate responsibility for the ongoing maintenance and operation of common open spaces and other facilities, must begin early—in the initial steps of the design process. The proper legal structure for each development will be unique to that development and must evolve in response to the design solution.

Two exhibits are provided, setting forth the legal framework for both the condominium and homeowners' association forms of community associations. In either case, the purpose of the legal documentation is to set forth the following specifics, responsive to the needs of the development:

- to define what is owned and by whom, including the specific location and parameters of the individual unit and the

9-4   Although each building cluster is phased as a separate condominium, all of the common elements are operated and governed by one association in this Florida project.

ownership interest of the owners or the association in the common elements;
- to establish a system of interlocking relationships binding each owner to all other owners for the purpose of maintaining and preserving what is owned and used in common;
- to establish an array of protective standards or restrictions designed to place limits and to assure that a certain level of appearance is maintained;
- to create an administrative vehicle to manage those elements shared in common and to enforce standards;
- to provide for the operation and financing of the association; and
- to assess the process involved in affecting the transfer of control of the association and responsibility for the common elements of the developer (existing owner) to the unit owners collectively.*

Just as this publication does not provide detailed discussions of engineering or subdivision documentation, it does not attempt to provide detailed understanding of legal elements for the community association. However, it should be pointed out that a competent legal counsel who is familiar with association legal documents that will translate the community's design into a workable association is an important participant in the overall development process. His participation should prove valuable from the very first embryonic design analysis through development and marketing.

*Creating a Community Association, p. 27.

CONDOMINIUM ASSOCIATION LEGAL DOCUMENTS

PURPOSE OF CONCEPTS	**Description** to define what is owned by whom. **Restrictions** to establish the interlocking relationships of all owners and establish protective standards. **Administration** to create the association of owners and provide for the operation of the association. **Financial** to provide funding for the association. **Transition** to establish the process by which the developer transfers control of the association to the owners.	
LEGAL BASIS	• Roman law • Specific state condominium enabling legislation • Nonprofit corporate law	
BASIC DOCUMENTS	• State enabling statute	**State enabling legislation** defines the ownership percentage, the obligations of the owners, and the dissolution of the condominium.
	• Subdivision or condominium plat	The **condominium plat** describes the location of the common elements and the units.
	• Condominium declaration	The **condominium declaration** defines the units, common elements, and limited common elements, the basis for and the percentage of interest, and voting rights. It also provides for automatic association membership, the proportional obligation for assessments, and the limited use restrictions.
	• Individual unit deeds	The **unit deeds** (individual) assign a percentage of ownership interest in the common elements.
	• Articles of incorporation (occasionally)	The **articles of incorporation** (usually not required for a condominium) contain a legal description of the property, define the association membership and the powers of the association, and create the board and the voting procedures.
	• Bylaws	The **bylaws with articles of incorporation** delineate the meetings process, election procedures, powers and duties, board meetings, committees, insurance requirements, and most use restrictions. The **bylaws without articles of incorporation** include the above with the addition of the legal description, association membership, the powers of the association, the creation of the board, and the voting procedures.
	• Rules and regulations	The **rules and regulations** include operational provisions or use restrictions adopted by the board upon initiation by the association.

Source: *Creating a Community Association*, p. 39.

HOMEOWNERS' ASSOCIATION LEGAL DOCUMENTS

PURPOSE OF CONCEPTS	**Description** to define what is owned by whom. **Restrictions** to establish the interlocking relationships of all owners and establish protective standards. **Administration** to create the association of owners and provide for the operation of the association. **Financial** to provide funding for the association. **Transition** to establish the process by which the developer transfers control of the association to the owners.	
LEGAL BASIS	• English common law • State corporate law or nonprofit corporate law	
BASIC DOCUMENTS	• Subdivision plat	The **subdivision plat** describes the location of the common elements, and describes the common elements.
	• Property deeds	The **property deeds** are made up of the individual lot deeds and the common property deeds.
	• Declaration of covenants, conditions, and restrictions	The **declaration of CC&Rs** gives perpetual easement to the common elements. It also provides for automatic association membership, voting rights, and certain use restrictions. It also gives power to the association to own and maintain the common property, and to make and enforce the rules.
	• Articles of incorporation	The **articles of incorporation** designate the powers of the association, create the board, and establish the voting procedure.
	• Bylaws	The **bylaws** delineate the meetings process, election procedures, powers and duties, board meetings, committees, insurance requirements, and limited use restrictions.
	• Rules and regulations	The **rules and regulations** include operational provisions or use restrictions adopted by the board upon initiation by the association.

Source: *Creating a Community Association*, p. 30.

Association Development Process

The process of designing and developing a community association is integral with the design and development of the project itself. Association development may be divided into five general areas: predesign, design, start-up, transition, and governance. The accompanying chart relates these five phases of association development with development phasing.

Just as soon as the need for an association is determined, the developer should assemble a community association development team, just as he has assembled a team for the design of the project. Many specialists will participate on both of these teams—the architect, land planner, attorney, and marketing specialist. However, these people must also be augmented by the following specialists for the association team: an association manager who, based on experience, will help create the proper structure for an association that may be successfully managed; an insurance specialist, since this area of concern is most crucial to community associations where the existence of common elements requires a special insurance package covering not only fire but also liability and insurance for the governing board; and a financial counsel familiar with the financial management of associations (this may well be the same individual as the association manager). On the association team it may also be appropriate to include the lender, since concepts and responsibilities for the association structure may affect a lender's willingness to finance the project.

Association Development Process

9-7

ASSOCIATION PHASE:	Pre-Design			Design	
DEVELOPMENT PHASE:	Choice and Evaluation of Site	Design Assessment	Market Approach	Financing the Project	Marketing the Project
ASSOCIATION-RELATED DECISIONS OR ACTIVITIES	Assessment of natural features or barriers, and of common property. Decisions about clustering and land conservation. Decisions about housing type.	Selection of common areas and open space. Determination of common facilities. Decisions about major capital items requiring long term maintenance. Decisions about whether to develop all at once or in phases.	Acceptance of design and project by market. Exploration of alternative approaches to ownership of common property: • association • joint ownership • private club • dedication to local entity • funded trust. Decide on condominium or HOA community. Acceptance of design and development by municipal officials. Assemble team of talents. Initiate preparation of association legal documents.	Complete the preparation of the legal documents. Make sure the project conforms with requirements of FNMA, FHLMC, VA, FHA, and other lending-related institutions. Prepare the initial association budget and management procedures. Submit preliminary association management and sales program to lender.	Explain the association concept as a sales tool. Inform the salesforce about the legal aspects of selling a home with an association. Prepare the homebuyer and homeowner brochures.

Source: *Creating a Community Association*, pp. 22-23.

| Management | Start-Up | | Transition | | Governance | |
	First Phase of Construction (pre-sale and sales) up to 25 Percent of Closings	Second Phase of Construction with 26 to 75 Percent of Closings	Final Phase of Construction with 76 to 90 Percent of Closings	Operational Project with Construction Completed and 91 to 100 Percent of Closings	Operational Project with Sales Completed	
Finalize the management procedures and program. Designate the management approach. Refine the initial budget and set initial assessments. Arrange for maintenance. Prepare financial and administrative management programs. Record the legal documents. Appoint (elect) initial board which will meet to adopt the budget, management approach, assessments, and rules. The board will let outside contracts for maintenance, etc., and contract for insurance.	Advise prospects of the nature and requirements of association living. Distribute homebuyer brochure with appropriate data and documents. Distribute homeowner information including association legal documents, budget, and brochure. Solicit homeowners for involvement and participation in association. Identify potential association leaders. Initiate association committees. If an HOA community, deed the common elements before the first closing.	Continue association-related sales activities. Management functions should be as follows: • owners on committees • annual membership meetings conducted • officers and board members elected • some, if not a majority of owner seats on board • most administrative and financial functions assumed by owners.	Continue sales program. Owners control association and proceed with management, with increasing emphasis on: • an architectural review committee • establishing firm administrative procedures and systems • owner-controlled committees • owner review of budget and assessments • finalization of transition process with common area inspections, and transfer of books, records, plans, and specifications. Developer continues minority position on board and key committees.	Continue sales program. Owners assume all management functions. Owners control all financial, physical, and administrative functions.	Owners prepare annual budget and set assessments. All committees are owner-controlled and functioning. Owners control capital improvement programs.	

Design Considerations

As the design of the project progresses, the following questions should be constantly tested in relationship to the obligations of the community association:

- What areas will be held in common ownership or under control of the community association and, therefore, are the association's responsibility to maintain, manage, and operate?
- Can the future operation and maintenance costs of the planned common areas, including open space, recreational amenities, gatehouses, fences, fountains, landscaping, water features, etc., be comfortably borne by the residents?
- As the design decisions are made, to what extent will the projected annual maintenance costs for the common areas have an impact on the market potential of the dwellings?
- Is there a proper balance between the amenities/common open spaces and the number of units that would be required to support their maintenance and operations?
- Is each of the amenities properly sized for the anticipated level of use?
- Should the association take on the responsibilities for such traditional public services as road maintenance, trash removal, and security?
- What use controls need to be developed to assure long-term quality of the community?
- What architectural controls need to be developed for the same purpose?

- What management structure will be required to properly manage the selected amenity package?
- What other social functions should be included in the association's structure to enhance the livability of the community?
- Will the project be developed in phases and thus will the number of common facilities be properly distributed between phases?
- Can the association adequately support the costs of maintenance and operation of common areas and facilities if the project is terminated after one or more phases are completed?

Many of these same questions have also been addressed in other sections of this book.

Special Issues

Architectural Controls

As a developer creates and markets a complete home package, many a developer and new homeowner are surprised by the imagination of certain homeowners in tacking on improvements to the exteriors of their homes. It is most important to the long-term maintenance of condominium or townhouse value to establish clear, reasonable, understandable, and enforceable architectural controls. Individuality is an important element of every homeowner's psyche. For example, it may be very desirable to encourage individual creativity in entrance patio areas, landscaping, patio sunscreens, privacy fences, and other elements adjacent to the individual unit. Establishing clear, reasonable architec-

tural control guidelines at the beginning of the association's operation may avoid many bitter conflicts as new homeowners start to move in and individualize their particular units. For example, to simplify the architectural approval process, design guidelines or architectural details for commonly anticipated modifications could be made available by the developer to the homeowners' association in advance of the first request for such modifications. In an era of rapidly expanding interest in communications, certain appurtenant structures related to television, radio, and CB sets may create difficult community management problems if allowable accessories are not clearly outlined from the beginning.

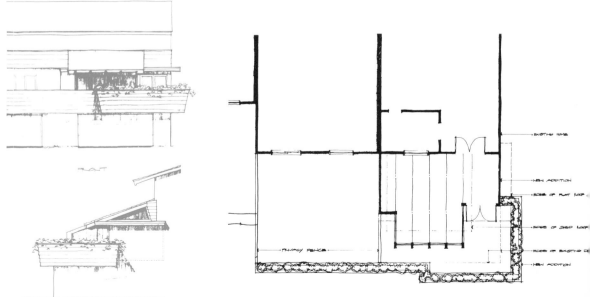

Even "For Sale" signs or such activities as yard sales or garage sales need to be considered in relation to community association design. If considered inappropriate, garage sales may be prohibited, even though local community laws might allow them. "For Sale" signs on resale properties may be limited in size and location or prohibited if it is deemed to be in the best interest of the community.

Every aspect of overall community appearance may be made subject to specific controls within the community association structure. It is important to recognize that most new residents of townhouse and condominium projects come from a different ownership environment. As a result they may see many of the architectural controls as constraints against their freedom of choice. Therefore, each control that is considered for a community association must be tested in terms of validity and importance before it is included in the final elements of the community association design.

9-9 (above) Avoid "For Sale" signs; they may give the impression that everyone wants to move. A kiosk or bulletin board is sometimes used in place of "For Sale" signs on the property.
9-10 (below) Arbors and sunscreens improve a deck's function and provide individuality. The association's architectural control committee will often have a set of approved architectural details.

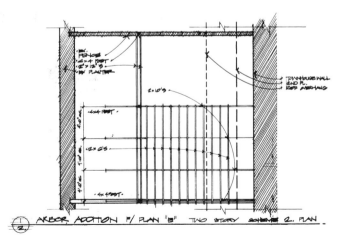

9-8 (left) This room addition improved the overall appearance of the building and enabled the owner to stay in the community when additional living space was required.

199

Phasing

There are a variety of reasons why townhouse or condominium projects may be divided into phases of development. One may be the overall size of the site; another the rate of market absorption; a third the requirement of lending institutions.

As soon as the concept of phasing is identified in the design process, there is a need to look at the association's legal design so that it may accommodate that phasing plan. There are several possible alternatives. A project could be divided into several associations, each responsible for its own common open space. An expandable association may be created whereby there is a single association responsible for the entire project, originally consisting of the first phase, with legal provisions for additional phases, thus expanding the association to a larger site area and project. The third alternative is to have a master association with responsibility for community-wide open space and facilities and sub-associations with specific responsibilities unique to their common interest in particular phases of the project.*

Since the options for community association legal structure in phased development are varied, it is very important that the proper

*For further discussions of community association structures or phased development, see: Residential Development Handbook, pp. 284-285; Condominium and Homeowner Associations That Work, pp. 11-18; and Creating a Community Association, pp. 4-7.

legal design be married to the needs of the physical design. Again, this emphasizes the importance of coordinating and integrating the community association design process with the physical design and development process.

Private Streets

As discussed in the design sections of this book, frequently a community's standard street configuration requirement suggests the use of private streets, owned, maintained, and operated by the community association. Further, the provision of private streets may allow the development of a more secure community. However, private streets and the concommitant community association responsibility for long-term maintenance, repair, and replacement may create a significant financial burden for the community association. This design option and the alternative of public dedication then need to be carefully evaluated in relation to community association cost, which must ultimately be shared by assessments to each of the property owners.

Division of Maintenance Responsibilities

While one of the major selling features for townhouse and condominium development has been freedom from property maintenance responsibilities, it is important to recognize that when these tasks are performed by the community association they must be

paid for as a part of the monthly assessment to each property owner. Therefore, it is important, during the design process, to carefully evaluate the appropriateness of the division of maintenance responsibilities between the community association and individual units. Should individual unit owners be responsible for the maintenance of their private front and rear yard patio areas? Who should perform exterior painting and other regular maintenance chores? What will the market preference be between total freedom from maintenance responsibility and the payment of a fee for this service versus partial maintenance by the individual owner?

Design for Maintenance

Within those areas that are defined for common maintenance and operation by a community association, the design team needs to continually concern itself with the selection of low-maintenance and easy-maintenance alternatives. For example, the landscaping design should not require the use of specialized gardening skills not normally available to maintenance crews. The major problem of community association budgets is the cost of labor. It is important to evaluate design solutions in search of those that will minimize this cost. Additionally, the servicing, repair, and replacement of sophisticated mechanical equipment may be equally burdensome to a community association.

It is fair to conclude that the decisions made during the design process are inexorably

9-11 Homeowner satisfaction and value are enhanced by well-maintained exterior grounds.

Marketing a Community Association

Just as the individual unit plans of a townhouse or condominium development must be marketed, the community association must also be marketed. The sales force must be able to actively portray the purpose, function, duties, costs, and legal responsibilities of the association to prospective buyers and must be familiar with the assessments, common elements, replacement reserves, architectural controls, covenants, and other terms basic to understanding the community association.

Two key concepts in conveying the community association to prospective buyers are disclosure and communication. Part of the sales force training should include education on the basic understanding of the community association as a form of mini-government that is important to the overall success of the project. First the sales force needs to be sold on the advantages of the association concept. Only in this way can the buyers be sold on the inherent value of the community association as a part of the new lifestyle they are purchasing in a townhouse or condominium project.

One of the display elements within the model homes area should be a clear and understandable description of community associations in general, and the specifics of the community association that will serve the community being marketed. As a part of the package of sales materials, the developer should prepare a homebuyers' brochure—a basic guide written in simple lay language which briefly describes the association to the buyer. The Community Association Institute has prepared for the Veterans Administration such a publication which is widely used in the development industry. This booklet clearly explains the role of a community association, the homeowners' responsibilities, and generally introduces buyers to the entire concept.

The developer may decide to augment this kind of a booklet with an attachment containing specifics on the particular development. The elements that might be included in a custom homeowners' manual would be:

- a description of the association in general;
- governance and finances;
- operations and management;
- the use of common elements;
- individual unit upkeep;
- reprint or synopsis of legal documents;
- operational forms for such items as architectural modification, clubhouse reservation, etc.; and
- local orientation guide.

The marketing of the community association for a townhouse or condominium development is not a simple task. It demands a knowledgeable sales force and an ambitious association education program as well as the developer's confidence in the association concept and in the product.

tied to the financial stability of the community association over time. Experience clearly shows that community associations that undergo financial difficulty are frequently those that are burdened by a physical design solution that precludes efficient, economical, cost-effective operation, maintenance, and management. For example, scattered amenity elements may require greater numbers of supervisory personnel than the same amenities concentrated in a single centrally located complex. Improperly sized clubhouses, swimming pools, and other components of the amenities package may place unnecessary financial burdens on the association. Poor choice of finishing materials may dramatically increase the requirements for repetitive maintenance over more durable and maintenance-free materials.

Managing a Successful Community Association

There are many pitfalls for the developer beginning a new community association. Principally, the problems seem to derive from a failure to recognize the community association as a separate entity from the development organization—even though the original association board is usually comprised of members of the development staff. A successful community association begins with the developer running it as it will be run later on, under the management control of the board elected by the homeowners. This is true of its business meetings, financial records, assessment collection practices, accountability for maintenance of common areas (even though these are still the responsibility of the developer in the early stages of development), and relationships to the homeowner members of the association. Again reference is made to a variety of publications dealing with the successful management of community associations.*

*See ULI and CAI joint publications, particularly *Managing a Successful Community Association*.

Building a Sense of Community

Developers have a unique opportunity to build a sense of community in the way they initiate the activities of the community association. A responsible and effective leadership may begin with the association when the first resident moves into a townhouse or condominium. By the time 25 to 50 homes have been occupied or perhaps even sooner, depending on the size of the project, the developer-controlled community association should begin structuring of ad hoc committees of resident members to provide communication between the developer and the community association. Perhaps the most effective initial developer tools are a newsletter keeping new owners informed of development progress and developer interest in assisting residents toward a strong community association leadership.

The developer may be the catalyst for social activities to further the sense of community. Organizing a single bridge party, teen party, adult get-acquainted party, or whatever may be a catalyst for the formation of continuous small group activities within the structure of the association. Most importantly, the developer may encourage a feeling of cooperation and mutual concern for the development of the best possible community, furthering the compatibility of his and the residents' objectives.

Within the development team, the developer needs to have an organized, efficient mechanism for responding to inquiries from individual residents and from the community association. A clear distinction needs to be made between the problems of an individual unit purchaser and problems related to the common elements, and therefore of interest to the community association.

9-12 (top) and 9-13 (middle) Special celebrations or events like this 4th of July celebration are part of the community spirit in a well-planned townhouse or condominium community. 9-14 (bottom) In larger developments, a small community association clubhouse adjacent to the swimming pool provides for a variety of social activities.

Resident Control

The transition from developer to resident control of a community association is one of the most sensitive areas of community association development. "Surveys indicate that the problems typically arising for the developer during the transition period usually are a result of:

- failure to recognize in the design phase the importance of planning for a smooth transition of operational controls to the owners;
- failure to orient buyers to the association process;
- failure to identify and involve resident leaders;
- failure to coach owners in the operation of the association;
- failure to complete or faulty construction of common elements;
- incomplete association financial records;
- turning over the association to the owners either too early in the sales period or too late in the occupancy period;
- developer and management indifference to violations of the rules or covenants, and their failure to uniformly enforce them."*

In areas where the developer may have a bonding agreement with the municipality for the installation of utilities and streets, the bond release should not be dependent upon the acceptance by the community association of common areas and common area improvements.

Avoidance of these problems and, therefore, the road to the successful creation of a community association for townhouses and condominiums requires skill, patience, and continuing attention to the community association during the development process.

Creating a Community Association, p. 63.

10 Marketing, Sales and Design

The site plan was magnificent, taking advantage of the bluff overlooking the creek valley. The architecture was striking, with details executed to perfection. Creative engineering had saved an existing stand of mature trees by installing the utilities with care and special grading instructions. The landscape architecture had complemented the existing natural features. City officials were proud of their rapid approval process. The builder was delighted with his accomplishments. In fact, he had already received an award from the local chapter of the Tall Oaks Club. The advertising agency was gleeful in marking up invoices as the potential buyers came and went. There was only one thing wrong with the project . . . buyers did not buy. The magnificence of it all was humbled by the lack of sales, and the good architecture did not seem so good anymore. The maturity of

10-1 Having the information, sales, and development office in a house is one approach to a marketing program. Later, as the development progresses, the home is sold and the office is located in a new phase of the development.

the landscape was now judged an immature design judgement on the part of the designer. The lending institution discovered it had a problem. The builder's award was tarnished and the advertising agency discovered that a 17.65 percent markup of zero sales was disastrous. What could have gone wrong?

Although the reasons may sometimes be more complex or difficult to isolate, in a case like the above the typical reason for failure is a lack of understanding of the market and a neglecting of the marketing program during the design process. The interrelationship of design decisions and the marketing program has been covered in earlier chapters. Some of the elements of a successful marketing program/sales environment are further referenced here, with an emphasis on those design elements that may be positively influenced by the marketing program.

Perhaps the most important element of a townhouse/condominium marketing program is the creation of confidence in the product. Prospective purchasers are concerned with the future resale value of the homes, the developer's reputation, and his ability to complete the development. They also require information about the future operation and assessment fees of the community association and want an assurance that the amenities and other details will be completed in accordance with the representations made by the marketing literature and sales staff. Creating confidence by providing assurances and completely accurate information is the first step in a successful marketing campaign that emphasizes the benefits of townhouse/condominium ownership.

How Many Home Types?

Given half a chance, an architect may bury a developer with too many floor plans. Requiring townhouse/condominium plans to be appropriate to the developer's market may cut down the number of plans but it does not precisely answer the first basic architectural question: "How many home designs are necessary?"

Obviously, the number of plans the developer needs must depend upon the various types of buyers anticipated for a development. For instance, a developer may intend to sell almost exclusively to one price range. On the other hand, he may intend to provide homes for different types of buyers. Contrasted to a development of single-family detached homes, it is easier to intermix different home sizes and price ranges within a townhouse/condominium development.

In the absence of more detailed design information, it is best to start from one's own general knowledge about people in deciding how many floor plans to include. Some reasonable guidelines are (1) most potential buyers lose track of home distinctions if there are too many to remember; (2) people are most comfortable and secure in a human-scale environment they can understand—large complexes with extensive options are confusing; (3) people need a sense of identity and desire an environment with character and variety, particularly in a townhouse/condominium community.

These general guidelines usually suggest building three to five floor plan types—enough home options to permit some interesting variety and price variation, while at the same time a small enough quantity to permit clear distinction and fairly easy recollection. Four floor plans is a common number; five is a good number if the project is large enough. Normally, three to four floor plans with several options is enough.

The developer building for a number of different markets—people of different purchasing capabilities, employment types, or age levels—should provide at least one plan for each different market. Saying this is one thing, being able to do it is quite another. Fortunately, surprises often occur when a plan type initially designed for one market, becomes a best seller to another market within the community as well. For instance, a one-story unit included in a model line as a price leader became most popular not just for budget reasons, as was originally anticipated, but for older people, because it had living all on one level.

It is important to have equally desirable plans for various grade conditions in order to ensure continuous sales and construction flow. There is, however, often an evolution of plan types once sales begin, more a reaction to the market than a quickly achieved goal. It is extremely difficult to come up with three, four, or five equally desirable plans and op-

tions at the outset of a development without buyer input.

Some considerations for model line plans are:

- Try to hit your target market with at least one specific plan.
- Don't build models of all plan possibilities unless the project is over 100 units.
- Graphically display options and alternatives. Keep the number of floor plan models to a quantity that permits the homebuyer to recall their distinctions.
- One way of minimizing the number of models is to have optional plan arrangements—like a two-bedroom plan that is also available with three bedrooms. A common and expensive mistake is to have too many models.
- Unfortunately, basic floor plans that are available but not displayed in a model complex usually do not sell well. Townhouse and condominium buyers, often coming from larger homes, like to imagine how furniture will fit into a home plan. What is therefore anticipated to be the most appealing plan should be included in the model line.
- Where plats must be recorded in advance of construction, try to have some plans that are interchangeable within the block envelope.

10-2 Too many models create confusion, not sales. Usually three or four models will be adequate.

The Printed Image

By the time the concept plans have been completed, a name, logo, and type style for the development should have been prepared. The architect, landscape architect, or other design professionals will often use their graphic abilities to assist the developer with these items. The name should be descriptive and have favorable but not misleading connotations. For example, Forest Hills Estates, if located on flat, open farm land, is likely to give the visitor arriving at the site a letdown; whereas Stonegate also has favorable connotations without the resultant disappointment. For media considerations, it is best to use a short name, because it is easier to use in radio commercials and display advertising. Naturally, if the site has some historical lineage that may be used in a name and theme, so much the better. The name selected for a community may be converted into a landscape architectural reality.

The early development of the logo saves expense and provides continuity that ranges from the working drawing base sheets to the entrance marker, brochures, signage, and advertising. Moreover, a carefully designed name and logo add distinction to a development. Care should be taken, however, to avoid using the advertising campaign for promoting a logo or name at the expense of more direct selling messages. The following guidelines may prove useful:

- If the builder is well known and has successful, completed projects, tie in the project name and logo with the builder's name.
- If the builder is new or new to townhouse/condominium development, promote the project name and logo, giving the builder's name secondary importance.

10-3   A professionally prepared logo should communicate a development's theme or dominant amenity as well as express a feeling of quality. It should then be repeatedly used in promotional literature.

10-4   A development's identification/marketing sign should convey an image of quality and good design.

The Model Home Center

During the concept or preliminary design stage, the developer and the design team should choose which building(s) will serve as the model home center. Selecting the home and environment that will be presented to those people who may ultimately buy is no light matter. Some developers have been successful without a carefully prepared sales area, or feel they cannot recoup the cost of a completed model center. But in an era of great consumer skepticism, the developer of today's residential community may no longer expect his potential customers to accept his promises without seeing the built reality. The dramatization of a model home environment will give a marketing advantage to a builder's townhouses or condominiums. Since it is the particular lifestyle that motivates townhouse/condominium buyers, it is important to show an actual planned area, giving a picture of the total community. More than the buyer of single-family detached homes, the townhouse buyer will have difficulty getting a feeling for the finished product—the average buyer will not be able to visualize the relationship of unfinished buildings and clusters to open space. That is why the provision of a model home center is so necessary. The construction of condominium model home centers may be a more complex task because of high initial costs and ongoing construction. Therefore, the use of visual displays may have to suffice to illustrate a finished condominium development.

The selection of the phase-one construction area and, more specifically, the area of the

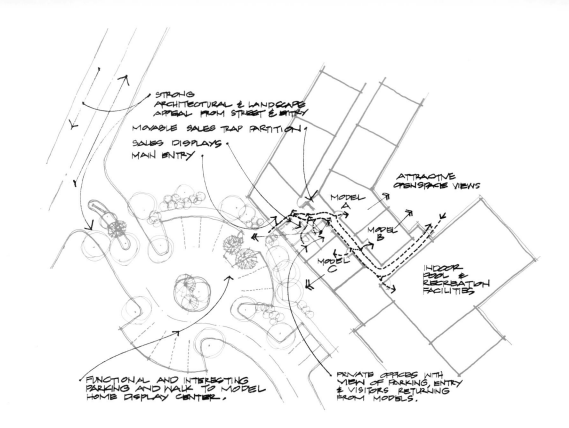

first addition, block, or building, is based upon a number of factors. Perhaps most important, this area should have both direct visual and physical access to the project entry road. There are, however, many successful projects where proper signage and off-site advertising have permitted a higher amenity, internal location area for the sales office/model home center. This is a good tactic where the primary natural or constructed amenities appear on the project's interior. In selecting the sales area and the extent of development, choices must be made to obtain the greatest impact for the lowest investment. Balancing the installation of amenities and special design features with the cash flow capabilities of the developer

will help ensure solvency and marketability of the project.

For a townhouse model center, the model block should be separate from other blocks that will be immediately sold to homebuyers. Using the cluster site planning concept and building a minimum of two or preferably three blocks, it is possible to enclose a landscaped space to achieve the feeling of a completed community. If the builder is unsure of the market and desires to "test the water" by building only one model block, it is likely that the buyers will perceive some of this uncertainty. In addition, they will not be able to understand or visualize the environmental quality of the new community. This, of

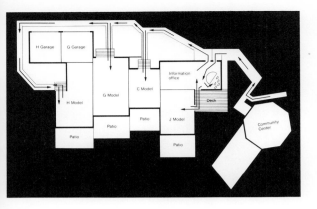

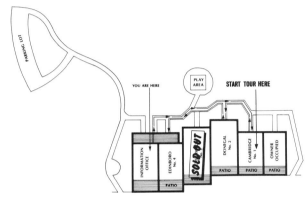

10-5 (left), 10-6 (above), and 10-7 (right) A sales tour should expose buyers to the homes as well as to other positive aspects of a development.

10-8 For a model center to be effective, it must create a sample of the finished townhouse or condominium environment.

10-9 A separate access for construction traffic increases the residents' enjoyment of their new homes and aids the marketing program.

course, may lead to a slowed sales pace and a greater chance of failure. Most builders favor making a commitment to building a series of two, three, or four blocks with the undesirable but practical "back door" alternative of a rental in the event of sales resistance.

The model center area selected must separate construction traffic from prospective homebuyer and new owner traffic. This should not interfere with the ideal construction strategy of having the initial complex of blocks under construction when the model center opens. With some of the blocks in various stages of construction, the momentum and excitement of a new development is

emphasized. However, having to cope with looking at and driving through a construction area for months or even years, is a common source of aggravation among new homeowners and a deterrent to potential homebuyers. Early land planning should take into consideration a staging plan that permits the splitting of construction traffic. Normally, this is accomplished by directing construction traffic on a portion of the project's roadways not utilized by the first homeowners. Another way to minimize inconveniences for the new homeowner in a large development is by designing small mini-neighborhoods, which may be completely finished and separated from later construction activity.

There are a number of basic site planning principles that should be applied to preliminary model home center designs:

- In most regions of the United States, the model block should be oriented to permit maximum admission of afternoon sunlight into the model homes. The light adds cheerfulness during the "Open for Inspection" hours.
- The sales office area should be visually adjacent to the rest of the model home center and model homes.
- Normally, a loose enclosure of fencing and planting is appropriate. In some locales, however, a more restrictive fence may be necessary to prevent thefts of model furnishings.
- Attention to detail is of utmost importance; walkways, signs, handrails, plant material, groundcover, and so on, all must be complete and well done—

this is the potential homebuyer's first contact with the community.

- The specific model homes should have good views of the open space and other amenities provided on the site.
- The path from the model home sales office to the separate home plans should be routed via the most pleasing exterior views of the homes and should leave the homebuyer with the image of a completed, livable community environment.

Model Homes

Model homes provide a precise example of the builder's workmanship and specifications. More importantly, they enable the consumer to visualize room sizes and floor plan relationships, so that a plan suitable to the buyer's individual needs may be found. The models should be surrounded by a reason-

able landscape representation, and visitor traffic flow should duplicate the approach a homeowner would use. Shortcuts through patios, or worse yet through common walls, should not be considered.

The furnishings and details selected for model home interiors should relate to the targeted market. The interior designer who selects furniture in scale with the room sizes as well as styles that will appear comfortable and appealing to the targeted market, provides valuable sales assistance. Furnished models are not meant for eventual occupancy by an actual family. Rather, the purpose of furnishings is to illustrate the livability of the home to a particular market and to help the prospective purchaser visualize what it might be like to live there. To that extent, the furnishings and accessories might suggest the ages of the fictitious family members who occupy the model home,

10-10   Private outdoor spaces should be decorated to reflect the lifestyle a buyer might have.

alluding to their activities, hobbies, and life-styles. These design ideas should provide the buyer with some furnishing possibilities for his own unit. As third or fourth bedrooms are commonly not used as sleeping areas but as TV rooms, studies, or sewing rooms, they may be shown that way in the model homes—particularly if the targeted market will include few or no children.

Most salespeople prefer to price as standard those items which a buyer normally expects in a home of a given price range. For example, a dishwasher would be a standard item in a higher-priced home but may be optional in a moderately-priced home. Displaying numerous "nice but not necessary" options, such as a built-in vacuum system, in the model homes is a needless sales distraction and hinders the conveyance of accurate information about more standard features.

Sales Offices

The sales office should be oriented so that the salespeople may see visitors approaching the model center. A traffic flow plan should be integral to the landscape design and conveniently route visitors into the sales office on their way to and from the model homes. A "sales trap" that channels prospective buyers through a pre-planned route winding up at the sales office is desirable but should be as inconspicuous as possible—use of landscape features like planters and plant material, combined with walkways and modest fencing, will avoid the "fenced in" feeling. Around model home areas, the use of rope, decorative single-chain fencing, or split rails is often an economical solution. This loose confinement helps to qualify prospective buyers—most salespeople recognize that the "rope jumpers" come only to look at the interior deco-

10-11 (top) and 10-12 (upper middle) Avoid covering model home windows with curtains or blinds; it replaces the effectiveness of a properly oriented home displaying open space and natural light. 10-13 (lower middle) and 10-14 (bottom) Channel buyers through a preplanned route, enabling a salesperson to discuss the homes after inspection. The route should have a subtle enclosure.

rating. A sales trap gives the salesperson an opportunity to talk to the visitors after they have completed the model homes tour, to point out features not readily apparent by merely inspecting the model homes. Misconceptions may often be clarified by questioning a sales representative. A buyer might find out, for example, that the home is not on a flight or landing pattern—that the plane just heard overhead must have been a lost Air National Guard pilot.

Depending on the size of the development and the sophistication of the competition in the market area, the sales office may be one of four types (listed in ascending order of expense):

Sales office within the model home is the most economical but also the least functional type. When a sales office is located within a particular model floor plan, the sales of that plan suffer from traffic confusion. Nevertheless, for small developments this option is a way of minimizing the merchandising expense.

Sales office within a partially completed model involves omitting some of the interior walls and postponing the installation of the kitchen or other area until the model is sold.

This is usually a one-story plan that permits private offices for more than one salesperson, while still providing adequate display space.

The double garage sales office is the most popular type of sales office around the country. It provides a separate sales area without impairing the salability of a floor plan model. The major design decision is whether or not a private office is to be included within the limited available space. A semi-private informal sitting area may become the substitute for the private office. Many salespeople then use another room within the model center complex as the closing office. It is necessary that the salesperson have private space that is separated from visitor traffic for discussions with buyers.

The biggest disadvantage of the garage sales office is initial expense and the subsequent remodeling expense. Also, in many developments, the sales office originally planned to be amortized over 200 homes ends up being used for 100 homes with a new model center constructed for the balance of the development. Using an additional attached garage to give a larger sales office is an alternative which provides a more elaborate and expensive sales facility with private offices for one or more additional salespeople.

A large detached sales center is usually used in the more sophisticated market areas and is located in a building planned for community association use at a later date. Being the most expensive, this type of sales office provides more display space. It may be the most feasible type when a community space is a required amenity; however, it should not be used as a rationalization for building an unneeded clubhouse. Further, it may have the limitation of being in the wrong place when a second model center is necessary for a growing project. Initial land use planning should anticipate the positioning of the detached sales center/clubhouse in later stages of the project by clustering "fingers" of later development phases around it.

It is very important to design the floor plan of a clubhouse which will include a sales center in such a manner that resident use will not interfere with the sales activities. A jointly used, smooth-running clubhouse/sales center will be a valuable sales asset, but evidence of clashes between the sales operations and the owners/users will spell sales disaster!

Displays

Effective sales displays will help to communicate the livability of the new environment to prospective buyers. The most commonly used displays are listed below.

Scale Models

A scale model that shows topographic relief, buildings, and vegetation is an effective catalyst for an introductory sales discussion as well as an excellent way of helping the buyer to visualize the completed development. However, a quality model is an expensive sales tool. The designer should phase the scale model similar to the phasing of the development—only the homes available for sale should be detailed on the scale model, with subsequent phases labeled as future additions. A scale model showing 200 detailed homes over the entire developed acreage is needlessly overwhelming at the beginning of the selling period and may create the temptation for the buyer to wait until a desirable looking future location is completed. The scale model becomes an excellent place to greet the visitor and give a brief introduction to the model center complex while asking some qualifying questions. An economical alternative to the scale model is a rendered site plan.

10-15 (above) A model or a rendered plat is an excellent place for salespeople to introduce themselves and briefly discuss the project, while evaluating the buyers. 10-16 (top) and 10-17 (bottom) A model may help buyers to visualize the character of buildings and open space.

Mel Jacobsen

213

Floor Plans

Floor plan displays showing the various models plus optional variations provide the buyer an opportunity to review the model home plans and give the salesperson an opportunity to point out features that may have been missed during the model homes tour. These plans are usually on a ¼ inch to ½ inch equals 1 foot scale. The displays should be located near the door through which people return from the model homes.

The same artwork that is used for the sales brochure may be used for the floor plan displays. One of the most economical methods of constructing these displays is to mount photostats on display board. For a modest additional expense, they may be covered with transparent plexiglass. One type of more elaborate display has the floor plan silkscreened on plexiglass. Renderings and perspectives of building exteriors may also complement the floor plan display. Prices could range from $100 per floor plan to over $300 each. Quality rendering artwork begins at over $100 per unit, with an additional mounting or silkscreening cost.

Sales Plat

The sales plat is often a photostat of the site plan addition currently available for sale. Mounted on a wall visible to the potential buyer, "Sold" stickers and buyers' names on a sales plat create interest and buyer confidence in the prospective project. At the beginning of the selling period, some optimistic salespersons will label tentative unit holds as "Sold." In addition to conveying the sales pace, the sales plat is a functional tool for the salesperson, showing the available locations for the various plan types.

Storyboards

A townhouse/condominium storyboard will usually show photos of other developments completed by the builder or photos of typical developments completed by others. It is a mood setter that builds confidence by showing details of developments that are enjoyed by other owners, especially if these developments have a history of proven resale value. A builder board might include a photo of the builder with a listing of past accomplishments, such as completed developments and awards.

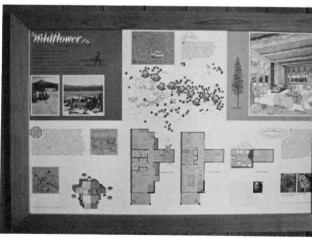

Environmental Photographs and Sketches

These displays act as decorative items, adding character to the sales office. Actual photos will also assist the busy shopper in understanding existing natural features and installed amenities elsewhere on the site.

Site Locator Map

This display shows the site in relation to major streets, municipal services, natural features, and other community amenities. Labeling these features on an aerial photo is an effective way of constructing this display. A more common method is to prepare a stylized map in keyline form. This same keyline may then be used at a reduced scale for a brochure insert.

Tour Guide

A tour guide shows the model center layout, gives some general information, and provides the visitor "something in hand" for the model homes tour. Upon completion of the tour, visitors must return to the salesperson for a more general brochure.

Brochures

Brochures are a necessary sales tool, which give the prospective purchaser factual information and a visual reminder of the development. A tastefully done, well-designed, one- or two-color brochure will usually accomplish the purpose as well as an expensive four-color, "coffee-table" quality brochure.

Some guidelines for designing brochures are:

- Don't bind floor plans permanently into the brochure. People always want the floor plan that is sold out and is no longer available.
- Don't put in prices. Prices continually change . . . and without including them the prospective buyers have a good reason to talk to the salespeople.
- Don't put the square footages on the plan . . . of course, square footage is a very competitive advantage. A well-designed 1,200-square-foot home may be more functional and livable than a competitor's 1,300-square-foot home.

Other Materials

An important sales aid for the townhouse/condominium development is a written explanation of the community association, often done in a question and answer format. Another handout that should be available upon request is the realistic projection of the community association operating expenses.

In addition to the display and distribution materials mentioned, sales representatives will require a variety of other materials. These may include price breakdown sheets, construction work orders, change orders, and buyer information sheets.

In general then, the design and layout of the on-site merchandising displays and collateral materials should reinforce the efforts of the sales staff to have the prospective buyer leave the development with a "tentative buying decision."

10-18 (top) Cover future phases of development to avoid confusion at the beginning of sales. 10-19 (upper middle) A rendered site plan is an economical display. 10-20 (lower middle) Floor plans and exterior elevations are frequently used displays. 10-21 (bottom) Additional photos or perspectives of local features and services may help to set the feeling of the community as well as show its convenience to surrounding facilities.

Media Plan

The media plan lays out the proposed advertising expenditures for a 12-month period. It is then relatively easy for the marketing manager to say no to the barrage of special media promotions that are constantly being requested after the expenditures are estimated. The result is that advertising dollars are utilized for quality impact rather than being lost to numerous insignificant special media uses. Media plans should reflect a pre-sale expenditure of the elements necessary for obtaining initial momentum at a grand opening, which should be staged to correspond with the optimum selling season. The media plan will usually take a risk in spending as much as 60 percent of the budget during the best selling season, which is typically February through May.

Signage

Visually attractive, on-site signs utilizing the approved project name, type style, and logo, direct the visitor to and throughout the model center. The designer should consult with the sales staff regarding the content and placement of signs. The locations should then be included in the model center site plan. Off-site signs may be the best advertising buy in the media budget. The designer should assist the developer by including off-site sign requests as part of the public approval process.

Sales Strategy

A basic question regarding sales personnel is whether to use an on-site new homes sales staff or a local realtor organization. In the larger metropolitan markets, builders usually prefer to have their own staff, controlled by and accountable to the development organization. An exception would be the use of a real estate company that specializes in townhouse/condominium sales. In smaller market areas, with populations of less than 100,000, serious consideration should be given to using one or more realtor firms as the sales staff or sales referral system.

Planning and design consultants may provide valuable sales training assistance by thoroughly explaining to the sales staff the rationale for the land plan and home designs. This is one of the best, but frequently neglected, ways of ensuring marketing success.

10-22 (above) Displaying "Sold" signs communicates the popularity of the project, maintaining sales momentum and the sense of urgency to buy. 10-23 (right) Marketing signs should convey a feeling of quality as well as communicate information.

Design Feedback

The salesperson is in direct contact with the consumer and is, therefore, an excellent source of input for evolving design changes. However, changes should be carefully considered. Chaos will result if plans are hastily changed based on the comments of the last casual visitor. If the salesperson suggests that a door and closet be moved, builders should generally ignore the comment the first time it is mentioned, listen more carefully the second time, and change the design if the comment persists. The developer should always consult with his designers to consider complications before making changes.

On larger-scale projects, the buyers-turned-homeowners, acting through their community association, may be expected to influence the design of later phases. Pressure to maintain the same kind of site and design of units is a common request. This may be a problem as prices escalate—necessitating design changes to maintain marketability. As new buyers will add their reactions—positive and negative—to the design review process, everyone on the design team should listen well. The sales personnel are in the best position to accumulate suggestions and criticisms and should attempt to express them during the review process in an unbiased manner.

As potential homebuyers visit the development, the accuracy of original market research and guidelines should be reevaluated. Are the interested people those who were expected? Repeated requests for something different than what is available may begin to change the design for subsequent phases.

10-24 Sound design and planning, quality, and cost-conscious construction, coupled with a well-conceived marketing plan, may send a design/development team in search of the next new community to build.

Appendices

Appendix A
Buyer Likes and Dislikes—A Minneapolis-St. Paul Survey

In 1973, ULI–the Urban Land Institute and Dr. Carl Norcross conducted an extensive buyer opinion poll of 49 different townhouse and condominium developments in California and the Washington, D.C. area. Due to budgetary limitations, the sample was restricted to these two geographical areas. Nearly 1,800 responses were received, with the results tabulated and published in the ULI publication, *Townhouses and Condominiums: Residents' Likes and Dislikes*. When properly interpreted, the results of the opinion poll provide an important source of data for making design, marketing, and development decisions.

The data presented in this appendix is from a survey by ULI—the authors intended to expand the base of buyer information presented in the Norcross publication, which should be consulted to enlarge the comparative spectrum. This 1975 buyer study is called the Minneapolis-St. Paul Survey, although samples are taken from only some of the townhouse communities of one developer in the Twin Cities market. It is likely that many of the same buyer characteristics and attitudes are typical of other market areas.

The buyer opinion poll was taken for three reasons:
1. to provide midwestern buyer input;
2. to update the base information (given in the Norcross study) with a current sample; and
3. to provide a sample of buyer reaction to developments that include many of the planning and design principles advocated in this book.

A summary of some of the buyer responses is presented in this appendix. Due to the great number of extremely favorable responses to the survey, the percentage of dissatisfied responses was generally not substantial enough to make significant conclusions or to warrant extensive discussion in this appendix. A

complete summary of the questionnaire results is contained in Appendix B.

Sampling Technique

The sample is taken from six townhouse developments in the Minneapolis-St. Paul metropolitan area that were developed while the authors of the survey were associated with Pemtom, Inc., a builder/developer. The sampling technique involved sending a mailed questionnaire and a cover letter from ULI, a copy of which is shown in Appendix B, to a mailing list of 921 townhouse owners in the six developments. The sizes of the developments range from 41 to 324 townhouses.

A total of 356 completed questionnaires were returned, giving a response of 38.5 percent. This high rate of questionnaire return is similar to the 37.7 percent return received for the Norcross sample. After discarding as invalid certain questionnaires such as those that were filled out on only one side, a net sample of 332 responses was tabulated. Although 332 responses were usable for the tabulation, some of the 332 respondents did not answer all the questions. Therefore, the number of responses (N) to any given question may be less than 332.

In order to compare the Minneappolis-St. Paul sample with the California/Washington, D.C. sample, the survey questions were left virtually intact. An important new question (Question 50) was added regarding security, as well as a new question on attitude toward the size of the development (Question 51). Using the previous format proved meaningful in providing comparison data, but has limited refinements of the questionnaire.

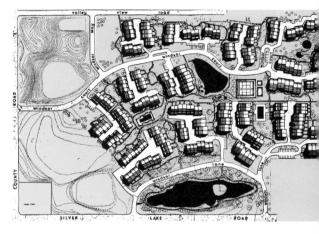

Windsor Green
Windsor Green was the first major "For Sale" townhouse development in the Minneapolis-St. Paul market. Started in 1965, 236 townhouses were built on a 40-acre site. Two ponds were built in areas of poor soil. These ponds provide a pleasant entrance approach and a visual amenity in the center of the development. The one- and two-story townhouses all have a basement and a two-car garage. The original sales prices of $17,900 to $23,000 have more than doubled in value. Several owners have added an additional room to obtain more living area.

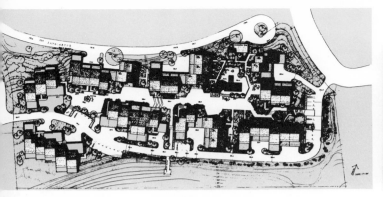

Cedarview

Cedarview is an "in-town" townhouse development of 41 homes on a site of approximately 4 acres of buildable area. The site was formerly used as a gravel pit and is bounded on two sides by railroad tracks and office/commercial construction. An intensively landscaped mall was developed as a focal point. Cedarview has a superb view of the Minneapolis skyline. The sales prices in 1970 were in the 40s and 50s. The re-sale values 8 years later about doubled the original sales prices.

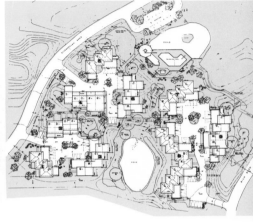

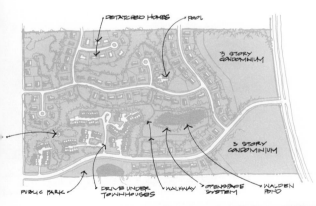

Walden Townhouses

Walden is a 100-acre planned unit development (PUD) of 100 single-family detached lots, about 150 condominium apartments, and 86 townhouses. The 86 townhouses were started in 1967 on a 16.5-acre portion of the site. A decade later, the original sales prices, starting at $22,000, had more than doubled. Flexibility in locating buildings was permitted by the city of Burnsville, thereby giving the developer an opportunity to adjust building grades with the terrain and to preserve existing trees and vegetation.

Scarborough

Scarborough is located in the city of Bloomington, Minnesota, a second tier suburb of Minneapolis. Eighty-nine townhouses were developed between 1971 and 1973 on a 16.5-acre site. The development was part of a 63-acre PUD that also included single-family detached lots. The 1971 sales prices ranged from $42,000 to $59,500. For additional data, see: Volume 3, Number 11, ULI's Project Reference File.

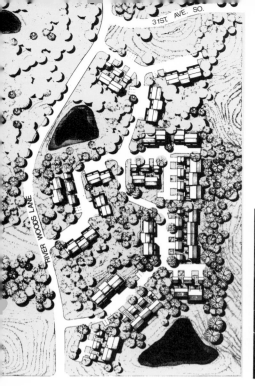

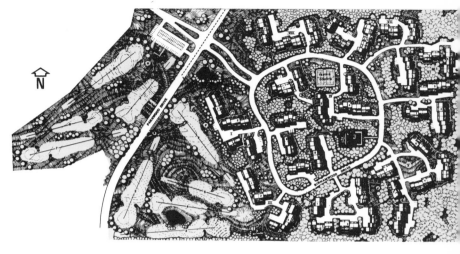

Riverwoods

Riverwoods is a PUD of townhouses and single-family detached homes. The 342 townhouses were built at an overall density of approximately four units per acre. Preservation of existing trees and vegetation provided a marketing advantage at Riverwoods, where the sales models were opened in February of 1972. Located in the third tier suburb of Burnsville, the one- and two-story homes were designed to appeal to the first homebuyer, with prices starting at $21,900.

Birnamwood

Birnamwood is a 43-acre development of 222 townhouses in the Minneapolis suburb of Burnsville. The gross density is 5.1 dwelling units per acre. The 1971 base prices ranged from $36,000 to $50,000. A pleasant entrance approach is provided by a single divided lane entrance. For additional data, see: Volume 1, Number 2, ULI's Project Reference File.

Common Design and Development Elements

Some of the design and development elements that are common to all six developments surveyed are listed here without comment to assist the reader in interpreting the implications of the opinion poll results.

- Platted lots, rather than condominium ownership
- Medium density
- Double garages
- Basements
- Private outdoor patios or decks
- Functional land plans
- Variety of plan types, including one- and two-story plans
- Public dedication of major streets
- Municipal cooperation
- Adequate landscape budgets
- Outdoor swimming pool, tot lots, and lighted walkways
- Wood and brick exteriors
- Flexibility to change unit mix
- "Sample of the environment" completed at the start of marketing process
- Aggressive marketing programs
- Attractive entrance approaches
- Efficient and well-managed community associations

Buyer Profile

The developer is most interested in who buys a townhouse in order to formulate a planning, design, and marketing program that will direct his product to the logical market. The experienced developer will start with general data, such as the material presented here, to guide his program, but adapt this data to suit his particular market and development needs. Municipal planning commissions and council members usually have quite an interest in buyer profiles, to evaluate their impact on local schools and municipal services.

The typical buyer in the Minneapolis-St. Paul sample has a managerial or professional occupation with a higher than average income, is between 30 and 59 years of age, and married. One-half of the buyers previously owned a single-family detached home.

Table 1 illustrates the trend of which experienced marketing people are well aware; namely, that there has been a nationwide increase in townhouse and condominium ownership by single people. In the Twin Cities sample, 30.2 percent of owners were either single, widowed, or divorced. This updated survey illustrates an increase over the East-West Norcross sample, which showed a combined 16.5 percent single, with 11 percent single buyers in the East and 27 percent in the West.

The average number of adults per home is shown in Table 2, indicating that 24.0 percent of the respondents have one adult living in the home. The largest market segment or 71.7 percent consists of two adults living in the home. Based on age of the head of the family (Table 3), somewhat surprisingly the greatest part of the market, or 32.3 percent, falls between ages 30 and 39. This figure corresponds with the Norcross East-West sample, which showed a similar age breakdown. It should be mentioned, though that the sample may be somewhat skewed by the number of under 30 buyers who purchased a townhouse as a first residence and liked it so well that they decided to stay.

Table 1—Marital Status (N = 331)

(Question 40)

Married	69.8%
Single	16.3%
Widowed	6.3%
Divorced	7.6%
	100.0%

Table 2—Adults, Age 20 or Over, Per Home (N = 325)

(Question 42)

	Percent	Total Adults
One	24.0	78
Two	71.7	466
Three	4.3	42
Four	0.0	0
	100.0	586

Table 3—Head of Family Age (N = 325)

(Question 44)

Age	Percent
20-29	11.1
30-39	32.3
40-49	17.8
50-59	24.6
Over 60	14.2
	100.0

Table 4—Persons Under 20 Per Household (N = 332)

(Question 43)

	Relative Percent	Total Children/ Young Adults
One	17.8	59
Two	13.9	92
Three	3.0	30
Four	1.5	20
None	63.8	0
	100.0	201

Table 5—Total Family Income (N = 321)

(Question 48)

Under $10,000	1.6%
$10,000-$14,999	13.7%
$15,000-$19,999	14.6%
$20,000-$24,999	19.3%
$25,000-$29,999	16.2%
$30,000 or over	34.6%
	100.0%

Table 6—Previous Residence (N = 325)

(Question 36)

1-family home you owned	51.3%
1-family home you rented	2.2%
A rented apartment	36.3%
A rented townhouse	4.0%
A townhouse you owned	3.7%
Other	2.5%
	100.0%

Table 4 shows 201 persons under age 20 in the homes of the 332 respondents, or an average of 0.6 children/young adults per home. The under 20 age category causes some problems in determining the number of school age children. Many of the children will be of pre-school age. Also, it is well known that many townhouse buyers decide to purchase about the time their last child graduates from high school. It is estimated that the number of school age children per household is about 0.4.

Over 50 percent of homeowners had a total family income of over $25,000. The high income levels are a reflection of the initial and re-sale home prices, the professional type of occupations held, and also the fact that 51 percent of married couple's wives worked.

A single-family detached home was the most common previous residence, with 51 percent of the sample previously owning their own home.

Reasons for Buying

"Why people buy" is fundamental marketing information for a townhouse/condominium developer. Experienced marketing directors know that it is easier to satisfy the needs of a given market than to create a new market and that advertising dollars may be stretched if they are directed toward that target market.

Table 7 illustrates the answers to Question 2, "Why did you buy your present home instead of another type of home or (renting an) apartment?" Up to three items were mentioned by each respondent.

The results of the Minneapolis-St. Paul survey show that maintenance-free living is by far the most important reason for purchasing. Table 7 shows that 298 out of 332 respondents checked freedom from house and yard maintenance as one of the reasons for purchasing. An interpretation of the response might suggest that freedom to travel and leave the home unattended is as important as the physical freedom of not having to mow the lawn. The second most frequently checked reason for buying was an improved living environment (35 percent), followed by recreation facilities (33 percent), and equity reasons (32 percent).

Interestingly, for this question the Minneapolis-St. Paul sample closely follows the results from California in the buyer's likes and dislikes survey. Seventy three and seven-tenths percent of the California residents rated freedom from maintenance as a reason for buying as compared to 44.3 percent in the East. It should be noted that while maintenance-free living may be a strong marketing point in some markets, in other markets it may not be as important. For example, in the Florida market many retirees prefer to maintain a small lot of their own.

Opinion polls are subject to many interpretations. With this in mind, a conclusion may be drawn from the comparative buyer surveys that economic reasons for buying a townhouse are a much more important motivator in the East than in the West or Midwest, where freedom from maintenance and improved living environment are more important. One of the reasons that a townhouse may be first considered as a low-cost housing alternative in the East is, for example, that some of the suburban townhouse developments in the Washington, D.C. area lack privacy, garages, functional land plans, and attractive building design. These townhouses, therefore, do not have as good an image to-date as compared with other sections of the country—they are viewed as secondary, economical alternatives to buying a detached home on a lot. The reduced construction cost of slab-on-grade construction permits strong price competition for a townhouse or a condominium as compared with a single-family detached home.

Table 7 - Reasons for Buying

(Question 2)

	Times Mentioned	Percent of 332 Respondents
Friends are near when needed	11	3.3
Feel more secure	65	19.6
Environment is better	116	34.9
Recreation facilities	110	33.1
Costs less than 1-family	52	15.7
Privacy	38	11.4
Tired of paying rent and getting no equity	106	31.9
Freedom from house and yard maintenance	298	89.8
Other	60	18.1
	856	100.0

Owner Satisfaction

Owner satisfaction is perhaps the most important standard by which the developer, designer, and municipal officials measure the results of a financially successful development. The reasons for achieving a high level of owner satisfaction from a development are varied, because of the individual nature of each homebuyer. By satisfying various individual requirements, the developer builds an important source of referral business for subsequent developments.

Dr. Norcross used two questions to establish an owner satisfaction scale: "How do you appraise living conditions in your type home and neighborhood?" and "How do you rate your environment (what you see or hear from your windows, front door, rear yard)?" The results were tabulated individually and then combined to give an indication of the level of owner satisfaction. The results from the Minneapo-lis-St. Paul sample are shown in Table 8. The great number of positive responses may be interpreted as a validation of many of the planning and design principles advocated in this book. Interestingly, Cedarview residents gave a rating of 100 percent to both questions, with Cedarview being the development of the highest density and the only "intown" townhouse development. The lowest ratings were obtained from Riverwoods, the largest and most recent development. At Riverwoods, some design compromises were made in order to obtain construction efficiencies that resulted in very competitive market prices.

Dr. Norcross structured a simple scale for rating the 49 developments in his sample by averaging the combined percentages of the responses to the two questions (#1 and #3). Table 10 shows the relationship of the Twin Cities developments to the larger sample.

Table 8 - Living Conditions and Environment (N = 329)

(Question 1)

* How do you appraise living conditions in your type home and neighborhood?

	Windsor Green	Cedarview	Walden	Scarborough	Riverwoods	Birnamwood
Good	76 (100)	18 (100)	38 (92.7)	31 (93.9)	66 (93)	90 (100)
Fair	0	0	3 (7.3)	2 (6.1)	5 (7)	0
Poor	0	0	0	0	0	0

* Percentages are given in parentheses.

(Question 3) (N = 331)

* How do you rate your environment (what you see or hear from your windows, front door, rear yard)?

	Windsor Green	Cedarview	Walden	Scarborough	Riverwoods	Birnamwood
Good	67 (89.3)	18 (100)	37 (88.1)	30 (90.9)	57 (79.2)	87 (95.6)
Fair	8 (10.7)	0	5 (11.9)	3 (9.1)	14 (19.4)	4 (4.4)
Poor	0	0	0	0	1 (1.4)	0

* Percentages are given in parentheses.

Table 9 - Comparison of Living Conditions and Environment (in percent)

Living Conditions	East	West	Combined East-West	Minneapolis-St. Paul (N = 331)
Good	87.0	84.0	86.0	97.0
Fair	11.7	12.8	12.0	3.0
Poor	1.3	2.9	2.0	0.0
	100.0	99.7	100.0	100.0
Living Environment				
Good	67.9	68.6	68.1	89.4
Fair	28.8	25.0	27.6	10.3
Poor	3.3	6.4	4.3	0.3
	100.0	100.0	100.0	100.0

Table 10 - Owner Satisfaction

Development*	Gross Density	Rating
Cedarview	10.0	100.0
1.	3.9	100.0
Birnamwood	5.1	97.8
2.	6.0	97.0
3.	3.7	97.0
4.	10.0	96.0
5.	4.9	95.0
Windsor Green	6.0	94.7
6.	6.0	94.5
7.	6.7	93.0
8.	17.0	93.0
9.	4.0	92.5
Scarborough	5.5	92.4
10.	8.4	91.0
11.	7.3	90.5
Walden	6.0	90.4
12.	10.0	90.0
13.	11.0	88.0
14.	7.0	87.0
15.	4.0	87.0
16.	7.2	86.5
Riverwoods	4.0	86.1
17.	6.5	85.0
18.	6.9	84.5
19.	8.0	83.5
20.	7.7	83.0
21.	5.0	82.5
22.	4.4	81.5
23.	11.0	81.5
24.	6.4	81.5

Development *	Gross Density	Rating
25.	10.0	81.0
26.	9.0	81.0
27.	6.0	79.0
28.	10.0	79.0
29.	10.0	78.0
30.	5.5	75.0
31.	11.8	75.0
32.	10.0	75.0
33.	8.5	74.0
34.	9.3	73.7
35.	10.0	73.0
36.	6.8	72.5
37.	9.4	72.0
38.	9.0	71.5
39.	11.0	69.0
40.	10.5	68.5
41.	10.0	68.0
42.	10.0	68.0
43.	8.0	67.0
44.	10.0	64.5
45.	12.0	64.0
46.	8.0	62.5
47.	12.0	59.0
48.	10.0	54.0
49.	15.0	39.0

* Numbers 1 through 49 indicate the various East-West developments in the Norcross survey.

It may be observed that most of the developments that received the higher ratings in the East-West sample have lower densities than the developments that received the lower ratings. In the Twin Cities sample most of the developments have a gross density of about six homes per acre.

Other survey questions that relate to owner satisfaction include how long residents expect to remain in their present residence (Question 38) and what type of future residence they prefer (Question 39). In the Minneapolis-St. Paul sample, two-thirds of the buyers expected to stay 5 years or longer and over one-half expected to buy a townhouse when they make their next move.

Owner Dissatisfaction
Several items in the questionnaire are directed at determining sources of dissatisfaction. The responses to Question 6, "How could the arrangement (of houses in rows or clusters) be improved?" are shown in Table 11.

As shown in Table 12, the guest parking facilities were a big source of dissatisfaction. In most cases, this may be a valid complaint due to a design emphasis on daily enjoyment by the residents, rather than on excessive guest parking which disrupts the land plan. Several respondents qualified their responses by saying they would rather have trees and landscaping than the blacktop for extra parking.

Appendix B should be consulted for other negative responses, such as objections to noise and traffic.

Table 11 - How could the arrangement be improved?

	Times Mentioned	Percent
More spacing between buildings	19	5.7
Smaller clusters of units	11	3.3
Stagger units (less common wall space, break up long, straight patterns, garages, etc.)	10	3.0
Avoid units (or decks, patios, etc.) that face one another	20	6.0
More enclosure for units (fencing, shrubbery, etc.— more privacy from front and rear)	6	1.8
Prefer garage in rear—away from access	3	0.9
More parking interspersed in development	5	1.5
Miscellaneous (wider driveways, etc.)	22	6.6
No improvement needed or no response	236	71.2
	332	100.0

Table 12 - How do you rate car parking facilities for you and your guests? (N = 327)

(Question 21)

	Percent
Good	47.7
Fair	37.0
Poor	15.3
	100.0

Extra Storage

None of the developments in the Minneapolis-St. Paul survey has a designated storage area for boats and recreational vehicles—the community associations have taken a firm position of prohibiting permanent outside storage. A double garage with each home tends to subdue the need for outside storage. With this information in mind, 56.4 percent of the respondents rated extra parking area for recreational vehicles as not important.

Table 13 - How important is a parking area for boats, campers, trailers, etc.? (N = 321)

(Question 24)

	Percent
Very	14.6
Fairly	29.0
Not important	56.4
	100.0

Size of Development

The developments in the Minneapolis-St. Paul survey range in size from 41 to 324 units. Two questions examined the attitude toward the size of the development. The conclusion seems to be that if the buyers are otherwise satisfied with their development, that whatever size it happens to be is the right size. For instance, Windsor Green has 236 homes, yet 90.7 percent of the buyers say they would not enjoy the development more if it were smaller. One of the reasons stated on some of the questionnaires was the ability of the present size to protect the surroundings from the intrusion of undesirable traffic or land uses.

Riverwoods, the largest development of 324 homes, does have a significant buyer reaction against the size. As Riverwoods is also the most recent development, with construction activity still in progress at the time the opinion poll was taken, the reader may speculate as to whether the adverse reaction is due to the prolonged construction activities or to the number of homes in the development. There may be disadvantages to a development size that would exceed a 3-year construction period; a 2-year construction period, or around 150 units, may be a better alternative.

Recreational Facilities

A modest approach to recreational facilities was used in all of the developments surveyed. An outdoor swimming pool, tot lots, and walking paths are common to all six developments. The four largest developments have two tennis courts. Table 16 shows the buyers' opinion of recreational facilities. For this specific market, an outdoor swimming pool, tennis courts, and walkways are the most popular recreational combination. Listed are Questions 15 to 18 and the tabulation of the responses.

Table 14—Would you enjoy living there more if the development was smaller? (N = 327)

(Question 8)	
Yes	18.3%
No	81.7%
	100.0%

Table 15—*How do you rate the size of your development? (N = 330)

	Windsor Green	Cedarview	Walden	Scarborough	Riverwoods	Birnamwood	All
Too large	5 (6.6)	0	1 (2.4)	4(12.1)	28(38.9)	5 (5.6)	43(13.0)
Too small	0	1 (5.6)	0	0	0	0	1 (0.3)
About right	71(93.4)	17(94.4)	40(97.6)	29(87.9)	44(61.1)	85(94.4)	286(86.7)

*Percentages are given in parentheses.

Table 16—Recreational Facilities

Q-15 Please list the recreation facilities in your development which your family use most, in order of popularity:

Q-16 Which additional recreational facilities would you like?

Q-17 Which recreational facilities that are provided could you do without?

Q-18 Which features (like a sauna) were sales attractions when you bought, but which you don't use?

Number of Times Mentioned (N = 332)

	Q-15	Q-16	Q-17	Q-18
Swimming, wading pools	293	1	27	28
Play areas, (tot lots, swings)	38	16	7	3
Tennis	188	30	34	31
Paths (walk, jog, bike)	112	6	3	-
Water—ponds, streams	8	-	1	-
Golf	34	5	1	4
Clubhouse activities	14	24	1	1
Basketball	4	5	4	-
Skating (ice and roller)	5	2	1	-
Baseball—barbeque	-	12	-	-
Jacuzzi whirlpool	-	-	-	-
Sauna	-	4	-	-
Volleyball	7	4	4	-
Gym and health club	-	6	-	-
Riding horses	-	-	-	-
Billiards, pool	-	-	-	-
Adult activity area	2	-	1	-
Indoor pool, tennis, etc.	-	37	-	-
Horseshoes	1	-	2	-
None	8	80	92	140
All	-	-	15	1
Shuffleboard	-	3	-	-
Racketball courts, handball	1	5	1	-
Garden space	3	1	-	-
Kitchen equipment in recreation center	-	1	-	-
Field and track	-	1	-	-
Paddle tennis	4	-	14	4

Security

A new question regarding security was added to the Minneapolis-St. Paul opinion poll. The results show that a townhouse community may offer residents an increased sense of security. No gatehouses or other complex security systems are involved. Rather, the increased security is obtained through a land plan that provides limited access into the neighborhood and the surveillance provided by other homeowners. For instance, Birnamwood has a single divided entrance that serves the 222 homes. Two-thirds of the buyers said they felt more secure than in their previous residence.

After the initial tabulation, a cross-run was made to determine the attitude regarding security based on the previous type of residence. As Table 18 indicates, previous apartment residents and single-family homeowners felt significantly more secure in their new townhouse environment.

Table 17—Security (N = 329)

(Question 50)

More secure	214	65.1%
Less secure	6	1.8%
About the same	109	33.1%
	329	100.0%

Table 18—Security Based on Previous Residence

(N = 323)

	Single-Family Homeowners	Single-Family Homeowners	Apartment Renters	Townhouse Renters	Townhouse Owners	Others
More secure	101	4	85	7	7	5
Less secure	2	0	4	0	0	0
About the same	63	3	28	6	5	3

Appendix B
Questionnaire Results

October, 1975

To Owners of Townhouses or Condominiums in Minnesota:

We need your help and ideas.

In 1973, ULI–the Urban Land Institute published a book, *Townhouses and Condominiums: Residents' Likes and Dislikes* by Carl Norcross. That book relied very heavily on 1800 surveys from people like you who live in townhouse and condominium communities. Their advice has helped many builder/developers, architects, planners, and public officials in their efforts to build townhouse and condominium communities that would be good places to live.

Now, two years later, with the concern over "problems" with condominiums having received the attention of Congress, we felt it was time to conduct another survey in another market using the same survey as in 1973 to find out if residents' likes and dislikes had changed. The results of this survey will be incorporated in a new ULI publication, *Planning and Design of Townhouses and Condominiums*. By filling out and returning the enclosed survey, you will help influence those who will design and build townhouse and condominium developments in the future.

How do you like your community? What is right with it? What is wrong? How could it be improved? Answering this survey will only take a few minutes of your time, and you will be making a contribution to better housing and a better environment in many cities.

Do not sign your name. Answer carefully and completely. And please use the return envelope enclosed for your reply.

We wish to complete the survey work by November 30th, 1975 in order to meet our publication deadlines. Don't wait to fill out the questionnaire; we are anxious to receive your opinion.

With many thanks,

Frank H. Spink, Jr.
Director, Technical Publications Division

Enclosures

ULI–the Urban Land Institute is an independent, non-profit, educational organization which conducts research; interprets current land-use trends in relation to the changing economic, social, and civic needs of our society; and disseminates pertinent information leading to the best and most efficient use and development of land.

OPINION POLL

Name of Development _____
Addition or Phase (if known) _____

1. How do you appraise living conditions in your type home & neighborhood?
   a. ☐ Good
   b. ☐ Fair   (Check One)
   c. ☐ Poor

2. Why did you buy your present home instead of another type of home or apartment? (Check the 3 most important reasons)
   a. ☐ Friends are near when needed
   b. ☐ Feel more secure
   c. ☐ Environment is better
   d. ☐ Recreation facilities
   e. ☐ Costs less than 1-family
   f. ☐ Privacy
   g. ☐ Tired of paying rent & getting no equity
   h. ☐ Freedom from house & yard maintenance
   i. ☐ Other

3. How do you rate your environment (what you see or hear from your windows, front door, rear yard)?
   a. ☐ Good
   b. ☐ Fair
   c. ☐ Poor

4. How could the environment be improved for your family?
   _____
   _____
   _____

5. Is your arrangement of houses (in rows or clusters) the best possible?
   a. ☐ Yes
   b. ☐ No

6. How could the arrangement be improved?
   _____
   _____

7. Do you feel there are too many families living too close to you?
   a. ☐ Yes
   b. ☐ No

8. Would you enjoy living there more if the development was smaller?
   a. ☐ Yes
   b. ☐ No

9. How often do you hear neighbors from your yard or patio?
   a. ☐ Often
   b. ☐ Occasionally
   c. ☐ Almost never

10. Can you hear your neighbors through the inside walls?
    a. ☐ Often
    b. ☐ Occasionally
    c. ☐ Almost never

11. How much do neighbors' noises bother you?
    a. ☐ Very much
    b. ☐ Somewhat
    c. ☐ No bother

12. Is car traffic near you a bother?
    a. ☐ Yes
    b. ☐ No

13. Have you enough outdoor space for family activities?
    a. ☐ Yes
    b. ☐ No

14. (If you have children) Are there proper places for children to play?
    a. ☐ Yes
    b. ☐ No

15. Please list the recreation facilities in your development which your family use most, in order of popularity:
    a. _____
    b. _____
    c. _____
    d. _____

16. Which additional recreational facilities would you like?
    _____

17. Which recreation facilities that are provided could you do without?
    _____

18. Which features (like a sauna) were sales attractions when you bought, but which you don't use?
    _____
    _____
    _____

19. Do you know your half-dozen nearest neighbors by name?
    a. ☐ Yes
    b. ☐ No

20. Is it easier to make friends here than in other places you've lived?
    a. ☐ Yes
    b. ☐ No
    c. ☐ About the same

21. How do you rate car parking facilities for you & your guests?
    a. ☐ Good
    b. ☐ Fair
    c. ☐ Poor

22. How could car parking be improved?
    _____
    _____

23. Rows of cars close to your door help spoil the environment. For better appearance, how far will you walk to a parking lot?
    a. ☐ 25 yards
    b. ☐ 50 yards
    c. ☐ 75 yards
    d. ☐ 100 yards
    e. ☐ We have garage or carport
    f. ☐ Prefer parking close as possible

24. How important is a parking area for boats, campers, trailers, etc.?
    a. ☐ Very important
    b. ☐ Fairly important
    c. ☐ Not important

25. If you remember the name or number of your floor plan, write it here:
    _____

26. How could your floor plan be improved for your family?
    _____
    _____
    _____

27. If you were buying again, which floor plan or model would you choose?
    a. ☐ The same one
    b. ☐ Which other model? _____

28. Which type of patio do you prefer?
    a. ☐ Open on three sides
    b. ☐ With side fences, open rear
    c. ☐ All enclosed

29. Do you regard a patio as:
    a. ☐ Very valuable
    b. ☐ Fairly valuable
    c. ☐ Not valuable

30. How do you rate the organization and operation of your condominium or homes association?
    a. ☐ Good
    b. ☐ Fair
    c. ☐ Poor

31. Are the monthly charges fair for the services you receive?
    a. ☐ Yes
    b. ☐ No

32. How could the set-up of the condominium or association be improved?
    _____
    _____

33. What have turned out to be the 3 best features of townhouses or condominium living for you?

_____
_____
_____

34. What are the 3 poorest features?

_____
_____
_____

35. In buying a townhouse or a condominium *in another location*, if you had a choice of several different neighborhoods within a development, which geographical or environmental features would be most important?

_____
_____
_____
_____
_____

To help developers, land planners and architects do a better job with townhouses or condominiums, we need to know more about families now living in them. Please tell us:

36. What kind of home did you live in just before you moved here?
   a. ☐ 1-family home you owned
   b. ☐ 1-family home you rented
   c. ☐ A rented apartment
   d. ☐ A rented townhouse
   e. ☐ A townhouse you owned
   f. ☐ Other (specify) _____
   _____

37. How long have you lived here?
   a. ☐ 1-6 months
   b. ☐ 7-12 months
   c. ☐ 13-18 months
   d. ☐ 19-24 months
   e. ☐ over 2 years

38. How much longer do you expect to remain here?
   a. ☐ 1-11 months
   b. ☐ 1 year
   c. ☐ 2 years
   d. ☐ 3 years
   e. ☐ 4 years
   f. ☐ 5 years or more

39. When you next move, what type of home will you probably move to?
   a. ☐ Buy a 1-family house
   b. ☐ Buy a townhouse or townhome
   c. ☐ Rent a townhouse
   d. ☐ Rent an apartment
   e. ☐ Other (specify) _____

40. Your marital status is:
   a. ☐ Married
   b. ☐ Single
   c. ☐ Widowed
   d. ☐ Divorced

41. Sex: M ☐   F ☐   Couple jointly ☐
   (of person filling this out)

42. How many adults, 20 or over, live in your home?
   a. ☐ 1
   b. ☐ 2
   c. ☐ 3
   d. ☐ 4

43. How many persons under 20?
   a. ☐ 1
   b. ☐ 2
   c. ☐ 3
   d. ☐ 4 or more

44. Age, principal wage earner.
   a. ☐ 20-29
   b. ☐ 30-39
   c. ☐ 40-49
   d. ☐ 50-59
   e. ☐ 60 +

45. Occupation, principal wage earner.

_____

46. Does wife have an outside job?
   a. ☐ Yes
   b. ☐ No

47. Wife's occupation_____

48. Your total family income. This is important because it gives us a clue to the price of houses that should be built. This is completely anonymous, so the figure remains your secret. We will appreciate an answer.
   a. ☐ Under $10,000
   b. ☐ $10,000-$14,999
   c. ☐ $15,000-$19,999
   d. ☐ $20,000-$24,999
   e. ☐ $25,000-$29,999
   f. ☐ $30,000-or over

49. Original price range when built? _____
   Present Value? _____

50. Compared to your previous residence, do you feel:
   a. ☐ More secure
   b. ☐ Less secure
   c. ☐ About the same

51. How do you rate the size of your development?
   a. ☐ Too large
   b. ☐ Too small
   c. ☐ About right

Minneapolis-St. Paul
Townhouse Residents Opinion Poll
Questionnaire Results

Development Key:
1 ..Windsor Green
2 ....Cedarview
3 ....Walden
4 ....Scarborough
5 .....Riverwoods
6 ....Birnamwood

Sample: The sample consists of six townhouse developments in the Mpls.-St. Paul area. 921 questionnaires were mailed. A total of 356 completed questionnaires were received, or a response of 38.5
percent. There were 332 useable questionnaires
used in the computer tabulation.

Note: In the following tables, the first number is the absolute frequency of responses (total respondents);
the second number (in parentheses) is the ad-
justed frequency percent (percent of responses
with missing cases excluded). Relative frequency
percent, when used, indicates the percent of total
respondents including those who gave no answer.

Q-1. How do you appraise living conditions in your type home and neighborhood?

	Windsor Green	Cedar-view	Walden	Scar-borough	River-woods	Birnam-wood	
	1	2	3	4	5	6	Total
a. Good	76(100)	18(100)	38(92.7)	31(93.9)	66(93)	90(100)	319(97)
b. Fair	0	0	3 (7.3)	2 (6.1)	5 (7)	0	10 (3)
c. Poor	0	0	0	0	0	0	0
							329

Q-2. Why did you buy your present home instead of another type of home or
apartment?

	Times Mentioned	% of 332 Respondents
Friends are near when needed	11	3.3
Feel more secure	65	19.6
Environment is better	116	34.9
Recreation facilities	110	33.1
Costs less than 1-family	52	15.7
Privacy	38	11.4
Tired of paying rent and getting no equity	106	31.9
Freedom from house and yard maintenance	298	89.8
Other	60	18.1

Q-3. How do you rate your environment (what you see or hear from your windows, front door, rear yard)?

	1	2	3	4	5	6	Total
a. Good	67(89.3)	18(100)	37(88.1)	30(90.9)	57(79.2)	87(95.6)	296(89.4)
b. Fair	8(10.7)	0	5(11.9)	3 (9.1)	14(19.4)	4 (4.4)	34(10.3)
c. Poor	0	0	0	0	1 (1.4)	0	1 (0.3)
							331

Q-4. How could the environment be improved for your family?

	Absolute Frequency	Relative Frequency %	Adjusted Frequency %
Lower density	1	0.3	(0.7)
More privacy (soundproofing, patio screening, arrangement of windows, play areas separated from homes, walks not so close to living room area, etc.)	18	5.4	(11.6)
Better landscaping (more trees, screening, drainage, etc.)	22	6.7	(14.2)
Better site development (views, sun exposure, arrangement of homes, lay-out of walkways, alleys, streets, etc.)	20	6.0	(12.9)
Better land use controls over surrounding areas	19	5.7	(12.3)
More recreation facilities	23	6.9	(14.8)
Better maintenance	16	4.8	(10.3)
Better security	4	1.2	(2.6)
Miscellaneous (more parking, larger units, pet control, human inter-action problems, etc.)	32	9.7	(20.6)
No improvement needed or no response	177	53.3	—
	332	100.0	100.0

Q-5. Is your arrangement of houses (in rows or clusters) the best possible?

	1	2	3	4	5	6	Total
a. Yes	66(93)	17(94.4)	31(77.5)	28(87.5)	52(74.3)	86(94.5)	280(87)
b. No	5 (7)	1 (5.6)	9(22.5)	4(12.5)	18(25.7)	5 (5.5)	42(13)
							322

Q-6. How could the arrangement be improved?

	Absolute Frequency	Relative Frequency %	Adjusted Frequency %
More spacing between buildings	19	5.8	(19.8)
Smaller clusters of units	11	3.3	(11.5)
Stagger units (less common wall space, break up long, straight patterns, garages, etc.)	10	3.0	(10.4)
Avoid units (or decks, patios, etc.) that face one another	20	6.0	(20.8)
More enclosure for units (fencing, shrubbery, etc.—more privacy from front and rear)	6	1.8	(6.3)
Prefer garage in rear—away from access	3	0.9	(3.1)
More parking interspersed in development	5	1.5	(5.2)
Miscellaneous (wider driveways, etc.)	22	6.6	(22.9)
No improvement needed or no response	236	71.1	—
	332	100.0	100.0

Q-7. Do you feel there are too many families living too close to you?

	1	2	3	4	5	6	Total
a. Yes	5 (6.6)	0 (0)	3 (7.1)	3 (9.1)	16(22.2)	4 (4.4)	31 (9.3)
b. No	71(93.4)	18(100)	39(92.9)	30(90.9)	56(77.8)	87(95.6)	301(90.7)
							332

Q-8. Would you enjoy living there more if the development was smaller?

	1	2	3	4	5	6	Total
a. Yes	7 (9.3)	3(16.7)	4 (9.8)	5(15.6)	32(45.7)	9 (9.9)	60(18.3)
b. No	68(90.7)	15(83.3)	37(90.2)	27(84.4)	38(54.3)	82(90.1)	267(81.7)
							327

Q-9. How often do you hear neighbors from your yard or patio?

	1	2	3	4	5	6	Total
a. Often	5 (6.7)	1 (5.5)	3 (7.1)	2 (6.1)	9(12.5)	7 (7.7)	27 (8.1)
b. Occas.	45(60.0)	7(38.9)	32(76.2)	13(39.4)	34(47.2)	48(52.7)	179(54.1)
c. Almost Never	25(33.3)	10(55.6)	7(16.7)	18(54.5)	29(40.3)	36(39.6)	125(37.8)
							331

Q-10. Can you hear your neighbors through the inside walls?

	1	2	3	4	5	6	Total
a. Often	3 (3.9)	1 (5.6)	0 (0)	0 (0)	2 (2.8)	1 (1.1)	7 (2.1)
b. Occas.	24(31.6)	2(11.1)	11(26.2)	4(12.5)	23(31.9)	12(13.3)	76(23.0)
c. Almost Never	49(64.5)	15(83.3)	31(73.8)	28(87.5)	47(65.3)	77(85.6)	247(74.9)
							330

Q-11. How much do neighbors' noises bother you?

	1	2	3	4	5	6	Total
a. Very Much	1 (1.3)	1 (5.6)	1 (2.4)	1 (3.0)	4 (5.6)	2 (2.2)	10 (3.0)
b. Somewhat	15(20.0)	1 (5.6)	12(28.6)	4(12.1)	13(18.1)	15(16.5)	60(18.1)
c. No Bother	59(78.7)	16(88.8)	29(69.0)	28(84.9)	55(76.3)	74(81.3)	261(78.9)
							331

Q-12. Is car traffic near you a bother?

	1	2	3	4	5	6	Total
a. Yes	4 (5.3)	0 (0)	0 (0)	1 (3)	6 (8.3)	1(98.9)	12 (3.6)
b. No	72(94.7)	18(100)	42(100)	32(97)	66(91.7)	89 (1.1)	319(96.4)
							331

Q-13. Have you enough outdoor space for family activities?

	1	2	3	4	5	6	Total
a. Yes	72(96.0)	17(100)	39(92.9)	31(93.9)	54(75)	82(90.1)	295(89.4)
b. No	3 (4.0)	0 (0)	3 (7.1)	2 (6.1)	18(25)	9 (9.9)	35(10.6)
							330

Q-14. (If you have children) are there proper places for children to play?

	1	2	3	4	5	6	Total
a. Yes	42(95.5)	3(75)	8(44.4)	18(81.8)	19(38)	52(89.7)	142(72.4)
b. No	2 (4.5)	1(25)	10(55.6)	4(18.2)	31(62)	6(10.3)	54(27.6)
							196

Q-15. Please list the recreation facilities in your development which your family use most, in order of popularity:

a. _____ b. _____ c. _____ d. _____

Q-16. Which additional recreational facilities would you like?

Q-17. Which recreational facilities that are provided could you do without?

Q-18. Which features (like a sauna) were sales attractions when you bought, but which you don't use?

332 Respondents
Number of Times Mentioned

	Q-15	Q-16	Q-17	Q-18
Swimming, wading pools	293	1	27	28
Play areas, (tot lots, swings)	38	16	7	3
Tennis	188	30	34	31
Paths (walk, jog, bike)	112	6	3	—
Water—ponds, streams	8	—	1	—
Golf	34	5	1	4
Clubhouse activities	14	24	1	1
Basketball	4	5	4	—
Skating (ice and roller)	5	2	1	—
Baseball—barbeque	—	12	—	—
Jacuzzi whirlpool	—	—	—	—
Sauna	—	4	—	—
Volleyball	7	4	4	—
Gym and health club	—	6	—	—
Riding horses	—	—	—	—
Billiards, pool	—	—	—	—
Adult activity area	2	—	1	—
Indoor pool, tennis, etc.	—	37	—	—
Horseshoes	1	—	2	—
None	8	80	92	140
All	—	—	15	1
Shuffleboard	—	3	—	—
Racketball courts, handball	1	5	1	—
Garden space	3	1	—	—
Kitchen equipment in recreation center	—	1	—	—
Field and track	—	1	—	—
Paddle tennis	4	—	14	4

Q-19. Do you know your half-dozen nearest neighbors by name?

	1	2	3	4	5	6	Total
a. Yes	64(84.2)	15(83.3)	34(81.0)	30(90.9)	55(77.5)	75(82.4)	273(82.5)
b. No	12(15.8)	3(16.7)	8(19.0)	3 (9.1)	16(22.5)	16(17.6)	58(17.5)
							331

Q-20. Is it easier to make friends here than in other places you've lived?

	1	2	3	4	5	6	Total
a. Yes	24(32.9)	6(33.3)	10(25.0)	11(34.4)	24(33.3)	41(45.1)	116(35.6)
b. No	11(15.1)	2(11.1)	11(27.5)	2 (6.3)	10(13.9)	6 (6.6)	42(12.9)
c. Same	38(52.0)	10(55.6)	19(47.5)	19(59.3)	38(52.8)	44(48.3)	168(51.5)
							324

Q-21. How do you rate car parking facilities for you and your guests?

	1	2	3	4	5	6	Total
a. Good	49(64.5)	10(58.8)	25(61.0)	9(28.1)	5 (7.0)	58(64.4)	156(47.7)
b. Fair	25(32.9)	7(41.2)	14(34.1)	16(50.0)	31(43.7)	28(31.1)	121(37.0)
c. Poor	2 (2.6)		2 (4.9)	7(21.9)	35(49.3)	4 (4.5)	50(15.3)
							327

Q-22. How could car parking be improved?

	Absolute Frequency	Relative Frequency % (N=332)	Adjusted Frequency % (N=221)
More residents' parking	—	—	—
More guest parking	65	19.6	(29.4)
More parking (resident and guest)	52	15.7	(23.5)
More accessible parking	7	2.1	(3.2)
Larger garages	—	—	—
No complaints	29	8.7	(13.1)
No response	6	1.8	(2.7)
Better identification and enforcement	18	5.4	(8.2)
Other	44	13.3	(19.9)
	221		100.0

Q-23. Rows of cars close to your door help spoil the environment. For better appearance, how far will you walk to a parking lot?

	1	2	3	4	5	6	Total
a. 25 Yds	3 (4.3)				5 (7.5)		8 (2.6)
b. 50 Yds	3 (4.3)		1 (2.5)		2 (3.0)	5 (5.6)	11 (3.5)
c. 75 Yds	1 (1.5)		1 (2.5)	1 (3.2)	3 (4.5)	2 (2.2)	8 (2.6)
d. 100 Yds	2 (2.9)		1 (2.5)	1 (3.2)	1 (1.5)	1 (1.1)	6 (1.9)
e. Garage or car-port	60(87.0)	17(100)	35(90.0)	28(90.4)	51(76.0)	78(86.7)	269(85.9)
f. Prefer parking close as possible			1 (2.5)	1 (3.2)	5 (7.5)	4 (4.4)	11 (3.5)
							313

Q-24. How important is a parking area for boats, campers, trailers, etc.?

	1	2	3	4	5	6	Total
a. Very	11(15.1)	0 (0)	1 (2.5)	3 (9.7)	15(20.8)	17(19.5)	47(14.6)
b. Fairly	23(31.5)	3(16.7)	5(12.5)	4(12.9)	28(38.9)	30(34.5)	93(29.0)
c. Not Important	39(53.4)	15(83.3)	34(85.0)	24(77.4)	29(40.3)	40(46.0)	181(56.4)
							321

Q-25. If you remember the name or number of your floor plan, write it here: (Varied responses—not tabulated)

Q-26. How could your floor plan be improved for your family?

	Absolute Frequency	Relative Frequency % (N=332)	Adjusted Frequency % (N=168)
More storage space, cupboards, closets	20	6.0	(11.9)
Larger kitchen	10	3.0	(6.0)
Separate or more formal dining room	13	3.9	(7.7)
Have foyer	1	.3	(.6)
Bigger house, bigger bedrooms	38	11.4	(22.6)
More and better bathrooms	13	3.9	(7.7)
Better traffic pattern	2	.6	(1.2)
An improved basement, larger basement	18	5.4	(10.7)
More window area	5	1.5	(3.0)
More facilities on one floor (washing, family room, less stairs)	9	2.7	(5.4)
Miscellaneous	39	11.7	(23.2)
	168		100.0

Q-27. If you were buying again, which floor plan or model would you choose?

	1	2	3	4	5	6	All
a. Same	57(82.6)	12(80.0)	27(81.8)	25(80.6)	49(74.2)	69(83.1)	239(80.5)
b. Other	12(17.4)	3(20.0)	6(14.3)	6(19.4)	17(25.8)	14(16.9)	58(19.5)
							297

Q-28. Which type of patio do you prefer?

	1	2	3	4	5	6	All
a. Open on 3 sides	2 (2.7)	1 (6.3)	2 (4.9)	4(12.9)	8(11.4)	10(11.4)	27 (8.4)
b. W/side fences, open rear	42(56.0)	10(62.4)	36(87.8)	19(61.3)	46(65.7)	64(72.7)	217(67.6)
c. All enclosed	31(41.3)	5(31.3)	3 (7.3)	8(25.8)	16(22.9)	14(15.9)	77(24.0)
							321

Q-29. Do you regard a patio as:

	1	2	3	4	5	6	All
a. Very valuable	56(74.7)	11(61.1)	33(78.6)	26(78.7)	40(56.3)	71(79.7)	237(72.2)
b. Fairly valuable	19(25.3)	6(33.3)	8(19.0)	5(15.2)	26(36.6)	15(16.9)	79(24.1)
c. Not valuable	—	1 (5.6)	1 (2.4)	2 (6.1)	5 (7.1)	3 (3.4)	12 (3.7)
							328

Q-30. How do you rate the organization and operation of your condominium or homes association?

	1	2	3	4	5	6	All
Good	68(93.2)	16(88.9)	29(69.0)	26(78.8)	37(51.4)	82(90.1)	258(78.4)
Fair	5 (6.8)	2(11.1)	11(26.2)	6(18.2)	30(41.7)	9 (9.9)	63(19.2)
Poor	0	0	2 (4.8)	1 (3.0)	5 (6.9)	0	8 (2.4)
							329

Q-31. Are the monthly charges fair for the services you receive?

	1	2	3	4	5	6	All
Yes	73(96.1)	17(94.4)	39(97.5)	32(97.0)	56(77.8)	89(97.8)	306(92.7)
No	3 (3.9)	1 (5.6)	1 (2.5)	1 (3.0)	16(22.2)	2 (2.2)	24 (7.3)
							330

Q-32. How could the set-up of the condominium or association be improved?

	Absolute Frequency	Relative Frequency % (N=332)	Adjusted Frequency % (N=100)
Greater owner participation	25	7.5	(25.0)
Full-time or professional management	13	3.9	(13.0)
Better maintenance/full-time maintenance men	14	4.2	(14.0)
Present board needs improvement: more qualified members needed, needs to be more responsive to suggestions, etc.	9	2.7	(9.0)
Better communication for meetings/activities	11	3.3	(11.0)
Promote better understanding of association among owners: better preparation by developers, clearer understanding of covenants, etc.	2	.6	(2.0)
Equal treatment/enforcement of rules	6	1.8	(6.0)
Revise covenants, especially the selection of board members and limit power of board to act independently	1	.3	(1.0)
Miscellaneous: better funding, less social functions, etc.	19	5.7	(19.0)
		100.0	100.0

Q-33. What have turned out to be the 3 best features of townhouses or condominium living for you?

	Absolute Frequency	Relative Frequency % (N=332)	Adjusted Frequency % (N=259)
Ease of lifestyle (no exterior maintenance, etc.)	244	73.5	(32.2)
Recreation facilities	70	21.1	(9.2)
People of the development (interesting, good neighbors)	48	14.5	(6.3)
Privacy, quiet living, no heavy traffic	71	21.4	(9.4)
Safety—security from crime	57	17.2	(7.5)
Beauty of grounds (trees, nature)	78	23.5	(10.3)
Financial equity—price	45	13.6	(5.9)
Good for children	11	3.3	(1.4)
A sense of belonging (community)	12	3.6	(1.6)
Low heating costs (lower cost for services)	17	5.1	(2.2)
Advantages of single-family home (attached garage, basement, garden space, etc.)	17	5.1	(2.2)
Other	89	26.8	(11.8)
	759		100.0

Q-34. What are the 3 poorest features?

	Absolute Frequency	Relative Frequency % (N=332)	Adjusted Frequency % (N=268)
Not enough living space	16	4.8	(6.0)
Not enough storage space (basement)	3	0.9	(1.1)
No garden area	10	3.0	(3.7)
Too many children	7	2.1	(2.6)
Too many pets, lack of control	24	7.2	(9.0)
Poor parking	37	11.1	(13.7)
Lack of privacy—too many disturbances	23	6.9	(8.6)
Uncomfortable with association regulations or lack of complete freedom over own house or yard	13	3.9	(4.9)
Impact of inconsiderate neighbors is greater in townhouse developments	21	6.3	(7.8)
Multi-level living	6	1.8	(2.2)
Not enough windows	4	1.2	(1.5)
Poor entrance facilities	5	1.5	(1.9)
Poor maintenance or high cost of maintenance	34	1.0	(12.7)
Abuse of facilities by others	18	5.4	(6.7)
Association dues—no limit on how assessed	4	1.2	(1.5)
Not enough space for children's play	20	6.0	(7.5)
Poor street identification	3	0.9	(1.1)
Too much uniformity	5	1.5	(1.9)
Poor fire protection	1	0.3	(0.4)
Detached mailbox	3	0.9	(1.1)
Density too high	7	2.1	(2.6)
Other	4	1.2	(1.5)
	268		100.0

Q-35. In buying a townhouse or a condominium *in another location,* if you had a choice of several different neighborhoods within a development, which geographical or environmental features would be most important?
(Varied responses—not tabulated)

To help developers, land planners and architects do a better job with townhouses or condominiums, we need to know more about families now living in them. Please tell us:

Q-36. What kind of home did you live in just before you moved here?

	1	2	3	4	5	6	Total
a. 1-family home you owned	39(51.1)	10(55.5)	23(54.7)	19(59.3)	20(28.6)	56(63.6)	167(51.3)
b. 1-family home you rented	1 (1.3)	0	0	2 (6.3)	2 (2.9)	2 (2.3)	7 (2.2)
c. A rented apartment	24(32.0)	6(33.3)	18(42.9)	7(21.9)	43(61.4)	20(22.7)	118(36.3)
d. A rented townhouse	4 (6.3)	1 (5.6)	1 (2.4)	2 (6.3)	3 (4.3)	2 (2.3)	13 (4.0)
e. A townhouse you owned	4 (5.3)	1 (5.6)	0	1 (3.1)	1 (1.4)	5 (5.7)	12 (3.7)
f. Other	3 (4.0)		0	1 (3.1)	1 (1.4)	3 (3.4)	8 (2.5)
							325

Q-37. How long have you lived here?

	1	2	3	4	5	6	Total
a. 1-6 months	0	1 (5.6)	2 (4.8)	0	5 (6.9)	2 (2.2)	10 (3.0)
b. 7-12 months	1 (1.4)	1 (5.6)	3 (7.1)	0	13(18.1)	5 (5.5)	23 (6.9)
c. 13-18 months	3 (3.9)	4(22.2)	2 (4.8)	2 (6.1)	18(25.0)	9 (9.9)	38(11.4)
d. 19-24 months	2 (2.6)	3(16.7)	1 (2.4)	6(18.2)	5 (6.9)	5 (5.5)	22 (6.6)
e. Over 2 years	70(92.1)	9(49.9)	34(80.9)	25(75.8)	31(43.1)	70(76.9)	239(72.1)
							332

Q-38. How much longer do you expect to remain here?

	1	2	3	4	5	6	Total
a. 1-11 months	5 (6.9)	0	1 (2.6)	2 (6.7)	11(15.5)	4 (4.7)	23 (7.3)
b. 1 year	1 (1.7)	0	2 (5.1)	1 (3.3)	6 (8.5)	4 (4.7)	14 (4.5)
c. 2 years	2 (2.8)	0	4(10.3)	1 (3.4)	12(16.9)	12(14.0)	31 (9.9)
d. 3 years	3 (3.9)	0	1 (2.6)	3(10.0)	8(11.3)	6 (7.0)	21 (6.7)
e. 4 years	0	2(12.5)	1 (2.6)	1 (3.3)	6 (8.5)	5 (5.8)	15 (4.8)
f. 5 years or more	61(84.7)	14(87.5)	30(76.8)	22(73.3)	28(39.3)	55(63.8)	210(66.8)
							314

Q-39. When you next move, what type of home will you probably move to?

	1	2	3	4	5	6	Total
a. Buy a 1-family home	12(16.9)	0	5(15.6)	1 (3.9)	31(44.9)	11(15.9)	60(21.2)
b. Buy a townhouse or townhome	37(52.1)	9(56.3)	14(43.7)	17(65.4)	26(37.7)	49(71.0)	152(53.6)
c. Rent a townhouse	1 (1.4)	0	0	0	2 (2.9)	0	3 (1.1)
d. Rent an apartment	9(12.7)	0	2 (6.3)	5(19.2)	2 (2.9)	2 (3.0)	20 (7.1)
e. Other (specify)	12(16.9)	7(43.8)	11(34.4)	3(11.5)	8(11.6)	7(10.1)	48(17.0)
							283

Q-40. Your marital status is:

	1	2	3	4	5	6	Total
a. Married	53(69.7)	15(83.3)	26(61.9)	21(63.6)	47(66.2)	69(75.8)	231(69.8)
b. Single	11(14.5)	2(11.1)	10(23.8)	8(24.2)	17(23.9)	6 (6.6)	54(16.3)
c. Widowed	6 (7.9)	1 (5.6)	3 (7.1)	4(12.2)	1 (1.4)	6 (6.6)	21 (6.3)
d. Divorced	6 (7.9)	0	3 (7.2)	0	6 (8.5)	10(11.0)	25 (7.6)
							331

Q-41. Sex: (Of person filling this out)

	1	2	3	4	5	6	Total
Male	24(31.6)	8(44.4)	14(33.3)	13(40.6)	33(46.5)	31(34.1)	123(37.3)
Female	25(32.9)	3(16.7)	12(28.6)	12(37.5)	14(19.7)	21(23.1)	87(26.4)
Couple Jointly	27(35.5)	7(38.9)	16(38.1)	7(21.9)	24(33.8)	39(42.8)	120(36.3)
							330

Q-42. How many adults, 20 or over, live in your home?

	1	2	3	4	5	6	Total
a. 1	14(18.7)	3(16.7)	12(29.3)	11(33.3)	20(28.6)	18(20.5)	78(24.0)
b. 2	57(76.0)	14(77.7)	29(70.7)	19(57.6)	50(71.4)	64(72.7)	233(71.7)
c. 3	4 (5.3)	1 (5.6)	0	3 (9.1)	0	6 (6.8)	14 (4.3)
d. 4 or more	0	0	0	0	0	0	0 (0)
							325

Q-43. How many persons under 20?

	1	2	3	4	5	6	Total
a. 1	12(24.5)	3(20.0)	5(20.0)	7(30.4)	17(34.7)	15(22.1)	59(49.2)
b. 2	12(24.5)	1 (6.7)	1 (4.0)	5(21.7)	12(24.5)	15(22.1)	46(38.3)
c. 3	4 (8.2)	0	0	0	1 (2.0)	5 (7.4)	10 (8.3)
d. 4 or more	0	0	1 (4.0)	0	3 (6.1)	1 (1.5)	5 (4.2)
							120

Q-44. Age, principal wage earner.

	1	2	3	4	5	6	Total
a. 20-29	4 (5.5)	1 (5.6)	2 (4.8)	1 (3.1)	26(36.1)	2 (2.3)	36(11.1)
b. 30-39	20(27.0)	6(33.3)	8(19.0)	8(25.0)	29(40.2)	34(39.1)	105(32.3)
c. 40-49	14(18.9)	2(11.1)	7(16.7)	7(21.9)	11(15.3)	17(19.5)	58(17.8)
d. 50-59	18(24.3)	7(38.9)	16(38.1)	11(34.4)	4 (5.6)	24(27.6)	80(24.6)
e. 60 +	18(24.3)	2(11.1)	9(21.4)	5(15.6)	2 (2.8)	10(11.5)	46(14.2)
							325

Q-45. Occupation, principal wage earner.
(Varied responses—typically professionals, teachers and managers)

Q-46. Does wife have an outside job?

	1	2	3	4	5	6	Total
a. Yes	27(50.0)	14(87.5)	11(42.3)	7(31.8)	32(65.3)	32(45.1)	123(51.7)
b. No	27(50.0)	2(12.5)	15(57.7)	15(68.2)	17(34.7)	39(54.9)	115(48.3)
							238

Q-47. Wife's occupation _____
(Varied responses—not tabulated)

Q-48. Your total family income. This is important because it gives us a clue to the price of houses that should be built. This is completely anonymous, so the figure remains your secret. We will appreciate an answer.

	1	2	3	4	5	6	Total
a. Under $10,000	3 (4.2)	0	1 (2.5)	0	1 (1.4)	0	5 (1.6)
b. $10,000-$14,999	12(16.4)	0	6(15.0)	2 (6.5)	16(22.2)	8 (9.2)	44(13.7)
c. $15,000-$19,999	11(15.1)	0	4(10.0)	2 (6.5)	26(36.1)	4 (4.6)	47(14.6)
d. $20,000-$24,999	9(12.3)	2(11.1)	11(27.5)	6(19.4)	12(16.7)	22(25.3)	62(19.3)
e. $25,000-$29,999	13(17.8)	3(16.7)	6(15.0)	2 (6.5)	7 (9.7)	21(24.1)	52(16.2)
f. $30,000-or over	25(34.2)	13(72.2)	12(30.0)	19(61.1)	10(13.9)	32(36.8)	111(34.6)
							321

Q-49. Original price range when built?
Present value?

Responses showed an average increase in property value of $12,500 per home for all developments. The older developments had an average increase of $15,000 to $20,000 per home. The rapid escalation of prices since the survey was taken has raised the re-sale prices of many homes to double their initial sales price.

Q-50. Compared to your previous residence, do you feel:

	1	2	3	4	5	6	Total
a. More secure	52(69.3)	11(64.7)	30(71.4)	22(66.7)	44(62.0)	55(60.4)	214(65.1)
b. Less secure	0	1 (5.9)	1 (2.4)	0	4 (5.6)	0	6 (1.8)
c. About the same	23(30.7)	5(29.4)	11(26.2)	11(33.3)	23(32.4)	36(39.6)	109(33.1)
							329

Q-51. How do you rate the size of your development?

	1	2	3	4	5	6	Total
a. Too large	5 (6.6)	0	1 (2.4)	4(12.1)	28(38.9)	5 (5.6)	43(13.0)
b. Too small	0	1 (5.6)	0	0	0	0	1 (0.3)
c. About right	71(93.4)	17(94.4)	40(97.6)	29(87.9)	44(61.1)	85(94.4)	286(86.7)
							330

Selected Bibliography

Babcock, Richard F., and Bosselman, Fred P. *Exclusionary Zoning, Land Use Regulation and Housing in the 1970s*. New York: Praeger Publishers, 1973.

California Public Outdoor Recreation Plan Committee. *California Public Outdoor Recreation* Part 2. Sacramento, California: author, 1960.

Chermayeff, Serge, and Alexander, Christopher. *Community and Privacy*. Garden City, New York: Doubleday & Company, Inc., 1963.

Green, Isaac; Fedewa, Bernard E.; Johnston, Charles A.; Jackson, William M.; and Deardorff, Howard L. *Housing for the Elderly, the Development and Design Process*. New York: Van Nostrand, Reinhold Company, 1975.

Hanson, William A., and Bigelow, Frans. *Lake Management Case Study: Westlake Village, California*. Technical Bulletin 73. Washington, D.C.: Urban Land Institute, 1977.

Highway Research Board. *National Cooperative Highway Research Program Report #121*. Washington, D.C.: author, 1971.

ITE Trip Generation. *Institute of Transportation Engineers*. Topics 200-270. Arlington, Virginia: author, 1976.

Jacobs, Jane. *The Death and Life of Great American Cities*. New York: Vintage Books, 1961.

Jones, Rees L., and Rando, Guy L. *Golf Course Developments*. Technical Bulletin 70. Washington, D.C.: Urban Land Institute, 1974.

Maricopa Association of Governments. *Trip Generation by Land Use*. Maricopa County, Arizona: author.

National Association of Home Builders. *Cost Effective Site Planning: Single-Family Development*. Washington, D.C.: NAHB, 1976.

Norcross, Carl. *Open Space Communities in the Market Place*. Technical Bulletin 57. Washington, D.C.: Urban Land Institute, 1966.

———. *Townhouses and Condominiums: Residents' Likes and Dislikes*. Washington, D.C.: Urban Land Institute, 1973.

Real Estate Research Corporation, Council on Environmental Quality. *The Costs of Sprawl*. Washington, D.C.: CEQ, HUD, EPA, 1974.

Robinette, Gary O. *Landscape Architectural Site Construction Details*. Reston, Virginia: Environmental Design Press, 1976.

———. *Plants/People/and Environmental Quality*. Washington, D.C.: U.S. Department of the Interior, National Park Service, 1972.

Sagalyn, Lynne B., and Sternlieb, George. *Zoning and Housing Costs*. New Brunswick, New Jersey: Rutgers University, 1972.

Siegan, Bernard H. *Land Use Without Zoning*. Lexington, Massachusetts: D.C. Heath & Company, 1972.

Simonds, John Ormsbee. *Landscape Architecture*. New York: McGraw-Hill Book Company, Inc., 1961.

Smith, Barry. "New Forms for Cul-de-Sacs." *Journal of Home Building*. National Association of Home Builders Report #2. 15 February 1968.

State of California Department of Transportation. *Tenth Progress Report on Trip Ends Generation Research Count*. San Francisco: author, 1975.

Sternlieb, George. *Housing Development and Municipal Costs*. New Brunswick, New Jersey: Rutgers University, 1973.

Stone, Dave. *How to Sell New Homes and Condominiums*. New York: House & Home Press, 1975.

Tourbier, Joachim, and Westmacott, Richard. *Lakes and Ponds*. Technical Bulletin 72. Washington, D.C.: Urban Land Institute, 1976.

Urban Land Institute. *Adaptive Use: Development Economics, Process, and Profiles*. Washington, D.C.: ULI, 1978.

———. *Homes Association Handbook*. Technical Bulletin 50. Washington, D.C.: ULI, rev. ed. 1966.

———. *Project Reference File*. Washington, D.C.: ULI, 20 innovative projects per year, since 1971, covering all land use types.

———. *Residential Development Handbook*. Washington, D.C.: ULI, 1978.

Urban Land Institute, American Society of Civil Engineers, National Association of Home Builders. *Residential Erosion and Sediment Control: Objectives, Principles, and Design Considerations*. Washington, D.C.: ULI, ASCE, NAHB, 1978.

———. *Residential Storm Water Management: Objectives, Principles, and Design Considerations*. Washington, D.C.: ULI, ASCE, NAHB, 1976.

———. *Residential Streets: Objectives, Principles, and Design Considerations*. Washington, D.C.: ULI, ASCE, NAHB, 1974.

Urban Land Institute and Community Associations Institute. *Creating a Community Association: The Developer's Role in Condominium and Homeowner Associations*. Washington, D.C.: ULI, CAI, 1977.

———. *Financial Management of Condominium and Homeowners' Associations*, 2nd ed. Washington, D.C.: ULI, CAI, 1976.

———. *Managing a Successful Community Association*, 2nd ed. Washington, D.C.: ULI, CAI, 1976.

U.S. Department of Housing and Urban Development. *HUD Condominium/Cooperative Study*. National Evaluation, vol. 1. Washington, D.C.: HUD, July 1975.

Walker, Theodore D. *Site Design and Construction Detailing*. West Lafayette, Indiana: PDA Publishers, 1978.

Wards 1978 Automotive Yearbook, 14th ed. Library of Congress #40. Detroit: Wards' Communications Inc., 1978.

Whyte, William H. *Cluster Development*. New York: American Conservation Association, 1964.

———. *The Last Landscape*. Garden City, New York: Doubleday & Company, 1968.

Wolfe, David. *Condominium and Homeowner Associations That Work: On Paper and in Action*. Washington, D.C.: Urban Land Institute, Community Associations Institute, 1978.

Zion, Robert L. *Trees for Architecture and the Landscape*. New York: Van Nostrand, Reinhold Company, 1968.

List of Figures